RESTLESS
GENIUS

ALSO BY RICHARD J. TOFEL

Sounding the Trumpet: The Making of John F. Kennedy's Inaugural Address

*Vanishing Point: The Disappearance of Judge Crater,
and the New York He Left Behind*

A Legend in the Making: The New York Yankees in 1939

RICHARD J. TOFEL

RESTLESS GENIUS

GENIUS

Barney
Kilgore,
The Wall Street Journal,
and the
Invention of
Modern
Journalism

St. Martin's Press ✌ New York

RESTLESS GENIUS. Copyright © 2009 by Richard J. Tofel. All rights reserved. Printed in the United States of America. For information, address St. Martin's Press, 175 Fifth Avenue, New York, N.Y. 10010.

www.stmartins.com

Library of Congress Cataloging-in-Publication Data

Tofel, Richard J., 1957–
    Restless genius : Barney Kilgore, *The Wall Street Journal,* and the invention of modern jour-
nalism / Richard J. Tofel.—1st ed.
        p.   cm.
    Includes bibliographical references.
    ISBN-13: 978-0-312-53674-9
    ISBN-10: 0-312-53674-7
    1. Kilgore, Bernard, 1908–1967.   2. Journalists—United States—Biography.   3. News-
paper editors—United States—Biography.   I. Title.
    PN4874.K534T74   2009
    070.92—dc22
    [B]

                                                                          2008029880

First Edition: February 2009

10   9   8   7   6   5   4   3   2   1

For Janice

CONTENTS

PREFACE

On the day his bid to take over *The Wall Street Journal* and its publisher Dow Jones & Company was announced, Rupert Murdoch told an interviewer that Barney Kilgore "really invented modern journalism." The *Journal*'s "editorial traditions" had been "laid down" by the "great" Kilgore during a period "in the '40's, '50's and '60's, when he took the circulation from 30,000 to over a million." Whatever one thinks of Rupert Murdoch, he is well versed in this history: Much of what was worth five billion dollars to Murdoch in 2007 had been built by Kilgore forty or more years earlier.

This is the story of Bernard Kilgore, known to all during his lifetime as "Barney." It is the story of how he saved *The Wall Street Journal* from the narrowness of its origins and from the Great Depression and built it into the most profitable and most trusted newspaper in America—and, soon after his premature death, the largest in circulation. Beyond that, as Murdoch indicated, it is the story of the invention of much of what we have come to associate with modern newspaper journalism. A poll taken at the end of the twentieth century named Kilgore, overwhelmingly, as its greatest business journalist. More broadly, a *Columbia Journalism Review* article recently compared Kilgore's place in journalistic history with Sigmund Freud's role in the development of psychoanalysis.

This is also the story of a young man in a hurry, a man who had achieved success and wealth and power but whose obituary in the rarely repetitive and always word-conscious newspaper he built would three times describe him as "restless"; Kilgore's *National Observer* used the same word. It is the story of a man who, having triumphed in creating the most successful entrant in his chosen field, spent the last years of his life not basking in that triumph, but trying to top it with the *Observer,* a newspaper ahead of its time, a creation all his own, the nation's first general-interest national paper. That final effort, not then successful, may well point the way for serious journalism in our own time.

———————

Barney Kilgore was a columnist in *The Wall Street Journal* at the age of twenty-three. He had started and stopped two different columns before his twenty-fifth birthday. He broke new ground in forms and styles of newspaper writing, humanizing articles, making them more accessible, employing humor to tell stories. He crafted the *Journal*'s signature "What's News" summary—the archetype for the display of news on the Internet, a medium not then dreamed of, and not commercialized until nearly thirty years after his death—when he was just twenty-five.

Kilgore had not yet even begun to work full-time in Washington when President Franklin D. Roosevelt was already telling other reporters seeking to understand a complex economic story to read his work. His reporting on the New Deal helped business shape its attitude toward government, regulation, and stimulus in ways still being debated today—even as he drew his own perspective from the *Journal*'s editorial page, which soon became, and has remained, the leading voice of mainstream libertarian thinking in the nation.

From his first days as a journalist, Kilgore showed wisdom beyond his years and a startling capacity for precocious achievement and leadership. He became Washington bureau chief of the *Journal* at twenty-six, managing editor and inventor of much of its distinctive front-page format at thirty-two, general manager of its parent company at thirty-four.

As the *Journal*'s publisher, he and his associates finally achieved something of which others had only dreamed: building a truly national newspaper, expanding the financial paper they had inherited through regional editions based in Dallas and Chicago, and then spanning the continent with proprietary printing technology and the distribution network it made possible. Along the way, Kilgore and company rode the crest of the postwar economic boom to establish—and soon dominate—a market for national newspaper advertising to support their national editorial offering, leading ultimately to perhaps the greatest economic success in newspaper history.

Kilgore's *Journal* cemented its reputation for independence and integrity by facing down General Motors, then the nation's largest company, and the newspaper's largest advertiser, in a confrontation over who would decide what the news was. The result was a sharpening of distinctions between newspapers' "church" (their editorial content) and "state" (their business operations) that provides a gold standard, an aspiration for the industry and its progeny in newer media, which endures to this day.

I first worked with *The Wall Street Journal* as a young lawyer, and then was privileged to spend fifteen years at the paper, including stints as an assistant managing editor and ultimately as the newspaper's assistant publisher. Kilgore remained as well known in the newsroom he built as he was unknown elsewhere. His name was synonymous with high standards, integrity, and innovation.

But for all of that he remained a distant figure. Kilgore became real to me when I researched this book, and particularly when I read his published writing; the real story consistently surpassed even the myth. But he became truly human only when I became the first person outside his family to read a thirty-year correspondence he carried on with his father. Those letters, I hope, light up this book. As set forth more fully in the acknowledgments, I am deeply indebted to Jim, Kathryn, and Jack Kilgore for sharing this remarkable treasure with me.

Barney Kilgore was a practical man. He talked relatively little about the role of the press in our society. He believed in letting his work speak for itself. *The Wall Street Journal* is the embodiment of that work, one of the few truly great newspapers in our nation, one (at least until very recently) of the very few remaining truly independent voices of journalistic quality in our world.

That, in turn, is a bulwark of our freedom and our ability to govern ourselves in an ever-more complex and confusing world. The publication of this book roughly coincides with the centenary of Barney Kilgore's birth. I hope it makes clear why, Kilgore's modesty notwithstanding, that occasion should be marked with genuine and widespread celebration.

RESTLESS
GENIUS

INTRODUCTION

O N MONDAY AUGUST 25, 1958, a remarkable meeting took place in a quiet office in New York City. Three men convened to consider how they might save the *New York Herald Tribune.* The paper faced falling circulation and shrinking advertising; it was losing money and seemed headed toward losing much more. Their project had the express approval of Dwight D. Eisenhower, the president of the United States.

The *Herald Tribune* was the combination of the two dominant newspapers of the mid–nineteenth century, the *Herald* of James Gordon Bennett and the *Tribune* of Horace Greeley. For nearly three-quarters of a century, the newspaper had been controlled by the family of Whitelaw Reid, and had helped steer Republican Party thinking and policy. For much of the first half of the twentieth century, the *Herald Tribune* had contended with *The New York Times,* on more or less equal terms, for primacy in the country's largest city—and at the center of the country's political and social debates. But the postwar boom had been cruel to the Reids and their newspaper, and the Reid era was passing. At issue was whether the *Herald Tribune* could now be rescued, and, if so, how.

Two of the men at the meeting represented the new owner of the *Herald Tribune,* the United States ambassador to Great Britain, John Hay "Jock" Whitney, who would not even take control of the paper for three more days, and who had celebrated his fifty-fourth birthday just a day earlier. One was Walter Thayer, forty-eight, attorney and financier, managing partner of J. H. Whitney & Co., the first American venture capital firm, who would supervise

1

the newspaper until Whitney could return from London and advise on its business affairs thereafter. The other was Whitney's brother-in-law (their wives were sisters) and best friend, William Paley, fifty-six, the proprietor of CBS, the Columbia Broadcasting System, one of the nation's two dominant television and radio networks. Neither of them had experience in newspaper publishing, nor did Whitney.

On the other hand, the man to whom they now turned had spent his entire working life—nearly thirty years at that point—in newspapers. He was forty-nine years old at the time of this meeting and had led his own newspaper for seventeen years, first for a remarkable lightning-fast twenty-two months as its managing editor, when he had remade its content, and particularly its front page, then for fifteen years as its business head, revolutionizing those aspects of the paper as well—circulation, advertising, production, and distribution. His efforts on all of these scores had been wildly successful, and his newspaper's growth had been the most phenomenal in the industry since the rise of the tabloid picture press forty years earlier. The man's name was Bernard Kilgore, although everyone called him Barney, and his newspaper was *The Wall Street Journal.*

The advice Kilgore would offer the men at the meeting, and the succeeding months and years, was not the product of mere business philosophy. The advice was, instead, a distillation of concepts he had proved out over the course of twenty-five years crafting the *Journal,* broadening its offering and yet sharpening its appeal, extending its distribution while focusing its mission, building its readership and advertising base while making it truly distinctive.

Jock Whitney, Walter Thayer, and Bill Paley had approached Barney Kilgore about the possibility of his running the *Herald Tribune,* and Kilgore had not ruled that out—just as he had not ruled out earlier approaches from William Randolph Hearst, *Business Week,* and *Time* magazine, all of which had sought to hire him away from the *Journal.* But Kilgore was very well fixed at the *Journal* in 1958. He came to the meeting almost surely because newspapers, and how to improve them, intrigued him, *fascinated* him.

And he came with a five-page memo that began with a characteristically informal and parenthetical disclaimer: "(No strings attached to this)." Kilgore's memo offered lots of specific suggestions, and a few important general observations. He simply thought about the problems of newspapers in a different way than the other men with whom Whitney and his associates were consulting.

First, Kilgore thought about the project in terms of a ten-year time frame.

There were steps he would take quickly, he made clear, but a newspaper could not be remade overnight. Then it was essential to understand the particular newspaper's function in the lives of its readers—and who those readers were. "A newspaper has to set a course and create the impression it knows what it's about before it has much to sell." Success would come, if at all, from strong content that would attract new readers, who would, only then, prove attractive to advertisers. For now, as Kilgore said at the meeting that day, "The less said the better about changes." When Paley opined that the *Herald Tribune* needed a "hell of a good Promotion Department," Kilgore demurred: "You have got to get the *readers* talking about the newspaper."

Above all, in order to start this chain reaction, the paper needed to be distinctive. Editing the paper "with one eye on the *Times*" was insufficient, and ultimately self-defeating. Kilgore's summation of the *Herald Tribune* was damning, but in an unusual way: "It is not, as it now stands, a bad newspaper. But it is a little too much of a newspaper that might be published in Philadelphia, Washington or Chicago just as readily as in metropolitan New York."

Next, Kilgore urged that substantial resources be immediately put into research. He always wanted to know more about readers—current ones and potential ones as well—and while he treasured anecdotes, he had come, over the years, to find truth in data. In an anecdotal business, he was a statistical man. He warned, right off, that "research of this kind has its limitations and will not, by itself, provide all the answers. But it would, I think, give the right sort of editorial talent something to work with."

Not all of his suggestions were philosophical, however. The first thing that probably needed to be done, he wrote, was to cut costs, especially deadwood on the staff. A later memo underlined the essence of the thing: first, "Very useful newspapers are produced on budgets far below those of the *Trib*"; second, costs, if they were to be reduced, should be reduced quickly: "My father used to say it is a mistake to cut off the cat's tail an inch at a time. Doesn't help the cat."

Then the paper needed to be calmed down visually, not to "overdo" headlines, to favor white space over screaming black. Photos should be used more sparingly, but selected with an eye toward greater emotional impact. Color printing—then very unusual in newspapers—should be seriously considered. The news should be summarized on the front page, "boiled down," made more accessible to the average reader.

Kilgore had pioneered such work. He stressed the importance of summarization, but also that it took effort: "This will take two or three good men to produce. It isn't easy." Stories needed to be shorter; fewer needed to jump from one page to another; the weekday paper might be stronger if produced in a single section. As he later told Thayer, what he proposed was "the compact model newspaper. The economy model. . . . it may be better to have a good regiment than a weak division."

Whitney, Thayer, and Paley ultimately didn't take Barney Kilgore's advice for their newspaper—not when he first offered it in 1958, not after they chose a publisher on his recommendation in 1959, not when he repeated it in writing in 1961 after the publisher proved to be in over his head, not even after he served on Whitney's board. The *Herald Tribune* sank into a merger with the New York *World-Telegram & Sun* and the New York *Journal-American* in 1966; the combined *World Journal Tribune* was produced for less than eight months, before this combination of seven once-great daily newspapers ceased publication in May 1967.

Perhaps not even Barney Kilgore's idea for a highly distinctive, one-section, tightly summarized, reader-oriented, quietly displayed newspaper would have saved the New York *Herald Tribune*. We will never know.

But we do know that Kilgore had garnered the wisdom he sought to share with Whitney and his colleagues in the course of saving *The Wall Street Journal*. And not only saving it, but making it the best-respected, best-read, and most successful newspaper in America. This book, the story of Barney Kilgore's life, is the story of how he did so—and how, in so doing, he did, as Rupert Murdoch noted, invent much of modern journalism.

1

Hoosier Beginnings

Leslie Bernard Kilgore was born on November 9, 1908, in Albany, Indiana. (Neither he nor his parents seem ever to have used his first name, although his mother selected it to honor a family minister.) His father, Tecumseh Kilgore, was the local superintendent of schools. The family of his mother, Lavina Elizabeth Bodenhorn Kilgore, lived nearby, although they traced their origins to the Pennsylvania Dutch region.

Albany (not to be confused with the much larger city of New Albany on Indiana's southern border) was a small part of Delaware Township, in central Indiana's Delaware County. Albany's population actually shrank during the decade of Kilgore's birth, from about 3,200 people at the turn of the twentieth century to about 2,850 people—a decline of more than 10 percent—by 1910. The town is one-fifth smaller yet today.

The prospects of Albany, along with the arrival of his and Lavina's first child, seem to have prompted a career switch on the part of Tecumseh Kilgore. Before becoming superintendent of schools in Albany, he had taught school in nearby Muncie, after starting out as a teacher at age seventeen with his future wife as one of his students. But now he left education, moved his family to South Bend, Indiana, and became, in June 1909, just seven months after the birth of his son, an agent for the Union Central Life Insurance Company. He would remain at this work for the rest of his life. And South Bend was thriving: While the population of Albany had been contracting by a tenth in the first decade of the new century, that of South Bend had been growing by half again. Today it is twice what it was when the Kilgore family arrived.

Tecumseh Kilgore was born in 1875, and named after his father, who, in turn, had been named for the Shawnee Indian chief who had lived in Indiana and lost the battle of Tippecanoe to General William Henry Harrison, then governor of the Indiana Territory, and later (ever so briefly) president of the United States. The younger Tecumseh Kilgore attended Indiana University and married Lavina on August 15, 1897, in Madison County, just to the west of Delaware County, where the bride's family lived in the small town of Lapel. Lavina, at twenty, was two years younger than her husband.

Tecumseh's family had deep roots in Indiana. His great-grandfather, Obed Kilgore, was born in Pennsylvania, but lived most of his life in Kentucky, before coming to Franklin County, Indiana, on the southern border with Ohio, in 1819.

Obed's son, David Kilgore, who had been born in Kentucky in 1804, came to Delaware County in 1830, entered a homestead claim, and soon became active in Whig politics. The first of his several terms in the Indiana house of representatives began in 1833. He was a state court circuit judge for seven years and served as a leading delegate to the 1851 state constitutional convention before returning to elective politics. He was elected speaker of the house in 1855 as a member of the new Republican Party, and won two terms in the United States House of Representatives in the years just before the Civil War. He remained active in Republican politics throughout the war and the early years of Reconstruction.

David's son Alfred followed him into politics, also serving in the state legislature, and as United States district attorney for Indiana in the years just after the war, before dying at age thirty-eight. Alfred's brother, the first Tecumseh Kilgore, chose a different path. He was a doctor, practicing in Delaware County all his life, save time as regimental surgeon of the 13th Indiana Cavalry during the Civil War.

While the younger Tecumseh and Lavina decamped to South Bend, the upbringing they afforded Bernard—and, soon, his younger sister, Martha, as well—was traditional and Midwestern. Bernard enjoyed boxing and toy trains as a boy. He dug ditches for the local plumber and learned enough to later be able to pack the joint running to the dishwasher or to repair a faucet. He also painted the family house, learned to play the piano (a favorite lifelong pastime), and delivered newspapers.

But the atmosphere in the Kilgore home was also unusually intellectual, especially for its time and place. The boy, years later, recalled President Woodrow Wilson's campaign train coming through town when he was not yet eight years old and, as he later put it, "I can also remember how everybody thought he had lost the [1916] election, only he didn't."

Tecumseh was, throughout his life, an avid reader and amateur historian, always, as he put it, "mooching around among old papers and books." He worked hard with Bernard, who had a large vocabulary at a young age, using little cards to teach him to read before other children; the boy much later recalled that "that got me a head start in school." During a visit to his mother's family when he was only five and a half, Bernard wrote his first letter to his father. "Dear Papa, Do you want me to bring home a cat? Please answer. FROM BERNARD." Tecumseh kept the letter for the rest of his life.

Bernard eventually skipped a grade, and was a strong student in the public schools of South Bend. The central institutions in the town of Bernard Kilgore's boyhood were the Studebaker automotive factory—Studebaker moved its manufacturing operations to South Bend when Bernard was eleven—and the University of Notre Dame.

These were the early years of Knute Rockne, who arrived to coach Notre Dame football in 1918, when Bernard was not yet nine. In 1920, just weeks after being named Notre Dame's first All-American football player, George Gipp died at age twenty-four in a local hospital, but not before supposedly asking Rockne to someday have the team "win one" for him. Rockne's halftime speech conjuring up the ghost of the Gipper did not come until 1928, but he and Notre Dame won their first national championship, to enormous local acclaim, in 1924.

At home, young Bernard was less an athlete than a tinkerer. He built a model railroad, and hitched a sail to his favorite wagon. He was not much prone to extracurricular activities in high school, but was a member of the debate team. From the start, Barney (as he was soon known to peers and colleagues, although rarely to his family) was quietly competitive and markedly precocious. He won a Boy Scout birdhouse construction contest by creating a new category for entries—owl houses—getting the category officially sanctioned, and submitting the only entry. And, of course, he was simply intellectually ahead of those his age, having skipped that grade. Tecumseh overcame Lavina's objections that Barney was not yet ready for college when he graduated from the public high school in South Bend at the age of sixteen.

In early September 1925, Barney Kilgore, two months shy of his seventeenth birthday, set off to DePauw University, in Greencastle, Indiana. He traveled by train, by way of Indianapolis.

From this point in his life, we know much more than before, because he began a correspondence with his parents—mostly his father—that Tecumseh preserved. The elder Kilgore retained carbons of his own letters (which all began "Dear Son" and concluded "Love, Dad," and were invariably typed and precisely dated), and the original of his son's ("Dear Dad" or "Dear Mother," occasionally "Dear Folks"), beginning with the second letter home. The younger man's letters were signed "Love, Bernard," even when he had become nationally known as "Barney." There are gaps in the surviving letters, such as nothing from the spring semester of Barney's freshman year at college and little from his junior year, but the letters run from September 1925 through year-end 1954, by which time Tecumseh was seventy-nine. In all, the collection runs well more than a thousand pages. This cache of letters, generously shared with the author of this book by Barney's children, has never before been available to help tell Barney Kilgore's story. Without them, this book would not be the same, and might not have been written.

The university in which Barney Kilgore enrolled was, by the standards of the Midwest, quite venerable. DePauw had been founded in 1837 by the Indiana Methodist Conference as Indiana Asbury University, named for Francis Asbury, the first Methodist bishop in America. Asbury died in 1816.

The university was placed in Greencastle, then a town of 500 people (and only 10,000 today), when the town put up $25,000 for the privilege—the equivalent of about one thousand of today's dollars for each inhabitant. The school, it was clearly hoped, would put the town on the map.

Indiana Asbury enjoyed a relatively uneventful first fifty years, doing a credible job of educating young people, and opening its doors to women in 1867, but certainly not achieving any great distinction. By the mid-1880s it faced a financial crisis, and possible bankruptcy. The president of its board of trustees came personally to the rescue, offering to match, with two dollars of his own, each dollar contributed by others.

The president was a local industrialist named Washington C. DePauw, and the university was soon renamed for him. His gifts, which eventually totaled $300,000 (more than $7 million in today's dollars) went for more land, new dormitories for both men and women, and a new observatory with a state-of-the-art telescope. (The telescope, no longer state of the art, was still in use when Kilgore arrived on campus forty years later.) The new college song, "In Praise of Old DePauw" drew both words and music from Princeton's "In Praise of Old Nassau."

Beyond that, DePauw and his colleagues envisioned turning what had been essentially a small college into a true university. In quick succession, they launched schools of law, education, theology, music, and art. But disputes over Mr. DePauw's estate (he died suddenly in 1887) and losses from the Panic of 1893 soon limited their ambitions. A planned school of medicine never materialized. The university quickly ended its Ph.D. program and then its master's program as well; the law school lasted just ten years, the education school five, the theology school fourteen. The school of art limped along for twenty-six years, but was shuttered before the First World War. Only the school of music survived.

The school was not without distinguished students—historians Charles and Mary Beard graduated from DePauw in 1898, Margaret Mead attended for a year before transferring to Columbia University and beginning her studies in anthropology—and it hosted the first chapter of Phi Beta Kappa in the state of Indiana, but DePauw remained something of a backwater, led by a succession of mediocre Methodist ministers.

One area in which DePauw did stand out was journalism. *The DePauw Daily,* which was published from 1907 until 1920, made DePauw the smallest college in the country with a daily newspaper. (After 1920, and during Kilgore's student days, the newspaper appeared less frequently, and was known simply as *The DePauw.*)

In 1909 Sigma Delta Chi, still the national journalism fraternity (and now called the Society of Professional Journalists), was founded at DePauw. Sigma Delta Chi held its first national convention in Greencastle in 1912. Among the founders of both Sigma Delta Chi and *The DePauw Daily* was Eugene C. Pulliam, who dropped out after his junior year to go into the newspaper business, and ultimately built the Central Newspapers chain that included *The*

Indianapolis Star and *The Arizona Republic*. (One of Pulliam's grandchildren is Dan Quayle, former vice president of the United States.) Also on the staff of the *Daily* was Don Maxwell, later editor of the *Chicago Tribune,* and a young man named Kenneth C. Hogate, class of '18, who served as president of Sigma Delta Chi in 1921–22 and would later figure prominently in Barney Kilgore's life.

The 1920s were boom times at DePauw as they were in so many places in America. The student body, standing at 1,000 in 1919, had increased to 1,800 by the 1925–26 school year, Kilgore's freshman year. In 1919, Chicago lawyer and philanthropist Edward Rector, who had already contributed a new women's dormitory to the university, underwrote a new merit-based scholarship program offering a completely free education at DePauw to one hundred young men from each year's high school graduating classes across Indiana. DePauw's official history declares that the Rector Scholarships "had a revolutionary impact on the student population" and "sustained DePauw's continued growth while raising academic standards." Barney Kilgore received a Rector Scholarship; it may well have made the difference between his attending DePauw rather than Notre Dame.

And DePauw was beginning to loosen up. The Methodist-inspired ban on cardplaying was lifted after the Great War. The ban on social dancing was starting to fade, although "co-eds" needed written permission to attend school dances as late as 1935.

The transition to life at DePauw seems to have been smooth for Barney. By the second week, he was writing home that "college work does not seem very hard." He was already helping a sophomore in the Phi Gamma Delta fraternity house he had joined with the older student's trigonometry homework. Kilgore found the sophomore Spanish class into which he was placed too easy, and moved into junior Spanish. He played duets on the piano with the fraternity's house mother.

His own mother urged him not to work too hard, constantly sent him packages with food and candy, and received Barney's laundry by mail throughout his years at DePauw, washed it, and returned it to him the same way. His father, in contrast, constantly stressed diligence and even more frequently worried about finances. The Rector Scholarship did not cover room and board, which was $378 for the first semester, more than $4,000 today.

The resulting stress for Tecumseh was considerable. When, on November

15 of his freshman year, Barney had spent all of the eighty dollars (about $900 today) with which he had gone to school, his father refused him a further advance for the moment, even if it meant having to miss Thanksgiving at home. Tecumseh wrote, "I know it will be very inconvenient to be broke for I have had a lot of experience but you are still better off than I am because you have a place to sleep and three meals a day assured you while I have not."

A couple of weeks later, father pointed out to son that his spending was averaging seventy-eight and one-third cents per day, compared to an allowance of five dollars per week (or 71.4 cents). The older man was particularly displeased to see that the strict accountings on which he insisted revealed that "practically all your money is going for eats and dates. . . . The tall blonde from Iowa [that Barney had mentioned taking out a few times] must be some stepper[,] better get a brunette from Kentucky." Tecumseh did agree to buy and send his son a typewriter, but then quickly enjoined, "Buy ribbons for *it* instead of *her.*"

But not all of the lessons imparted were financial. Tecumseh Kilgore, whose love for his son shines through his stern lectures—and is always evidenced in how he treasured each word Barney sent home—also had things to say about the life of the mind. During Barney's second month at school, his father reminded him that

> *th[e] main thing is to train your mind in clear and straight thinking. The habits of thought you are forming now will stay with you as long as you live and will brand you either as a clear and careful thinker or as a careless and slovenly one. . . . It may be hard to decide as to the importance of some subjects but ther[e] is no doubt whatever that the most important is English because it is you[r] medium of exchange of ideas. You will get practically all your information through this medium and unless you live in a foreign country three fourths at least of the expression of your life will be through this medium.*

Nor were the exchanges between son and parents devoid of humor (at least from the son's side). More than once, when pleading for money, or the endorsement of a purchase, Barney addressed his letter "Dear Omnipotens." Frequently, throughout his life, he referred to his parents in the third person as "Hon. Pa" or "Hon. Ma."

Barney was an instant academic success at DePauw. A mix of B+'s and A's gave him the highest grades of any of the young men in his fraternity, and, he noted in a typewritten letter to his father, "I think my grades are the best in the Freshman class." In pen, he added, "In fact, I know so."

His first extracurricular interest was the debating team. He entered a school-wide competition as a freshman to join the team, and was one of twelve selected. Throughout his college years, he was a member of Mask & Gavel, the departmental club of the Public Speaking Department. The next year he tried out for the university's dramatic organization, Duzer Du, and continued to dabble in stage appearances during the rest of his time at DePauw.

This interest in public performance is particularly interesting given that Kilgore had a nervous twitch, apparently all of his life, which surfaced when he was under pressure. When the twitch struck, he would cock his head to the right, bob it quickly up and down two or three times, and repeat this sequence a couple of times at brief intervals. Neither Barney nor his father ever made reference to the twitch in their letters, but others remarked on it over the years, always linking it to moments of nervous tension.

In his sophomore year, Barney joined *The DePauw;* he had not worked on the newspaper in high school, so this was his first exposure to journalism. He sent copies of the newspaper along to his parents, noting that "I have been marking most of the stuff that I have written for no particular reason except to show that I am doing a little bit of something here this year." His father was encouraging: "We always enjoy the *DePauw* papers and then pass them on to the preacher and his family. We would like more of them."

Before long, Barney was also involved in the school yearbook, *The Mirage,* and his father was again worried that he was becoming overcommitted. Tecumseh sent his son a ruled sheet of paper and asked him to complete a very detailed account of his next two day's activities. Even when Barney's grades largely held up, his father always saw risks ahead. After the fall term of his son's sophomore year, Tecumseh wrote:

> *I got your grade card from the registrar the other day. The grades were very good but not quite so good as the last semester last year. They were just as you gave them to us four A's two B's and a D. The D is in Physical Education and I can guess that you go to the Gym just often enough to keep from flunking. You will leave the margin a little too close some time and will flunk.*

As sophomore year neared an end, Barney's extracurricular activities nevertheless accelerated. Debate remained his passion, but he also joined Sigma Delta Chi and was elected editor in chief of *The Mirage.* His interest in writing and publishing was clearly increasing, but it does not seem to have been terribly focused. He also submitted at least two short stories for magazine publication, neither successfully. He was on the staff of the *Yellow Crab,* a humor magazine published by Sigma Delta Chi. And he was named news editor of *The DePauw,* which he told his parents "is the third highest position on the paper staff."

At the same time, his grades were holding up, and he teased his father, who continued to frequently press him about money, about whether he would provide the sixteen-dollar initiation fee for Phi Beta Kappa if Barney was elected. Tecumseh hardly took the bait, noting, "You speak of Phi Beta Kappa. If you make it we will try to finance the deal but you have always said you would not make it on account of having so much outside work to do." But Barney continued to get A's in subjects ranging from science to French.

Barney had his first date at DePauw during his second week at school. The young woman was a fellow student from South Bend, and the date cost him twenty-five cents. He seems to have begun dating fellow student Margaret Rohwedder, a native of Davenport, Iowa, in the spring of sophomore year. Barney apparently liked her so much he went to church with her, something he otherwise seems to have done only when his parents came to visit. Margaret was sorority editor of *The Mirage* during Barney's editorship, and later society editor of *The DePauw* as he shifted his focus there. She was also elected May Queen at the end of their senior year.

The relationship with "the fair Margaret" lasted nearly five years, mostly at long distance, however. Barney spent the summers after his sophomore and senior years in Davenport, working for Margaret's father, O. F. Rohwedder, and his partner, George McClelland, at Mac-Roh Sales & Manufacturing Co., which billed itself as "Manufacturers and Distributers [*sic*] of the Rohwedder Bakery Bread Slicer." During his first summer he sold bread racks, but during the second the bread slicer was his focus. In fact, Otto Rohwedder was the inventor of the first mechanical bread slicer, the inventor, if you will, of sliced bread. Kilgore later wrote that he had been present, possibly during the summer of 1927, "when the first slicing machine was completed. It roared and clattered, but it did slice a loaf of bread."

For junior year at school, Barney obtained permission to have on campus and then acquired a Model T Ford he dubbed "Pandora." When it broke down and Barney lacked the funds to have it repaired, the car became the impetus for another money lecture from Tecumseh. This one, from a man whose letters never seemed to shout, was simple and direct: "DON'T SPEND YOUR MONEY TILL YOU GET IT AND THEN DON'T SPEND IT ALL."

In light of his many activities Barney cut his class load back to the minimum required fifteen hours, taking economics, political science, American history, French, and military science during the fall semester.

His military training in the Reserve Officer Training Corps was a continuing element of his DePauw experience, which required enrollment in ROTC; one of his first expenses as an arriving freshman had been for the rental of a military uniform. Kilgore spent the first half of the summer of 1928, after his junior year, at an ROTC camp in Kentucky. He graduated as a captain, between third and sixth in his military class, and was a member of the ROTC-linked Scabbard and Blade.

In April of junior year, with the help of Charles Robbins, his onetime roommate and most recent editor of *The DePauw,* Barney was selected to succeed Robbins as editor, the newspaper's top post. By the beginning of senior year, he seems to have gotten the rhythm of the three-times-per-week publication, and was expressing satisfaction and pride in his work on it in a letter he wrote to his parents on newspaper letterhead bearing his name in a place of prominence:

> The DePauw *is coming along better than it was going this time last year by quite considerable and it isn't nearly as much work for me as it was last year either. I have put you on the mailing list so you should get every issue of the paper. Please save them for me if you can because I'd like to keep a complete file and have them bound at the end of the year to show relatives and such.*

Tecumseh was overflowing in return: "You do not know how much we enjoy the DePauw. We read it every bit just as soon as we can get hold of it and Mother and I have some difficulty deciding who shall have it."

Barney's sister Martha joined him at DePauw as a freshman for his senior year. But by year's end, she was ill, with her pulse highly elevated, perhaps as a result of a heart condition or some sort of nervous collapse. Her father wrote Barney that "I am afraid her college work is over," although she did return to school for the spring term of 1930.

As his own time at DePauw neared an end, Barney's thoughts, of course, turned more toward the world outside. In early November of his senior year, he made his first trip east, to cover the Army-DePauw football game at West Point for his paper. (Army won, 38–12, with *The DePauw* story headlined "Tigers Score Twice on Powerful Army Eleven" as the subhead acknowledged, "Cadets Break Loose During Last Quarter." Rockne's "win one for the Gipper" speech came one week later at Yankee Stadium in New York City, as Kilgore's hometown team upset the same Army squad.)

Kilgore's role during the DePauw game at West Point was to take charge of the two young sons of DePauw president G. Bromley Oxnam, a leading pacifist and social reformer, during the trip by Pullman train car. Kilgore could then make his way back to Indiana by open rail ticket. He hoped to stop in New York City and Washington on the way, but no record of what must have been a memorable journey survives.

Increasingly, Kilgore seemed to think of journalism as a possible future. His salary of one hundred dollars (more than $1,100 today) for the spring semester from *The DePauw* probably encouraged him.

He also seemed to revel in his first controversy as a newspaper editor. On February 27, 1929, *The DePauw* published what Barney told his parents was "a rather rash student opinion." It attacked an evangelical preacher named E. Stanley Jones from India who had led one day's on-campus chapel service with what the writer called "the mysterious hocus-pocus of a second rate Billy Sunday," and also criticized President Oxnam for seeming to join in Jones's call for instant salvation. In the ensuing brouhaha, Kilgore noted, "Several professors . . . think that the student who wrote it and the editor of the paper should both be kicked out of school and they have told President Oxnam so. Oxnam just laughed about it and said that when he was in school he wrote articles that were stronger than that. He is all for more student expression even though he doesn't agree with it. So it seems that I will stay in school, although, I repeat, I wouldn't be here long if certain professors had anything to do with it." In fact, Oxnam told the paper he considered the flap "one of the most heartening signs I've seen since coming to DePauw" and that "I am very happy that there is one student in DePauw [the writer of the original commentary] who has ideas of his own and the courage to express them." It was a lesson about how to respond when a newspaper was under attack that Barney Kilgore would take to heart.

Kilgore also followed the progress of Charlie Robbins. While Kilgore was at ROTC camp, Robbins worked during the summer of 1928 at the Indianapolis *Star*. In February 1929, Robbins left for a job at DePauw alumnus Casey Hogate's *Wall Street Journal*. Not naming the paper, Barney put it this way to his parents: "Charles Robbins left for New York this week. He has what I would consider to be a good job at what I know to be a fair salary, considering."

Tecumseh and Barney had other plans, however. Edward Rector had now added graduate fellowships to the scholarships he had endowed, and both Kilgore men saw this as presenting an opportunity for Barney to attend Columbia University's Graduate School of Journalism.

But in May, Barney Kilgore, about to graduate Phi Beta Kappa, suffered a rare setback. He failed to secure one of the Rector Fellowships, and Columbia was now out of reach. Responding to a letter of sympathy from his father (one of the very few Tecumseh seems not to have retained), Barney wrote:

> *I really didn't expect to get one of the things very much—in fact not as much as several people around here expected me to. They did just about the usual thing and gave them . . . to deep students who no doubt are the best fitted for graduate work and who will become college professors and the like. Very fine. If you like that sort of a life.*

(More than a decade later, Barney wrote his father that "I've often thought . . . what a lucky break by not getting one of the Rector Fellowships in 1929 by which I could have gone to school for another year. That would have left me looking for a job just one year too late and maybe I would still be looking.")

With the end of college approaching, Barney immediately moved on to Plan B. He had written to Robbins's employer, *The Wall Street Journal,* asking about the possibility of employment, and had been told "they could find a place for me" in the fall of 1929, or after graduate school, sometime in 1930. Now, just a day or two after the fellowship rejection, he specified that he'd like to start in the fall. "So," he wrote his father, "that is settled."

> *It is a very fine opportunity to get into the best type of journalism and will be valuable experience if nothing more. The work pays better than the average, Robbins tells me, and is more pleasant than the general run of newspaper work. If I like it I will probably stay in newspaper work—if I don't there will still be time to go to law school a year later and at the usual age for entering law.*

With that, perhaps the greatest newspaper journalist of the twentieth century went off to his calling.

2

A Newspaper's Origins

ADDRESSING KILGORE AS EDITOR of *The DePauw,* Casey Hogate wrote that he couldn't "tell you just now about your probable duties but we will try to make it interesting for you. As to your starting salary, it will probably be some place around $40 a week." Hogate's job offer was firm, but fairly casual. He let Kilgore set his own starting date, and Barney wondered aloud through May and June 1929 whether it would be wiser to begin in September or October, before settling on an earlier date.

Kilgore considered his salary, which is nearly $24,000 today, "generous indeed."

> *Most of the Phi Gams [fraternity brothers] that have started to work in New York started at $25.00 per week—which of course isn't so much [just under $15,000 today]. $40.00 isn't a whole lot either, but if I have any luck at all there should be some raises. The other DePauw men there [at the* Journal*] have received them.*

By July, Charlie Robbins had been made the *Journal*'s bureau manager in Cincinnati, and Kilgore was further encouraged:

> *That certainly is a fine break for him because he [h]as a good job now. Of course he won't be in New York now when I go there, but I don't intend to stay in New York any longer than is necessary. I would*

like to do just what he has done, only of course I probably c[a]n't do it so fast.

Kilgore left his job selling Margaret's father's new bread-slicing machines and came to New York in the first days of September. He took a room at the new Phi Gamma Delta Club, on West 56th Street in Manhattan, just west of Sixth Avenue. The Club, which had opened in February 1928, contained about a hundred hotel rooms, a dining room, two lounges, a bar, a gym, and a library. Kilgore shared his room with another young man, a graduate of Yale working for the phone company and drawing $33 dollars a week. Kilgore took the top bunk, his roommate the bottom.

On Friday, September 6, 1929, Kilgore set off for work at the *Journal*'s office on Broad Street. He had breakfast first in the club dining room, paying twenty-five cents for orange juice and rice flakes. His subway ride on the local train took about a half hour and cost five cents. He left for work at about nine o'clock in the morning, and arrived at the *Journal*'s offices, walked up the half flight of stone steps from the street, past Uhl's drugstore in the lobby, and took the iron-cage elevator up to Casey Hogate's office. Hogate kept him waiting for instructions until nearly noon. But his adventure had begun.

Like many firms in that summer of 1929, the company Barney Kilgore joined seemed to be riding high. Like most American success stories of the time, its origins were modest.

The story of Dow Jones & Company actually begins with a man named John Kiernan, who got his own start, in the advertising business, at Albert Frank & Co. The Frank company dominated financial advertising (as well as advertising for insurance and marine services) in New York circa 1870. Kiernan, the junior ad man, saw an opportunity in the financial sector and split off from Frank to set up a financial news agency in the early 1870s.

New York's fledgling financial press quickly came to center on Kiernan, who churned through young journalists come to town to seek their fortunes. In 1880, Kiernan took on two more such young men, first Charles Dow and, soon after, Dow's friend Edward Jones. Both were New England boys: Dow was born on a farm in Sterling, Connecticut, where his father died when he was six years old; Jones was raised in Worcester, Massachusetts. Dow went to work early as a newspaper journalist, first at the *Daily Republican* in Springfield,

Massachusetts, under renowned editor Samuel Bowles, the man who advised reporters, "Put it all in the first line." Then, in 1875, Dow moved to Providence, Rhode Island, to work first at the *Press and Star,* then at the *Journal.* Jones enrolled at Brown University in Providence, as a member of the class of 1877, but dropped out to work at one newspaper after another in town, finally encountering Dow at the *Journal.*

The two men Kiernan hired had complementary skills. Dow was a natural creature of the market. Even as he pursued his work in publishing, he also became a partner in a brokerage firm, Goodbody, Glyn & Dow, and bought a seat on the New York Stock Exchange because his partner, Robert Goodbody, was an Irish citizen, and thus ineligible to own a seat. In short order he would become the leading market theorist of the nineteenth century. One colleague recalled Dow this way: "It would be less than just to say that I never saw him angry; I never saw him even excited." Jones, on the other hand, became a student of companies rather than markets, and was later described as "probably the first of the 'corporation analysts' in Wall Street."

Dow's ambitions soon left him feeling confined by the modest scope of the Kiernan News Agency, and he and Jones, in November 1882, set off on their own. They called the company they formed Dow, Jones & Company (only later would the comma between "Dow" and "Jones" be dropped). From the outset, they recruited a third partner as well, another Kiernan colleague, Charles Bergstresser, a college graduate (Lafayette, in his native Pennsylvania), who could supply some much-needed capital.

The new firm opened for business in the basement of 15 Wall Street—the same building in which the Kiernan Agency was housed—behind the soda fountain. Financial news bulletins were published by Dow, Jones on "flimsies" (multiple handmade carbon copies) and run around the Wall Street area to customers by messenger boys. The service averaged a cumulative 800 words per day at the outset; the charge was five dollars per month (nearly $1,200 per year in today's dollars). Dow was thirty-one years old, Jones twenty-six, Bergstresser just twenty-three. An early employee remembered them this way:

> *Dow was a tall, black bearded, slightly stooping man, with the grave air*
> *and the measured speech of a college professor. Jones was tall and ruddy,*
> *swift in his motions, high-strung as a race horse, tempestuous in temper and*
> *speech, with a mind quick as a lightning flash and a nose for "news" as keen*

as that of a thoroughbred bird dog. Bergstresser was of shorter build, but stocky, placid, imperturbable, with a thick brown beard, a photographic memory, a capacity for penetrating recesses where no other reporter could gain access, and an acquaintance with everyone of any importance in the entire financial district.

Dow and Bergstresser reported; Jones edited.

The volume of bulletins put out by the firm increased quickly. After a year in business, Dow, Jones began collecting each day's output in a printed summary sheet called the *Customer's Afternoon News Letter.* The charge for this service—"time-delayed" in today's parlance, as opposed to the "real-time" regular "flimsies"—was just $1.50 per month, about $350 annually in today's dollars; it was delivered free of additional charge, at day's end, as a supplementary reference tool to news service subscribers.

A young messenger much later recalled the office:

[There] was a small dark room (light on all day) without any attempt at painted walls or floor covering. On one side of the room a little space was walled off by a few plain pine boards and gave privacy of a sort to two desks, one for Mr. Dow and the other for an assistant. Mr. Jones' desk was at the far end. If Mr. Bergstresser had a desk I never knew where it was. The center of the room was taken up by copywriters. We boys—well, we were just there.

In 1884, Dow began publishing the first of his indexes of common stocks, a gauge of railroad stock performance. It was the forerunner of the Dow Jones Industrial Average, which he would launch in 1896. In 1885, the company brought to Wall Street the area's first printing press and installed it in new offices at 71 Broadway.

By 1889, Dow, Jones had grown to fifty employees—although most of these were employed as messengers for delivering the news bulletins to a growing customer base—and had relocated again, to 26 Broadway. On July 8, 1889, the *Customer's Afternoon News Letter* gave way to a full-fledged newspaper, four broadsheet pages in length, available in the early afternoon, and selling for two cents a copy. Bergstresser is said to have persuaded his partners to name it *The Wall Street Journal.*

The early *Wall Street Journal* of Dow, Jones, and Bergstresser is often portrayed as quaint and curious. But it was, not surprisingly, a product of its time.

The *Journal* began as an afternoon paper. Morning papers had been the norm through the 1870s, but by 1880, half the newspapers in the country were published in the afternoon. By 1890, just a year after the *Journal* first appeared, two-thirds of American newspapers were PM's.

The *Journal* ran front-page advertisements, but so, until 1892, did *The New York Times.* Dow, Jones had just one typewriter and one telephone in its offices as late as 1892, but the *Chicago Tribune* also had only one telephone at this time, and many metropolitan newspapers had not yet adopted the typewriter at all.

The *Journal's* first issue contained four unbroken vertical columns on each of the first three pages, and five such columns on the fourth page, which was largely devoted to market statistics. Not a single illustration marred the march of type.

On the front page, the left- and right-hand columns were devoted almost entirely to sixteen advertisements, most of them for bankers or brokers, but including one for Rand, McNally & Co. ("WE FURNISH MAPS"). The first words of the first news story in the second column drew on Dow's penchant for observing market movements and summarizing them in one of his indexes: Under the headline "Average Movement of Prices," it began, "The bull market of 1885 began July 2, with the average of 12 active stocks 61.40. The rise culminated May 18, 1887, with the same 12 stocks selling at 93.27. Prices gradually declined for about a year. . . ." It was a dry beginning for a dry presentation, and only slightly relieved by a couple of wire items elsewhere on the page reporting on a boxing match between John L. Sullivan and Jake Kilrain, the last bare-knuckle heavyweight title contest, which was held in a secret location that turned out to be Richburg, Mississippi, and ended with Sullivan victorious after seventy-five rounds.

On the third page the new publishers laid out their editorial approach. *"The Wall Street Journal,"* they began simply, "is another step in the development of our business." They knew what they intended it to be, and what they did not:

> *It will aim steadily at being a paper of news and not a paper of opinions. It will give a good deal of news not found in other publications, and will present in its market articles, its news, its tables and its advertisements a faithful picture of the rapidly shifting panorama of the Street.*

Distribution was envisioned, on a next-day basis, from Montreal to the north to Washington to the south, and as far west as Buffalo and Pittsburgh.

For news sources, the paper boasted of a "private wire to Boston" (to Clarence Barron's Boston News Bureau), "telegraphic connections" with Philadelphia, Chicago, and Washington, and correspondents around the country and in London.

The publishers had, they pointed out as well, a philosophy about their new business:

> *The fundamental principles in carrying on our news business are these:*
> *To get the news.*
> *To publish it instantly, whether bull or bear.*
> *No operator controls or can control our news. Any prominent man can say in our columns substantially what he pleases over his own name.*
> *We are proud of the confidence reposed in our work. We mean to make it better, and we mean to have the paper always honest, intelligent and unprejudiced.*

In 1892, ensconced now at 41 Broad Street, the partners were joined by Thomas Woodlock, who would eventually succeed Dow as editor, leave the paper, and later return to anchor its editorial pages. The company continued to expand, with the original news service remaining by far its largest business. In 1896, Dow launched the Dow Jones Industrial Average. The next year Dow, Jones began using electric news printers developed by Thomas Edison to deliver the news service; the first such Dow, Jones machines were bought from the Kiernan Agency when John Kiernan retired. In November 1898, with circulation of the *Journal* having reached 7,000 copies per day, the paper began printing a morning edition and circulation soon rose above 10,000 even as the cover price was raised to three cents. (The largest paper of the time, Joseph Pulitzer's New York *World,* had a circulation of 375,000 in 1892 and reached one million by 1897, but the *Journal* claimed to have twice the circulation "of any other financial newspaper in the United States." The paper had been positioned to be, in its own uncharacteristically immodest view of 1899, like the Dow, Jones news service, "in all things first, and in many things alone.")

The original partnership was drawing to a close, however. Jones, who was rumored to drink to excess and had grown estranged from his partners, left the company in early 1899 to join a stock brokerage. By 1902, after twenty years in business, Dow and Bergstresser decided to sell, and accepted an offer from their Boston (and Philadelphia) news supplier, Clarence Barron. The price: $212,000, or about $5 million today, although only $100,000 of this was paid in cash. Barron apparently got the money for the purchase from his wife, and the controlling interest in the company's shares became hers.

Dow remained on as editor and initiated an editorial column called "Review and Outlook," focusing mostly on the markets, but branching out also to opine on the 1902 coal strike; "Review & Outlook" remains the title under which *Journal* editorials are published today. But his health began to falter. Dow soon suffered what the *Journal* later called "a short illness following an attack of nervous prostration," and died in December 1902 at the age of fifty-one. The newspaper he had edited devoted its full front-page news space—the two middle columns of a black-bordered page—to his obituary. Its verdict: "his associates would to-day point to the work done in the name of the firm that he founded and say that, while others helped loyally and helped much, it was essentially 'Dow's creation' and 'Dow's work.'"

Now it was Clarence Barron's newspaper, and its future lay in his hands.

Clarence Walker Barron—often "C.W." to friends—was a contemporary of the founders of the company he bought, four years younger than Dow, one year older than Jones. He was born in Boston's North End, and grew up in its Charlestown neighborhood. His dreams of being a newspaper reporter began when he was fifteen years old. He soon went to work for *The Boston Daily News,* and then moved to the city's establishment paper of the time, *The Evening Transcript,* where he launched the financial coverage.

At the age of thirty-one, four years after the founding of Dow, Jones in New York, Barron took new lodgings as a boarder in the home of Jessie Waldron, a local widow four years his senior whose husband had died in 1882, leaving her the single mother of two daughters. In 1887, Barron began the Boston News Bureau, like Dow, Jones a local real-time financial news service, publishing bulletins of market news. Where Dow, Jones had waited a year to collect its bulletins in the *Customer's Afternoon News Letter,* Barron launched a newspaper under the same *Boston News Bureau* name two days later, as soon as he had material to compile. The Boston News Bureau almost immediately became the local affiliate of, and news provider for Dow, Jones. When *The Wall Street Journal* was founded two years later, its first issue noted the informal connection between the two organizations.

In 1896, Barron extended his publishing activities to Philadelphia, where he established the *Philadelphia Financial Journal.* In 1900, he extended his personal life, marrying his landlady of fourteen years. He was forty-five, five feet, five inches tall, and weighed 300 pounds, a man of enormous appetite; Jessie Waldron was forty-nine, and Barron soon adopted her daughters, Jane and Martha.

In 1902, as noted, Barron purchased Dow, Jones with Jessie's money. *The Wall Street Journal* soon picked up as its own the Boston News Bureau motto "The truth in its proper use," derived from a phrase of Emanuel Swedenborg, in whose Christian denomination Barron worshipped. Not only was the stock of the acquired company held in Mrs. Barron's name (a common tactic at the time, to avoid some of the perils of the bankruptcy courts), Jessie actually seemed to direct proceedings at Dow, Jones on Barron's behalf. For ten years after the purchase, it was she, not he, who attended company board meetings, she, not he, who named the editors.

The most important of the editors kept or put in place by Jessie Barron were Thomas Woodlock and William Peter Hamilton. Woodlock, Irish by birth and educated in London, arrived at the *Journal* in 1892 and led the news operation from 1899 until 1905, when he broke with Barron, returning as a columnist only after Barron's death many years later. Hamilton joined in 1899 to cover the stock market, and later developed the Dow Theory of stock market movements based on Dow's index work. Hamilton became the *Journal*'s "editor," that is, the leader of its editorial page (the *Journal* long used the title in this way), in 1909. The "Review and Outlook" column over which he presided continued to run on the newspaper's front page, where Dow had placed it, throughout Hamilton's life. Hamilton was later recalled by Woodlock as "a Scotchman who had lived mainly in England where as a clerk on the stock exchange and a very young man he had dabbled not a little in Liberal politics." It was Hamilton, remaining at his post until he died in December 1929, who set the course for *Journal* editorials, a course largely followed ever since. The page's lack of equivocation is his: "You can't write a fifty-fifty editorial," he once declared. "Don't believe the man who tells you there are two sides to every question. There is only one side to the truth." When the *Journal* editorial page refers to itself as "liberal" in the nineteenth-century sense of the word—as it often does—this is no coincidence, but part of its inheritance from William Peter Hamilton.

Things began to change on the business side of the paper, it seems, in 1906. In that year, Barron lured young widower Hugh Bancroft, a promising Boston attorney whose wife had died in childbirth, to Dow, Jones as the corporate secretary. By the next year, Bancroft had married Jessie's daughter Jane. In the financial market panic of that same 1907, Barron, always an avid speculator as well as energetic publisher, lost badly. He soon thereafter suffered some sort of physical collapse, likely a breakdown.

Hugh Bancroft gave up other business interests as business improved in 1908, and Jessie drew a record sum of $142,000 out of the company over the course of that year—roughly $3.1 million in today's dollars. But the fortunes of Dow, Jones and the *Journal* seemed to have peaked, and by 1911 Hugh Bancroft, who would periodically quarrel with Barron for the rest of the older man's life, left to head the Boston Port Authority. Barron, his health recovered from his 1907 collapse, and his fortune hanging in the balance, finally took control of Dow, Jones for himself.

By 1920, just about halfway in what would turn out to be his tenure at the head of Dow, Jones, Barron, Jessie, and the editors had managed to drive *Wall Street Journal* circulation from 7,000 in 1902 to 18,750, even as the cover price was gradually increased from three cents to seven. Barron was drawing $60,000 annually from the company in salary—nearly $600,000 in today's dollars—and another one-third as much in expenses. He was probably worth it. By the time Barron had completed his work, *The New York Times* would observe that, "to a large extent, he initiated the system of financial journalism in vogue today."

But the *Journal* and Dow, Jones were not Barron's only interests. He began to travel widely and to collect his impressions of people and places in at least four original books. He amassed a large collection of books and documents about the South Sea bubble of the early eighteenth century. And he kept up a furious pace. In addition to his financial market speculations, which Barron delighted in discussing, either orally or in writing, he launched a new weekly financial magazine in 1921. He modestly permitted his son-in-law to name it *Barron's*.

Throughout his fifteen years actively running Dow, Jones and the *Journal,* Barron seemed in perpetual motion. Edward Scharff notes that Barron

demanded personal service at all hours and for all manner of reasons. He was attended night and day by a team of two or three male secretaries. So long as he was awake and not otherwise engaged, Barron would dictate thoughts and questions to his secretaries in an unceasing staccato stream, and because of his obesity, Barron never slept more than a few hours a night. He would dictate over supper, in the barber's chair, or at stool. He would dictate from the bathtub, with his nose and navel forming twin peaks above the soapy water, and he would be dictating long after he had climbed into bed.

On his death, his secretaries estimated his lifetime output at two million words. Another secretary summed up his experience this way: "People worked for Mr. Barron—they didn't work with him." *Journal* columnist Vermont Royster later observed that Barron's "associates rarely knew from one day to the next whether he would be in Boston, New York or London."

Particularly after Jessie's death in 1918 (she left half the company to her daughter Jane, the other half in trust for her husband and then to be divided among her grandchildren), such a man as Barron needed a second, a protégé who could direct the enterprise during his absences and in his stead. Barron found such a person in Casey Hogate.

If Charles Dow and Edward Jones gave their company, and its newspaper, their start and their focus, and if C. W. Barron recast the enterprise as a family dynasty, it was Kenneth Craven Hogate who instilled a certain Midwestern cultural sensitivity at Dow Jones and *The Wall Street Journal*—as well as a soaring national ambition.

Hogate ("Casey" seems to have derived from his initials, K.C.) was a true child of the Midwest. He was a native of Danville, Indiana, a local newsboy for the Indianapolis *Star*, his father the editor and publisher of the weekly *Hendricks County Republican.* Casey graduated from nearby DePauw (Danville is just twenty-five miles from Greencastle), as did his wife.

Casey was Phi Beta Kappa and editor of the school paper, and made his way into journalism, first at the *Vincennes* (Ind.) *Sun,* then at the *Cleveland News Leader.* For years, he carried in his pocket a makeup rule once used in the print shop in Danville. He was fresh from having scored an exclusive interview with Henry Ford when Barron encountered him in 1921. Hogate was twenty-four years old and had already graduated from full-time reporter to copy editor at the Detroit *News.*

Barron hired Hogate away to work for the *Journal* in Detroit; he opened an office there and named Hogate to manage it. By the next year, Hogate was off to New York. At twenty-five, he had become the newspaper's managing editor; he was a vice president of Dow Jones and the *Journal*'s general manager before he was thirty.

Hogate and Barron were close despite—or perhaps because of—a great gulf in their temperaments. Maybe the only important thing they actually had in common, apart from a love of journalism, was a love of food; Hogate was nearly as rotund as Barron, already 280 pounds when he graduated from college, although, at six feet two inches, he was nine inches taller than his mentor. His weight led to his rejection from naval service in the Great War, after his early graduation from DePauw.

Hogate, Lloyd Wendt has written, was "patient, kindly, affable, slow in speech and slow to anger. He accepted the burdens of all who sought his help and uncomplainingly endured thoughtless slights and indignities from Barron since he was aware that Barron did love him." In 1928, on his thirty-first visit to Dr. John Kellogg's sanitarium in Battle Creek, Michigan, Barron's obesity finally overcame him and he died, at the age of seventy-three. Hogate, only eleven years older than Barney Kilgore, was already chief operating officer.

Forty years after it began publication, when Kilgore joined the newspaper, the aspirations of *The Wall Street Journal* were pretty much the same as those of Dow, Jones, and Bergstresser on the first day of its publication. So, unfortunately, was the newspaper's look and feel. Advertisements, in the last moment of giddy prosperity, had crept out to cover not just the right-and left-hand columns of the front page, but much of the rest of the lower half of the page as well. Twenty-four such ads ran on the fortieth anniversary of the *Journal*'s first issue (and nowhere, in the advertisements or elsewhere on the front page, was the anniversary noted). There were still no illustrations of any kind. Six columns of type marched up and down the page instead of four.

The world around the *Journal* and Dow Jones (Hogate would soon remove the comma between the two names) had changed, of course, and was about to change much more dramatically. The newspaper would ultimately have to change, too, if it was to survive. And the man who would end up changing it was due to arrive.

3

"Dear George"

Kilgore's first assignment at Dow Jones was to help monitor news tickers from the Dow Jones News Service, the news wire, and its chief competitor of the time, known within Dow Jones as "Tammany." This was the essence of the news wire business, and to some extent remains so today: In the stock market, where being first with a tidbit of information has significant economic value, the news wire services needed to keep score on when they had beaten the competition with a corporate earnings release or a new government statistic or some other market-moving event, when they had come second, and by how much. The results were used both for marketing purposes and as the bread and butter of internal controls, keeping score of how often Dow Jones won the race to publish. Today these reports are known as the "time-outs"; Kilgore's letters do not indicate what he called them.

But they do suggest that his role in the process was really by way of orientation. At the end of his first day at work, he wrote his parents:

There is another man who takes down the records, all I do is watch. My hours are just about anytime. The ticker [news wire] starts at eight and ends about four thirty but there is nobody around that long. At the end of these couple of weeks I will go on the copy desk which is where Charlie Robbins was, and Hogate told the city editor [Cyril Kissane, who ran the News Service, and had just been named the Journal's *next managing editor] to take care of me so that I would know enough to be sent out to a*

28

branch in six months and mentioned the difficulty they had in getting branch
managers. So far so good.

Most young men would have quickly complained of the boredom in this
role, but Kilgore made the most of the perch, and the time. He devoured the
material pumped out on the wires, learning an enormous amount about companies and the markets, and filled the hours reading books from the Dow Jones
library, and others he had sent from home, particularly books on economics.

On his second Saturday at work (Saturday was a half day for the stock market, and thus a workday at Dow Jones), Kilgore had his first encounter in more
than a week with Hogate and then remained behind when others departed
and took advantage of the leased wire to "chat" back and forth with Charlie
Robbins in Cincinnati. "It works just like a typewriter from either end," he explained to his parents, "and we had a great time."

Tecumseh had trained him well, and Barney watched his spending carefully,
taking care, now that he was living on his own and earning a decent salary, to
almost immediately begin to save money. He avoided restaurant tips by eating
in cafeterias, kept a daily record of expenses without having been asked to by
his father, and even took account of the need for a "sinking fund" for clothes.
He was still corresponding frequently with Margaret Rohwedder, but also beginning to date other girls. And he missed home, asking his parents to write
more frequently, something he had rarely if ever done while at college.

By his fifth week on the job, Kilgore had begun submitting small items,
known in company lingo of the day as "straws," for some of the *Journal*'s feature columns. The first one, his first original contribution to the newspaper,
ran in the second week of October and earned him an extra three dollars—
enough to pay for two days of food and transportation.

Meanwhile, the stock market had been slumping since Kilgore's arrival in
New York. Many of the reporters at the *Journal* actively played the market, but
Kilgore held off—in large measure, of course, because he had almost nothing
to play it with. On Sunday, October 20 he noted in a letter to his parents that

the stock market continues to go down tremendously. It appears as
though some other people were learning about it too, only it costs them more
than it is costing me. I don't propose to start tinkering with the market for a

good while yet—'tis an art all in itself that few seem to acquire. There are,
however, a couple of millionaires in the Journal *office who started there as*
office boys so I'm told. Not bad, not bad.

The eight days between that letter to his parents and the next can clearly be
seen to have marked Barney Kilgore's coming of age.

On Thursday, October 24, 1929, the stock market convulsed in a panic that
came to be known as Black Thursday. We do not know where Kilgore spent
the day, whether he left the *Journal*'s offices and walked the few steps to the
floor of the New York Stock Exchange. But he certainly saw the action on
Wall Street up close.

He had arrived in New York just fifty days earlier. He had not yet had an article published in his newspaper, and he was not yet a market expert. He confessed that "Dow Jones and Company, publishers of the *[J]ournal,* keep an
average based on 30 industrial stocks. Just exactly how it is calculated and
weighted I do not know as yet." But he had been paying very close attention,
and he saw things whole and clearly.

On Monday night, October 28, on the eve of what would come to be known
as Black Tuesday, the climactic day of the Great Crash, Barney Kilgore sat down
in his room in the Phi Gamma Delta Club and banged out a three-page singled-
spaced typewritten letter to his parents. It was, in large measure, the *Wall Street
Journal* article on the events in the market that he would have published if he
could have. He wrote it with a command of his subject, and a quiet confidence
in his own judgment, that seems particularly remarkable for a person of his station and experience.

One of the books he had absorbed from the Dow Jones library must surely
have been William Peter Hamilton's *Stock Market Barometer,* a series of essays
originally serialized in *Barron's* during its first year of publication, 1921.
Hamilton's thesis, following Charles Dow, was simple: "The market represents
everything everybody knows, hopes, believes, anticipates."

Inspired by Hamilton, Kilgore wrote:

I have . . . had the rather doubtful pleasure of seeing a lot of people lose
a lot of money, knowing full well that my resources, though meag[er],
were reasonably safe. That is, unless the Seaman's Bank goes busted,
which I don't think it will for a while yet at least.

Last Thursday was a real panic as far as the market was concerned and as far as several men in the office who had rather extensive holdings were concerned. There has been talk of closing the exchange, frantic talk at times, but nothing done about it and it wouldn't do any good anyway as far as I can see.

[T]he stock market has always been the most sensitive business barometer in the world, and the most reliable forecasting agent. If history repeats itself, business is due for an all-fired re[verbe]rating smash within the next six months. It has already affected the automobile trade, airplane business, and apparently some luxury lines. I have a feeling that my little forty dollars a week will be worth more before the year is over when it comes to buying anything.

If I were you I wouldn't take a note of anybody less than a bank president from now on— . . . it's going to be a long cold winter. . . .

You don't hear much about that, even around the Wall Street Journal, *and the reaction is "technical" and all that, but just the same, stocks don't come tumbling down without a reason, and their descent is usually well ahead of the reason.*

This may all be wrong, and President Hoover may be right, and Secretary Mellon may mean what he says which I doubt, but if things do get pretty well along toward Hades by spring, I'll say I told you so. Can't pick up a whole lot of information in two months, but if I were going to build a big factory just now, I wouldn't build it.

Put up a storm door to keep the wolf out and hang onto your shekels.

Some of his own colleagues, he soon noted, had lost everything, going from blithely driving Rolls-Royces to being unable to make the payments. "Everybody starts in again at scratch, it seems." As he had noted at the outset of the letter, Kilgore was "at scratch" anyway.

For all of his insight, Kilgore was still new to New York and its ways, a country boy in the big city. On November 9, a Saturday night, he was so delighted to have been invited to represent the *Journal* at a dinner marking the first meeting of the American Institute of Food Distribution at the Roosevelt Hotel that he sent the printed invitation back to his father in South Bend. He described it as a "six or seven dollar dinner," including "fruit cup (big one), nuts, olives and celery, soup, fish with mushrooms and shrimp, chicken peas and potatoes, fancy ice cream, salad, little cakes, rolls butter and demi tasse. All served in the utmost style of course."

He was particularly delighted because the previous day had been his birthday. But he wasn't drawing the connection for many people outside his family:

> *The possibility of my bragging about this birthday is limited considerably because no one around here knows how old I am and I don't think that it would do me any good at the office to break down and admit that I am now eligible to vote and all that. They might wonder what such a mere infant was doing around there.*

Kilgore was one of only two reporters at the dinner—the other represented the *New York Herald Tribune*—and he wrote up the dinner speeches of Farm Board member and former Nebraska governor Samuel McKelvie and R. W. Dunlap, an assistant secretary of agriculture, for the *Journal*. Eleven of the article's sixteen paragraphs consisted entirely of quotes from the two men's speeches, but, when it appeared on page 9 of the *Journal*'s edition of Tuesday, November 12, it was Barney Kilgore's first contribution of more than a "straw" to the *Journal*. Tecumseh proudly clipped the piece and kept it with Barney's invitation.

Just over two weeks later, on the day after Thanksgiving, Kilgore's fortunes took a much more momentous turn. He was told that Casey Hogate wanted to talk to him about the possibility of transferring to San Francisco. There was an opening on the staff there, and Hogate wanted to send someone from the New York office.

Hogate dreamed of a national financial newspaper. Today this may seem like an obvious concept—as so much of business, and nearly all of high finance, is conducted on a national if not a global basis. But the publishing landscape that Hogate surveyed was intensely local. Business itself was thought to be local, or regional at best. Independent stock exchanges dotted the nation. And in publishing, while the *Journal* was the leading financial paper in New York, Clarence Barron himself had built *The Boston News Bureau* and the *Philadelphia Financial Journal*. *The Wall Street Journal*'s principal, albeit fading, New York competitor, was the *Journal of Commerce*. An entirely separate paper, the *Chicago Journal of Commerce*, dominated financial publishing in Chicago.

As early as 1923, Hogate was writing that

> The Wall Street Journal *is in truth a national newspaper. It is as much interested in reporting crop conditions in the Northwest as in stock prices in New York; it is as much interested in general business in the South as in foreign exchange fluctuations; in fact, it is more interested in reporting business of most localities than are newspapers in that locality.*

But the reality was more prosaic. The *Journal* was printed only in New York, and largely circulated there as well. Hogate's first step toward this dream would be a Pacific Coast edition of the *Journal*.

With the economy and the markets seemingly booming, its appearance was set for the fall of 1929. The *Journal* announced the move on October 14. The Pacific Coast edition made its debut on October 21, the Monday before Black Thursday, and the night after Kilgore had written his parents that "[t]he stock market continues to go down tremendously."

The San Francisco post was just what Kilgore wanted, and it was coming faster than he had dreamed possible, even faster than Charlie Robbins's promotion to Cincinnati. While waiting to see Hogate, he wrote home that "if I do go it ought to be a better job than I have here, and perhaps more money. And being a new organization there ought to be a chance to work up to something good."

On Monday, December 2, Hogate and Kilgore finally had a chance to talk. The next morning Barney sent Tecumseh a telegram which began with the news: "AM GOING TO SAN FRANCISCO AS NEWS EDITOR MORE MONEY AND OPPORTUNITY I THINK LEAVE HERE FRIDAY." He had worked in the *Journal*'s New York offices for thirteen weeks.

Kilgore visited his parents on his way west, and was joined in South Bend by Margaret Rohwedder; she went with him as far as Chicago before he set out by train across the country. He arrived in San Francisco on Sunday, December 15, and went into the *Journal* offices on Bush Street to look around and write a letter home; his mother always worried when he traveled.

He was excited about his new post, calling it "exceedingly interesting. It looks like more of a real job than the work I did in New York." He was the *Journal*'s news editor in San Francisco, the number-two post in the four-man bureau, and was in charge of the copy desk for the Pacific Coast edition. His salary had been raised to $60 per week, or nearly $36,000 annually in today's dollars, and he almost immediately received a Christmas bonus of two week's pay at his new rate. His rent, at the Springer Hotel (now the Taylor) on Taylor Street was just $13 per week, and he could buy all of his week's meals for less than ten dollars. His money worries appeared to be at an end. He bought himself a Ford roadster and a Wurlitzer piano, paying for the latter at $5.50 each month.

His work sometimes began as early as eight o'clock in the morning, a difficult hour for a young man unaccustomed to early rising. He described the tasks with gusto, however:

> *I . . . sort out the copy that comes in by mail [from New York] and decide what is to be used and what kind of headlines are to be written. Then I start in on the stuff that is coming in all the time on the telegraph printer and try to get a paper out by six o'clock. It really is a lot of fun though. I have one fellow working for me all day and another one about half the day—both of them much older than I am but very agreeable and easy to get along with.*

Kilgore's boss was H. C. "Deac" Hendee, a veteran of the *Journal*'s Washington bureau and the Dow Jones News Service. Hendee, who was married and well settled in the Bay Area, showed Kilgore around the town and extended a warm welcome. It was Barney's first-ever Christmas away from home.

He took easily to the job, winning strong reviews from Hendee. The wires in the office hummed beginning at 5:30 A.M., an hour earlier during Daylight Savings Time, but Kilgore settled in to a routine of working from ten in the morning until seven at night. His work won favorable notice from Hogate on a visit west in February 1930. Kilgore thanked Hogate for the praise, and promptly asked for more money, his second raise in seven weeks. He got it— $70 per week, more than $42,000 annually today. If Hogate was offended, he did not show it. On the trip back east, stopping at DePauw, he told an acquaintance of Tecumseh's that Barney "is getting along swimmingly. If you have any more like him send them along."

Far from home, Kilgore was nevertheless increasingly surrounded by men who, like Hogate and himself, had DePauw in common. Robert Bottorff, who had served as sports editor, then associate editor, and "my right hand man" at *The DePauw* during Kilgore's year as editor, arrived in the spring of 1930. Kenneth Kramer, who had edited *The DePauw* two years before Kilgore, had preceded Kilgore to San Francisco and with whom Barney shared a room at the Springer, now left his job at a telephone company and joined Dow Jones as well. Hogate also sent word that he was hiring Kilgore's close friend and fraternity brother Ted Callis, former business manager of *The DePauw*.

His father's letters noticeably softened, and were filled with unabashed expressions of love and pride. And there is no question that Barney was having the time of his life. He played tennis himself, and watched Bill Tilden in a match; he rode horses in the park with Bottorff or took long drives on his free time, later frequently going boating with Hendee. He took finance courses at the University of California Extension Division.

In the summer of 1930, the *Journal*'s Pacific Coast edition seemed to be thriving, with advertising and circulation both growing nicely. Kilgore began writing movie and theater reviews, with the first a review of *Torch Song* at the Alcazar Theatre, appearing in June. The reviews were signed with the initials "B.K.," and Kilgore published at least twelve through April 1931. But the lighthearted atmosphere soon darkened. The market had peaked in the spring of 1930 (even Kilgore was fooled by the rally, and considered buying stocks), and it soon fell again, continuing down, almost relentlessly, for more than two years.

The depression that Kilgore had predicted on the eve of Black Tuesday began to take hold. His own rent was reduced in June 1931; Tecumseh wrote of a cut in their preacher's salary. Barney noted, in a letter home, that the American Trust Company in South Bend had "folded up"; his father's reply indicated that the local Union Trust Company had also collapsed following the suicide of the bank's president.

By August 1, Barney was worrying that the *Journal*'s Pacific Coast edition, never yet profitable, could be closed. He reassured himself and his parents with the thought that "even if it folded up I probably could go back to New York again."

The following spring, on a visit to San Francisco, Hogate indicated that Pacific Coast edition losses had begun to outweigh New York edition profits, which were "getting on [Hugh Bancroft's] nerves," and that active consideration had been given to shutting the paper. Instead, jobs were eliminated, as was Saturday publication of the Pacific Coast edition. The paper lived to fight another day, and Hogate repeated that Kilgore would have a job in New York in the worst case, but the younger man had become pessimistic about the Pacific Coast edition's prospects for succeeding.

Kilgore's own salary was cut, and he was no longer flush; he asked if his parents could afford to send him two hundred dollars. His salary would be cut twice more—the first cut had been by 10 percent, the second was 5 percent, then 10 percent again—bottoming out at about $54 per week in March 1932, although deflation meant his purchasing power was little changed. His parents, pressed as well, were not in a position to help him, and their correspondence flagged, not out of anger, but in a seeming familial hunkering down. Barney missed his sister's wedding to Stewart Lea of South Bend, in large part because he could not afford the trip. Barney may have snapped the family's dour mood when he bought his parents their first radio as a present for Christmas 1931.

Indeed, as the Depression deepened, Tecumseh took to telling Barney that he saw in its desperation an enormous opportunity for his son:

> *You got out into the world at a very fortunate time for your own benefit. You may not think so but you did just the same. You have practically nothing invested so you can lose nothing. Your wisdom will come from the other fellow[']s experience largely. . . .*
>
> *Some men will go through this depression and come out without much damage to their financial standing. Try to find out just what they did or did not do that made for their success. Many will come through the depression a complete wreck—try to find out just what they did or did not do that made the mess. If you can do this you will emerge from the crisis a wizard in your generation and it will not have cost you much to become one.*

Tecumseh took to repeating the point: "Don't forget. You are now seeing the biggest financial show the world ever put on. It is all for your benefit. If you don't get a lot out of it[,] it will be your own fault and just too bad."

Shortly before the first of these injunctions, Barney's four-plus years relationship with Margaret Rohwedder was coming to an end. The causes seem to have been the old clichés of time and distance. After his arrival in San Francisco, Barney had reported that Margaret was writing him nearly every day. She and Barney's mother were close, and corresponded separately; Tecumseh reported that Lavina considered Margaret "just about the cats whisker." Margaret was pursuing jobs in theater production and traveled for work from Michigan to Illinois to New York.

In a letter to his father in the fall of 1930, before hard times really set in, Barney wrote cryptically, "I have got to save money fast from now on if I am ever going to have a home of my own, which shouldn't be terrifically far away." Barney and Margaret saw each other during the summer of 1930 in Iowa, and again toward Christmas 1931 in San Francisco. But the last visit was not successful, with Margaret failing to get along either with the Hendees or the Bottorffs. Barney's weight had ballooned to 184 pounds, a gain of forty pounds in twenty-six months, more than filling out his five foot eleven inch frame, and his hair was "falling out in large batches," although then growing right back. In January 1932, Barney reported that "I fear that the fire has gone out. Which is all right with me." Just two weeks later Margaret announced her engagement to a man named Carl Steinhaur, a fellow native of Davenport. Perhaps it is a coincidence, perhaps not, but the weeks to come would be the most creative yet of Barney Kilgore's young career.

In February 1932, in his third year at the *Journal,* Barney Kilgore began a series of experiments with journalistic forms that would enable him to revolutionize journalistic content. Summary boxes, spotlighting key points in important articles, which Kilgore had pioneered in the *Journal*'s Pacific Coast edition, were picked up on the front page of the New York paper. Kilgore realized that the summaries were helpful not only to readers, but even to the reporters involved: "I get quite a bit of good out of writing some of those black boxes for stories, because it requires a bit of digging into the background of the thing."

His next, and much more significant vehicle, was a series of letters, headlined "Dear George" and identically addressed. They were signed "J.W.", and the origins of the choices of both "George" (in one column specified as "George Robertson") and "J.W." are lost. Readers seemed to be joining the correspondence in midstream; the first published letter opened with a reference to George's last missive to J.W. The letters began appearing in the *Journal*'s Pacific Coast edition on March 10, but starting on July 12, as Hogate had been promising since June, they were reprinted on the editorial page of the New York edition. An explanatory note, in italics, preceded each: *"This series of letters, in so far as persons mentioned therein are concerned, is fiction, of course. But the problems discussed are real."*

And the problems were real indeed. The subject of the first letter, and of many that followed, was the crushing deflation brought on by the Depression. Kilgore's language was both familiar and plain. He took a common concern and dealt with it squarely:

I can't see why you think the bankers and the Government are plotting an inflation campaign. All they are trying to do is to put a stop to this deflation that seems to gone out of all reason.

Did you ever stop to think what deflation is? It isn't a thing more than a bull market in money. . . .

Right now prices are low and dollars are high. And what that does to a lot of people is plenty.

Kilgore was delighted to see the letters used in the New York paper. He proudly noted that they were being reprinted even though already four months old: "It made me pretty cocky to think that they used it anyway. They took my headline and all—which I think is a good thing because when it comes to figuring out new kinds of headlines our New York office seems to be terrible."

To a considerable extent, the letters seem to have grown out of a remarkable exchange between Barney and Tecumseh, and out of the clear need to change the product in some way if the Pacific Coast edition was to survive. When Barney asked his father what he thought of the *Journal,* Tecumseh, in late February, replied with a long and thoughtful letter. Among his suggestions:

I would endeavor to have the first or the first two paragraphs of items . . . tell the story without figures if possible. Feed them the figures later. If they do not want to eat them they will still have a pretty good idea of what it is all about and how.

Barney well understood the necessity for this sort of innovation: "I believe that if we can just get a little something in every day that every subscriber can read and understand he will think that he is getting his money's worth." This was a call for a dramatic departure from the way in which financial journalism had long been practiced, and "Dear George" more than heeded the call.

"Dear George" was an extraordinary breath of fresh air in the musty precincts of financial journalism, and newspaper journalism generally. It immediately did two things differently: First, it used simple language—just contrast its "what that does to a lot of people is plenty" with the introductory note the editors of the *Journal* placed atop the column, "in so far as the persons mentioned therein."

Edward Scharff has written that George was addressed as "an uncomprehending friend, perhaps a son in his freshman year at college." But that misses the point, sells Kilgore short, and ignores the lesson of the three hundred letters received by the Pacific Coast edition seeking "Dear George" treatment of additional subjects. "George" was Barney Kilgore's peer, his friend. While dealing with complicated concepts such as deflation in a sophisticated manner, Kilgore's new column assumed that its readers were interested but not expert, eager to understand but currently confused, particularly as the economic order seemed to collapse around them. This second point would become the focus of all of Kilgore's work, and of most of his insights: Journalism was not about the writer, but the reader. As he put it in a letter home, "There are a lot of people apparently who don't know everything and are willing to learn."

And Kilgore didn't just offer his readers nostrums of supply and demand. He explained deflation and its effects in terms to which his readers could easily relate:

> *You wouldn't sell Radio [RCA] for $100 a share in 1929 because you were quite certain that it would reach $150 at least. [RCA stock had peaked at 114 in September 1929; its 1932 low point was below 3.] For the same reason the fellow who has the dollar that has gone from 100 to over 160 thinks it will go still higher. And he hangs onto it. That's what puts a stop to business.*

The first "Dear George" column ended with an invitation: "If you're interested we can talk this over more later. Write me again when you can find the time." Kilgore, it seems, suspected he was on to something.

His editors apparently agreed. The second "Dear George" letter to appear in the New York edition was dated on the forty-third anniversary of the *Journal*'s first edition, and published in New York the same week as the first. The forty-three-year-old newspaper's newest columnist was twenty-three years old.

In the second of what he called his "penny lectures" Kilgore tried to explain the relationship between bank deposits and the money supply:

> *When you deposit a dollar in the bank you make it possible for the country's banks, considered as a group, to assume safely, in normal times, a deposit liability of roughly ten times that much. They assume that additional deposit liability by extending loans. . . .*
>
> *But a dollar behind the mantel clock does no such thing. It is a dollar*

"in circulation," according to the weekly Federal Reserve reports, but that doesn't mean it is out passing from hand to hand doing useful work.

As the New York summer wore on, the letters to "George" ranged over the financial landscape, elucidating those weekly statements from the "Reserve" (not yet the "Fed"), explaining the impact of the Glass-Steagall Act, unpacking the accounting that caused companies to reduce their shares' par value, or charting relationships between companies' surplus and income accounts, tackling the Federal Reserve ratio in plain language. Kilgore's tutorials were straightforward, although somewhat abstract. Most of the statements were general, and there was almost no tie to the news of the day—in part because the pieces had been written four months earlier, and the topical references removed before they were republished.

But the columnist did show an occasional eye for aphorism: "The problem of inflation or deflation is not one of a condition but of a change in condition. . . . It is a change in the value of the dollar that wreaks havoc with the economic order." And he remained painfully aware that his readers did not live in a theoretical world. In discussing the subject of financial leverage "J.W." asked George to "suppose you and I have some money and want to go into the lumber business. That's not likely with conditions as they are, but supposing doesn't cost anything." The bottom line on leverage, and the last words of the letter on the subject, were clear: "When things go well they go very well, but when they are bad they are awful."

And at the time they were awful indeed. The scandals surrounding the excesses of the twenties had taken a toll on financial journalism as well as the markets. In April 1932, Congressman Fiorello La Guardia presented evidence at a Senate hearing that payoffs to Wall Street reporters to tout stocks had been a routine practice before—and even after—the Crash. La Guardia produced canceled checks to reporters at *The New York Times, Herald Tribune,* and *Post*—and two from *The Wall Street Journal,* Richard Edmondson and William Gomber. Up until the day before the hearing, Edmondson wrote the *Journal*'s "Abreast of the Market" column and Gomber its "Broad Street Gossip." The men's bylines disappeared from the paper, never to return, but the *Journal* said nothing about the matter, and Gomber, who had taken the money while working elsewhere, was still with the paper eight years later.

Kilgore was appalled, and for the first time in his career mused about leaving journalism:

> Well, such is life. If everything goes completely to pot I'll move back to Indiana and settle down on Uncle Sam's farm and raise enough corn and potatoes to live from year to year. No fooling, I expect to see a lot of people move back to farms. They can't pay the taxes on them at the present rates, but the taxes will come down or they just won't be collected.

But Kilgore soon picked himself up and, in his eighteenth "Dear George" column had occasion to make explicit what had only been implicit in his new approach to journalism. This column, published in the *Journal*'s New York edition on August 24, 1932, must be seen, three-quarters of a century later, as a quiet landmark, the first attempt at a declaration of new journalistic principles.

The column ostensibly addressed the stock market, but it ranged far beyond that. "J.W.," again reflecting the work of William Peter Hamilton, first took on a note he'd received from George:

> You say you are not interested in the stock market. The answer to that is that you probably are. I hear you muttering that you don't own any stock any more and don't intend to for a long while. That hasn't anything to do with it. There are other things of interest in the stock market besides quotations on shares that you might happen to own. . . .
> The stock market, in its important swings or "major movements" is one of the most valuable, accurate, cold-blooded barometers of modern business that has ever been discovered. Its record, traced back over a long period of time, is amazingly free from error.

Kilgore here was making a number of points. In the most narrow sense, he was making anew the case for the value of stock indexes, such as Dow Jones's own averages, which had been Charles Dow's greatest contribution, and had provided one of the foundations on which the company that employed him had been built.

More broadly, he was making a connection that few before him had made, and that his own newspaper had not yet fully grasped: the insight that finance and the financial markets were inextricably tied to the much wider world of business. Now he summed this up for "George," declaring that the stock market is "a place where all knowledge about everything that has the slightest thing to do with business and trade is brought to bear eventually upon the price of securities representing equities in that business and trade." Echoing the prescient letter he had written his parents on the eve of Black Tuesday, some thirty months earlier, he pointed out that the lesson had been learned relatively recently—and quite painfully:

> *Do you remember how many people said "business is sound" during the last few months of 1929 and early 1930? So it was, as far as many ordinary indications were concerned. But the stock market was saying that there were some hard winters ahead, and the stock market, as usual, was right.*

But Kilgore did not stop there. Not only was it imperative to look beyond finance to business generally, it was also essential to adopt the reader's perspective on what truly mattered in business. In a word, the explication of Federal Reserve money supply reports was not enough. "Statistics of trade and business are useful, of course. But they are more on the order of 'thermometers' rather than 'barometers.' They tell us of the present, but they are distinctly silent about the future." Stock indexes, as measures of the market—itself a leading indicator—"may be of considerable service."

Why does this matter? It was here that Kilgore had his critical insight. He pushed "George" on the point;

> *What business is going to be six months or a year from now is of considerable importance to you, isn't it? As a matter of fact* you'd rather have some good indication of the future than to be fully and statistically informed as to the present and recent state of affairs, *wouldn't you?* (emphasis added)

It was a rhetorical question. Kilgore had realized that readers, even readers of a daily newspaper, came to it more interested in insights into tomorrow than in news of yesterday.

The August 24, 1932, column probably did not strike Kilgore as the epiphany that it seems, in retrospect, to the modern eye. He likely saw it, instead, as one marker of his growing understanding of his craft. In any event, he turned back from its more personal tone, and implicit reflections on journalism and readers' interests to the day-to-day tutelage of "Dear George." Next up were five successive columns on the gold standard and one on foreign exchange.

There is no question that he was striking a chord. In early September, he told his father that the letters gave him "a little better standing with the paper." Hogate told another friend of Tecumseh's that Kilgore was "the best young man *The Wall Street Journal* had ever gotten." Kilgore soon received a letter from Hogate directly asking whether he would be interested in returning to New York to write a "daily column of financial news interpretation." Kilgore, delighted, immediately replied that he would be "more than willing." The opportunity would be huge, and he expected some additional money as well, if only to offset the higher cost of living in New York. Even in San Francisco, financial pressure had led him to freelancing for the *California Banker* magazine to earn more ("I wouldn't let them use my name on it because there was nothing really original in it"), and he was also exploring the possibility of radio commentary under the sponsorship of a local brokerage firm.

On October 20, with a missive on the French currency, the "Dear George" column, while continuing to be signed "J.W.," was bylined "By Bernard Kilgore." It was his first byline at the *Journal,* and the column no longer noted that it was reprinted from the Pacific Coast edition. Barney Kilgore had been promoted to the major leagues.

A few days later—two weeks before the election in which voters would choose between President Herbert Hoover and Governor Franklin Roosevelt—the *Journal* began running a six-part series by Kilgore "dealing with certain fundamentals of money and credit that have a direct bearing on the meaning and problems of deflation and inflation." Each of the pieces ran on the *Journal*'s front page, and they were not only bylined, but also bore a copyright notice, evidence of the value seen in them by Hogate and his colleagues. They had been written during the second half of September, and Kilgore considered them "more carefully worked out than the Dear George letters." He was thrilled with their placement.

The series was an attempt to build on "Dear George" by tying its somewhat abstract tutorials more closely to the news. In the first article, Kilgore summed up the country's economic plight: "For the past few years we have had a bear market in commodities, in securities, in labor. We have had a bull market in money, and money, under our present monetary scheme, is gold. Deflation, we can therefore say, is simply an excessive rise in the dollar's worth." Moreover, he indicated one of the factors that had brought things to this pass: "Some day someone ought to write a book entitled 'The Perils of Prosperity.' The subject of that book would be debt."

Kilgore, a political science major at DePauw who took only one college course in economics, nevertheless displayed an extraordinary sophistication about economic matters, both for his time and for his age. With respect to his time, it is important to understand that "Dear George" came "before there was any macroeconomics," that is, well before John Maynard Keynes's 1936 publication of *The General Theory of Employment, Interest, and Money*. And, as already noted, Kilgore was twenty-three at the time of "Dear George." Where, in such a period, did such a young man come by his economic insights?

It is hard to answer this question with certainty, but Kilgore did leave a string of hints in his own work. The hints point in one direction, that of the only economist Kilgore mentioned regularly during this period, Irving Fisher.

Irving Fisher is little remembered today, a name recognized only by students of the history of economics, and even then not universally. But in 1932, and throughout a life that ended in 1947, he was probably the best-known economist in the United States.

A graduate student and then professor at Yale, Fisher's 1891 dissertation, *Mathematical Investigations in the Theory of Value and Prices*, was later described by Joseph Schumpeter as "one of the greatest performances of nascent economics" and by Paul Samuelson as "the greatest doctoral dissertation in economics ever written." His biographer notes that Fisher was "the first American to come to economics from mathematics, and he was also the first American to use mathematics in economics." Fisher served as president of the more traditional American Economics Association in 1918, but also went on, in 1930, to be the founding president of the Econometric Society. Along the way, he explicated the utility theory of value, and "created the national accounting systems of the United States and other countries."

Fisher also rescued and refurbished the theory in monetary economics that goes back to the sixteenth century. He dressed up the quantity theory of money, put it in modern form, made it more rigorous, all the while improving it. Every economics textbook today employs the Fisher monetary equation. He named it the equation of exchange, relating money supply and its rate of turnover to prices and production.

Much of Fisher's pioneering came in the development and application of indexes. From the beginning of 1923 and thereafter, both *The Wall Street Journal* and *The New York Times* published Fisher's proprietary index of commodity prices each week.

A member, along with Frank William Taussig of Harvard and John Bates Clark of Columbia, of "the triumvirate who established modern economics in America," Fisher was ranked above them by contemporaries. By 1912 *The Wall Street Journal* called him "one of the most distinguished economists in this country, if not in the world." His 1930 book, *The Theory of Interest,* with its theory of interest and capital, "came close to providing a theory and model of the economy as a whole, a macroeconomic analysis before there was macroeconomics." Samuelson terms it a "classic." Schumpeter, who died in 1950, believed him "the greatest economist that America has produced." In an important sense, Fisher was "the first of the modern 'monetarists,' " the intellectual ancestor of such economists as Milton Friedman. But Fisher had no interest in fiscal policy, and was thus left behind by the revolution Keynes brought to economics, and to government economic policies.

Modern histories, if they mention Fisher at all, usually do so only ironically, and particularly to note Fisher's speech in Washington the evening before Black Thursday, the first great wave of the Crash of 1929, in which he answered the question "Is the Stock Market Too High?" in the negative.

But Kilgore was not distracted by this, nor by Fisher's quirky advocacy of causes far beyond economics, ranging from nutrition and fitness to Prohibition to eugenics. In October 1932, a "Dear George" column dwelt on the quantity theory of money, linking the money supply to prices levels, and noted, "I don't pretend to be original in this matter. A great many real honest-to-goodness economists have discussed the matter at great length—notable among them, Professor Irving Fisher."

Kilgore did not accept all of Fisher's prescriptions. In late 1932, he used another "Dear George" column to discuss, and ultimately reject, Fisher's scheme for a dollar tied not to gold but to a basket of commodities that Fisher believed would stabilize the currency. But while disagreeing with Fisher's recommendation, Kilgore implicitly accepted Fisher's most important point—that stability of the currency, and thus the money supply, was essential to the health of the economy. And he indicated a very substantial respect for Fisher overall:

> *Professor Fisher is not the inventor of index numbers, but he probably did more than any other individual to make the country "index number conscious." He has given a lot of people their first inkling that the* number *of dollars in the pay envelope was not so important as* what those dollars would buy. *He has shown definitely that the dollar can sometimes look like 50 cents or like 150 cents in comparison with its former self.* (emphasis in original)

Nor was Kilgore's awareness of Fisher's work apparently limited to the latter's work on indexes, or even one or two additional theories. An April 1933 column reference by Kilgore to "some of the textbooks on economics" suggests that he may have been familiar with Fisher's 1912 text, *Elementary Principles of Economics.* And this despite the fact that Taussig and others thought Fisher's book "too difficult for beginning students, and used [it] only with their intermediate and advanced students."

It is easy to see why Kilgore would have found Fisher not only intellectually compelling, but also temperamentally compatible. Like Kilgore, Fisher's "optimism and wishful thinking sometimes clouded his understanding of business conditions." Moreover, this was not confined to the moment of the Crash. Kilgore saw recovery always just around the corner in 1932, for instance, just as Fisher, even after his embarrassment at the time of the Crash, in early 1930 had lectured that "when stockholders realize that business is going along all right we should have a resumption of the bull market."

More important, like Kilgore in journalism, Fisher in economics was a man of short attention span, given to bursts of blinding creativity, but not to great statements of integrating worldview or synthesis. Indeed, Fisher is little remembered today, not necessarily because he was Keynes's intellectual inferior, but perhaps because he failed to follow through on his own work. Schumpeter's verdict was that Fisher had constructed the "pillars and arches of a temple that was never built."

The first article in Kilgore's money and credit series ended with a note that the second would "appear in an early issue" of the *Journal,* possibly because its editing for the New York edition had not been completed. In fact, it was published two days later. Subsequent installments in the series dealt with details of money supply and demand, including, importantly, the velocity of financial transactions. In 1929, Kilgore pointed out, money had changed hands with enormous speed; now, in the throes of Depression, it had become sluggish. "Probably the most important influence" was simply fear: "Depression, once initiated, is self-propagating. Apprehension of trouble often helps in bringing it about."

But the author was an optimist—it was a trait that seemed inveterate with him, and he would return to it constantly in his otherwise clearheaded columns. He acknowledged that the passage from mid-1931 to mid-1932 "so far as the banking structure of the country is concerned . . . was a thirteen-month period of trouble with a capital 'T.'" But the worst, he speculated, had passed. Inflation, and recovery, might be just around the corner.

Yet the series concluded on the Saturday before Election Day—without once having made reference to the election itself, or the candidates—on an un-characteristically uncertain note. The last paragraph began, "What will really happen? Nobody knows. During the next few months the credit situation—the value of the dollar—the supply of money—the basic money-credit equation—will take on a new significance." Had Kilgore been less intent on his own optimism, he might have seen in this painful uncertainty the roots of the banking crisis that would soon sweep the country, and threaten the collapse of the nation's financial system.

The New York edition of the *Journal* continued to publish the "Dear George" columns for the remainder of 1932. But just before Christmas 1932, with no warning or indication to readers, and after fifty-three appearances, "Dear George" ended its run. For Kilgore, a new chapter was beginning.

With a gap between them of less than four weeks, the new year of 1933 would see him launch another new column—this time originating in the *Journal*'s main edition, not as a reprint of a regional offering. It would be another experiment, another quick step down the path he was blazing.

4

COVERING THE GREAT DEPRESSION

O VER THE NEXT EIGHT years, roughly coinciding with Franklin Roosevelt's momentous first two terms as president of the United States, Barney Kilgore established himself as perhaps the nation's leading financial journalist. He continued to innovate in the columns of his own newspaper and planted the seeds of still more innovation to come.

His written output at the height of the Great Depression indelibly stamped both his own later business career and the future of *The Wall Street Journal*. A close look at this body of work, outlined in this and the next two chapters, and never collected in book form, reflects a clearheaded, realistic, contemporary assessment of a period in our history still subject to endless debate; for that alone it would be worth detailed examination. A close look reveals a portrait of a great reporter and columnist finding and then exercising his own voice, but also the making of a consummate editor and publisher.

The column that would bring Kilgore back to New York was Casey Hogate's idea. He first posed the possibility to Kilgore in a letter received in San Francisco in mid-September 1932. But the two men's minds, as would so often be the case, were running together. Hogate now wanted a column "of financial news interpretation." Kilgore had, just ten days earlier, written his father about a book he was thinking about writing, to be called *Reading the News*

About Money. The new column would be launched with the unwieldy name "Reading the News of the Day."

Kilgore almost immediately crafted a few sample columns and dispatched them to Hogate. Hogate thought they missed the mark and suggested a somewhat different approach, which Kilgore tried to take in a second set of samples. These Hogate liked, and a third set of samples was ordered up. By early November, Kilgore and bureau manager Hendee had been instructed by Hogate to begin arranging the younger man's transition out of the San Francisco bureau; by mid-November the move was set, and Kilgore wrote to his parents that he would be home for Christmas en route to New York. He sold his Ford for $100 and was on his way.

In New York, Kilgore took up residence again at the Phi Gamma Delta Club, although he soon moved to an apartment in the Palm, a residential hotel on Pierrepont Street in Brooklyn Heights. One of his two roommates was Buren McCormack, a member of the DePauw gang at Dow Jones. His new salary, which had been uncertain until his arrival in New York (Hogate had initially mentioned $70 per week, which was what Kilgore had been making before salary cuts began in 1931), was set at $85 per week, more by far than he had ever earned before, and about $66,000 annually in today's dollars. In fact, as the Depression continued to deepen, Barney was now called upon to send money to his struggling father, and did so in January 1933, and again in July.

The "Reading the News of the Day" column made its debut on January 17, 1933. Like "Dear George," it ran in the morning paper on page 8, the *Journal*'s editorial page. It bore Kilgore's byline, and was anchored at the top of the page, in the middle two columns.

It picked up where the 1932 series on money had left off, spinning out general lessons for readers on business, finance, and economics, but tying them closely to the news. But the new column brought two more elements to Kilgore's work: First, it conveyed much greater immediacy—it was, quite self-consciously, not just "Reading the News" but "Reading the *News of the Day*." Next, it also made more extensive use of reportorial skills. To make this scope possible, the column ran even longer than "Dear George," often ranging upward of 1,400 words. Keyed to daily announcements, "Reading the News" was quickly ramped up to appear in the *Journal* Tuesdays through Saturdays (the Monday paper would have had little news on which to draw), although even Kilgore was occasionally compelled to skip a Tuesday or Wednesday issue.

Just as "Dear George" had seemed to begin in the middle of a stream of correspondence, "Reading the News of the Day" began without introduction or fanfare of any kind. Neither Kilgore nor his editors sought directly to explain to readers what this new vehicle was about. Instead, they would let the column speak for itself. The first column began as matter-of-factly as possible: "Production in Germany, as reflected in the Statistical Office's Index, is running counter to the 1931 trend." Many columns dealt with a single subject, but most covered three, four, or more separate subjects, each squared away in a tight essay that sought to draw larger lessons from particular events. In that first column other subjects included domestic farm equipment sales, proposals for a moratorium on mortgage payments in the Midwest, and cotton prices and sales.

In a sense, Kilgore was creating a column whose subject was what we would now call macroeconomics, but the grist for which was microeconomic vignettes; it was a column that would comment on policy options, but would do so always in the context of facts on the ground. Thus, in the first column, news of lower cotton prices was quickly followed with the fruits of seemingly effortless (but, in fact in 1933, painstaking) research: basic facts about cotton production, the growing season, and consumption and export figures. But Kilgore did not stop there. "King Cotton," he noted,

> *rules ten southern states. The dependence of his domain on foreign markets to such a large extent is one of the best arguments that can be put forth against the talk of an "isolation" policy. . . .*
>
> *Hence the southerner had better think twice before he takes up the cry, "Buy American!" The northerner who expects to do business in the South might spend some time looking into the situation, too.*

The integration of these concerns in a single newspaper narrative was as novel as it was breathtaking, and the range of subjects marked Kilgore as a virtuoso. Hogate recognized the value of his new star columnist almost at once. After three weeks of "Reading the News" columns, the twenty-four-year-old Kilgore was given his own weekly radio program, a broadcast of "Economic Highlights" each Monday evening at 8:15. P.M. on Coytesville, New Jersey, radio station, WRNY, which shared frequency 1010 AM in New York City with Loew's WHN. The *Journal* ran display advertisements nearly every day promoting the show. Kilgore found the broadcasting work "fun, but putting the material together is the real job." The radio station, he noted, "want something as cheerful as possible" and were billing the program as devoted to "Business Recovery or something optimistic like that."

By April, he was making guest appearances on the NBC Red Network, and WHN had picked up the local show. His parents heard the national broadcast, and Tecumseh opined that Barney had "good Radio Delivery and a good Radio speaking voice. Mother was all thrilled to hear you."

By the column's second week, as it coincided with what would turn out to be the darkest moment of the Great Depression, Kilgore was vividly charting the nation's emerging banking crisis, noting that a report from the Reconstruction Finance Corporation showed the country's commercial banks requiring an average of $850,000 in net emergency financial aid each day in December 1932. Marking a year since an optimistic statement from Hoover on signing the act creating the RFC, Kilgore wrote:

> *A considerable quantity of water has gone over the dam since that time, and so have a good many banks, an insurance company or two, and a number of other important business enterprises including some railroads.*

Yet Kilgore's column would not surrender its optimism. Kilgore would, it sometimes seemed, seize on any straw in the wind to speculate that economic clouds might be lifting. One day it was a prediction by a previously successful speculator in railroad stocks, another an uptick in railroads' operating income, yet another General Motors' decision not to cut its dividend, then some modest rises in commodity prices.

Privately, Kilgore saw a darker picture. His father had warned him in early February that "I am looking for some kind of assault on our money system before long but do not know just what the nature of it will be." By the end of the month, as the Hoover administration entered its last days, Barney was expressing fears that "the banking situation in this country has now gotten completely out of control." But he acknowledged that "I haven't been able to write what I really think about some of these things. It's too much like playing around with nitroglycerine."

Even more than he had in "Dear George," Kilgore sprinkled history and basic factual background throughout his journalism—a daily story on the gold standard might note that Great Britain adopted it in 1816, for instance, while a piece on tire prices would note the state of industry concentration and the geographic distribution, within the country, of oil production and gasoline consumption. Auto industry sales were not just down, they were the lowest since 1915 for cars, since 1918 for trucks. When a bank holiday was declared in Michigan, Kilgore's readers were reminded not only that Nevada had taken a similar step the previous year, but that bank holidays had helped stem the Panic of 1907. The report of the Timber Conservation Board called forth the fact that 80 percent of all U.S. residences were made of wood, and that construction accounted for half of all timber orders. A column item on leather sales and leather company stocks described ancient Egyptian tanning practices and the use of leather as a money by the Greeks and Romans.

As usual, his father remained his most devoted reader, and his toughest critic. He was pasting every column in a scrapbook, but was not blinded by pride or loyalty. To his son, Tecumseh wrote of the first six weeks of "Reading the News" columns, "I think some of them fine, some pretty good and some pretty punk. The ones I do not like are the ones that seem to be nothing more than a restatement of the news item."

Urged on, Kilgore indulged his penchants for aphorism, pointed summary, and humor:

On bimetallism: *A silver dollar buys as much as a paper dollar, and for exactly the same reason—the government stands ready to redeem both in gold.*

On the history of sugar prices: *on July 28, 1914, somebody shot the Archduke Franz Ferdinand, heir to the Austrian throne, and it wasn't long until a lot of European beet sugar fields were used for other purposes.*

On industrial production: *If United States Steel Corp.'s gigantic organization were operating at capacity today it would be turning out more steel than Germany, France and Great Britain combined are now producing.*

On RFC loans: *They were in the nature of a bridge started across a chasm, when the other side was not in sight.*

On British trade practice: *John Bull became an international merchant because he had to. His homeland is small in area and none too fertile, but he has plenty of coal which can be converted into power for manufacturing.*

On the money supply: *The amount of money in circulation in the country is determined, not by the government or by the banks but by the people as a whole.*

On purchasing power: *The number of dollars in anybody's pay envelope is not the most important thing—the real point is what those dollars will buy.*

On dairy production: *The output per cow has fallen 5% below a year ago and the proportion of cows being milked now is smaller than a year ago.*
Apparently both the cows and the farmers have been discouraged somewhat by low prices for dairy products.

On the failure of agricultural tariffs: *The history of "helping the farmer" in the last few years has been a process of trial and error, with some pretty good-sized errors.*

On the American role at the international monetary conference in London: *Uncle Sam's position might now be compared with that of a man who ran into a telephone pole and wrecked his automobile on the way to a conference at which the removal of telephone poles from the highway was to be discussed.*

But Kilgore did not let his capacity for phrasemaking blind him to the confusing troubles surrounding his readers. The clarity of his thinking largely matched that of his prose. As the banking crisis deepened in February 1933, he wrote:

> *The biggest savings bank in the country limits new deposits and in five days turns down half a million dollars offered it. Boston banks shy away from new funds tendered by the U.S. Postal Savings system. Does that sound like depression? Yes, unfortunately—and, paradoxically—it does.*

The banks, Kilgore noted, couldn't reliably find investments that would return the interest they would be required to pay on new deposits. Similarly, J. C. Penney could find no better use for cash than retiring preferred stock. Kilgore could applaud General Motors for paying a dividend, but did not ignore the fact that 850,000 more cars were junked than purchased from manufacturers in 1931, with the number likely rising to two million in 1932. And he acknowledged that "the building industry, which once ranked second only to agriculture as far as the number of men and dollars employed was concerned, is practically flat on its back, with most of its workers unemployed."

His understanding of what was happening out in the country, beyond Wall Street, was no doubt enhanced by reports from home. His father reported on the failure of nearly all of the banks in South Bend beginning in mid-February. His birthday, he wrote, had been pleasant, despite the fact that the bank had closed the day before "with all my worldly possessions tied up except the few dollars I had in my pocket." He was reassured only because he owed the bank more than it owed him: "It is somewhat like a big dog having an inch of a little dog's tail in his mouth while the little dog has six inches of the big dog's tail in his mouth."

Barney wrote of taking money out of the bank and perhaps investing it in British pounds sterling. Tecumseh didn't favor that option, but did, just two days before Hoover was to leave office, write that "I would get some of my money out of the banks and keep it where I could get hold of it right away any how for your own safety as well as ours."

The younger Kilgore was conservative, hardly a New Dealer. His background dictated as much, and the *Journal,* where he felt very much at home, was staunchly Republican. But he quickly acknowledged the difference in tone that came over the country almost immediately after Franklin Roosevelt assumed the presidency. In his column of March 7, his first after Roosevelt's inaugural declaration that "the only thing we have to fear—is fear itself," Kilgore wrote that " 'Credit' is just another word for 'confidence.' "

He supported Roosevelt's drastic remedies of a national bank holiday and suspension of the gold standard;

> *It is easy enough to point out what should have been done months ago. But it wasn't done. Now it has come to the place where the country has to choose whether it will have a banking system or whether it won't. An answer in the affirmative involves unpleasant possibilities—but much less unpleasant than a negative reply.*

And he explained to readers why the bank holiday had, in the short term only accelerated the deflation it was, in the long term, intended to help curb:

Look at the money supply of the United States. It normally consists of bank deposits, now around 43 billion dollars, and currency, now outstanding to the extent of somewhat over seven billion. But what has happened to it now? For all practical purposes, the bank deposits are effectively tied up and the country is trying to do business on that portion of the seven billion dollars in currency that is outside the commercial banks.

In other words, the money supply is not 50 billion dollars, but less than seven billion. Naturally, this cannot last. However, as long as such a condition exists there is deflation on a grand scale. It is already seen in drastic temporary salary and wage cuts, which in turn mean reduced purchasing power, which in turn mean sharply reduced business activity and lower prices. People can't pay for things at a normal level with only one-seventh or less their normal money supply.

Nor was this simply an academic observation. On Wednesday, March 8, Dow Jones failed to make payroll, giving each employee just five dollars. Another fifteen dollars followed on Saturday the eleventh, although Kilgore expected regular payments to resume the following week.

When the bank holiday ended with congressional passage of emergency banking legislation, Kilgore acknowledged that it "must be taken as a manifestation of nothing less than implicit faith in President Roosevelt." With Roosevelt's first "fireside chat" a few days later, Kilgore marveled at

how big (or how small?) is a nation when its Chief Executive can sit down in a room at the White House and, without raising his voice above an ordinary conversational tone, speak frankly and convincingly to an audience composed of nearly half of his fellow countrymen?

FDR, he declared, had "struck a telling blow at the spectre of fear" that had threatened the banks. Beyond this, it is easy to imagine why Kilgore would be particularly admiring of someone communicating "without raising his voice above an ordinary conversational tone" and "speak[ing] frankly and convincingly." This is precisely what he was trying to do in "Reading the News of the Day." His father noted the parallel. Writing Barney about the first fireside chat, Tecumseh said,

I think the time for big high sounding words and phrases has passed for a while. The man who has something worth while to say and says it in a

plain simple and interesting way will not lack for an audience. The man who writes after this fashion will have a lot of readers. You started out this way and I hope you will never get away from it.

By March 16, less than two weeks into Roosevelt's presidency, Kilgore was ready to call a turn:

> *This bull market in dollars apparently reached a climax in the sudden rush only a few days ago, to turn everything—even bank deposits—as quickly as possible into cash. . . .*
>
> *Under these circumstances, it seems logical to conclude that—from a long term viewpoint—any substantial further increase in the dollar's value in terms of other things is not very probable.*

Yet the very same column made clear that Kilgore knew business was still suffering.

In such a situation, Roosevelt's candid experimentalism—the president had famously said during the 1932 campaign, "The country needs and, unless I mistake its temper, the country demands bold, persistent experimentation. It is common sense to take a method and try it: If it fails, admit it frankly and try another. But above all, try something"—appealed to Kilgore's own pragmatism and impatience. Writing of the administration's emergency farm bill, Kilgore observed, "President Roosevelt has frankly admitted that he doesn't know whether it will work. He must think the odds are pretty good, however, or he wouldn't sponsor the bill."

Kilgore himself was also constantly looking at possible experiments, ways to reflate prices. One column noted that even a small increase in the velocity of the money supply would have a dramatic effect ("Five dollars changing hands five times can do more work than $10 changing hands only once or twice"), another described what would happen if currency hoarders could be induced to purchase government bonds. But there were strict limits on how far he would go. He harshly ridiculed simplistic schemes for debt relief:

> *No matter how cold the weather might be, a man of average intelligence would think at least twice before he would burn down his house in order to keep warm. . . .*

Government credit is fundamental. It is the "house" which shelters and supports many other forms of vital economic activity. And "relief" for farmers, for debtors, for workers, for anybody, that endangers that credit is not "relief" at all. It is just a form of suicide.

With an increasing tone of self-confidence, Kilgore felt free to editorialize not only against what he regarded as foolish measures, but also in favor of those he thought sensible. On the issue of greater federal supervision of banking, perhaps accompanied by deposit insurance, he wrote, "It is becoming more and more apparent that unless the present emergency measures are followed up with some such change in fundamentals, sooner or later another lurid chapter in United States financial history will have to be written."

And he retained a strong sense of history—and history in the making:

Historians and economists, fifty or a hundred years from now, ought to have an interesting time analyzing and interpreting the swirling currents in world economic and political affairs set in motion by the reparations and debt arrangements created after the European war that began in 1914. They should be able to prove the folly of spending billions and billions of dollars in destructive combat and then treating that expenditure as though it were an "investment." They should be able to make an entertaining study of the efforts of Germany's victorious neighbors to grind that nation down and the surprise of those victors on finding out that desperate "bankrupt" sales make bad business for everybody.

When Kilgore moved on to "Reading the News of the Day" from "Dear George," and as the Roosevelt administration he was covering increasingly experimented with fiscal policy solutions, Kilgore began to leave Irving Fisher behind. In the relatively brief run of the column, Kilgore managed to mention Fisher three more times. But he was becoming a more discerning student: The first of these references noted that Fisher's commodity index, based as it was on wholesale price levels, was less powerful as an indicator of consumer behavior than, for instance, the National Industrial Conference Board's index of the cost of goods at the retail level. Two years later, and just six months before the publication of Keynes's *General Theory of Employment, Interest and*

Money, Kilgore wrote that "no book [has] yet been written . . . which will provide, once and for all, the elusive truth about depressions and recoveries." The student may have felt that he was growing beyond the teacher. A 1935 book review by Kilgore of Fisher's *100% Money* indicates that this process was largely completed, with Kilgore finding Fisher's prescriptions for restructuring the banking system increasingly unpersuasive.

All through this period, we can see in retrospect, Kilgore's vision of the *Journal*'s readers—and, perhaps more important, its *potential* readers—was being shaped. Repeatedly, he was struck by, and wrote about, the scope of shareholdings in major corporations. General Motors had 372,000 shareholders—enough so that if each one purchased a new automobile in a single year, it would account for 70 percent of the company's annual sales. U.S. Steel's 193,000 shareholders represented roughly a doubling in their number from 1901 to 1910, another doubling from 1910 to 1917, another from 1917 to 1926 and yet another from 1926 until 1933. This mass could form a population "nearly as large as Omaha, Nebraska." Both GM and U.S. Steel, Kilgore also pointed out, trailed AT&T (with 700,000 holders) and Cities Service (with 550,000) on this dimension. The contrast between these enormous figures and the *Journal*'s own paltry circulation, now down to 28,000, no doubt particularly impressed him.

And Kilgore was, for the first and only time in his life, beginning to play the market himself. He called it "stock market 'gambling,'" and doubled his $300 stake in six weeks. But he was modest about his investment skill, noting that "the country had to go off the gold standard for me to make any money in stocks."

By the end of March 1933, just ten weeks after launching "Reading the News of the Day," the burden of the column was beginning to wear on Kilgore. He sometimes now substituted five- to eight-line snippets, gathered under the subhed "Footnotes on the News," for the column's last daily item. Each of the "footnotes" made one point, but they were necessarily less analytical than the mini-essays they replaced.

In mid-April, Kilgore went on the road, taking advantage of an invitation to Charlie Robbins's wedding to report from outside New York for the first time since beginning the column. His first new dateline was Cincinnati, site of the wedding, where he sought to dig into the story of Kroger Grocery & Baking Co. earnings, and found that "[b]ack of the fact . . . is a story of a change in management, a change in business policies and a change in the trend line of net profits." It was the first "Reading the News" column that appears to have been based on firsthand reporting, rather than analysis of secondary sources, such as government reports and historical data. From Kroger in Cincinnati, Kilgore moved on to Chicago to report on the Board of Trade on his way to a visit in South Bend. The column was bringing him a measure of renown. One of his articles—the first of many—was being reprinted nationally in *The Literary Digest* and another was the subject of a Lowell Thomas radio broadcast. The format itself was now constraining his work. The near-daily run of "Reading the News of the Day" ended after just three months.

Kilgore's new venue was the *Journal's* front page. In effect, the column continued, although without a title, and the author remained just as prolific. After the last regular column appeared, he filed stories on the next two days, thus, at least initially, producing articles in the *Journal* five days a week. The new articles bore a one- to three-word title, from "Price Control" (the first installment, which ran the day after the last regular "Reading the News of the Day") to "Dr. Roosevelt" to "Securities Bill" to "Stabilization." They ran from the top of the page to the bottom, in the second column from the left. Given that the *Journal* ran advertisements on page one at the top of the left-hand and right-hand columns, this was the most prominent position in the newspaper.

Kilgore vied for this choice space each day with the editorial column written by *Journal* veteran Thomas Woodlock. Kilgore won the duel more often than not, but confessed an advantage in a letter to his parents: "The people who decide whether Woodlock goes on page one or not are friends of mine rather than friends of Mr. Woodlock, and that might make a difference." Woodlock was gracious about the competition, going out of his way to compliment the much younger man. For his part, Kilgore was impressed. Woodlock, he wrote, "is about 70 years old now [in fact he was sixty-six] and knows a lot of things."

Kilgore's articles remained explanatory in tone, but they were a bit more analytical, somewhat less opinionated, and generally longer. As momentous legislation poured out of Washington—the Securities Act of 1933, the Glass-Steagall separation of commercial and investment banking, federal deposit insurance, the National Industrial Recovery Act—most of the new pieces were tied just as closely to a current news development. As he wrote more, however, Kilgore seems to have had less time to report. Observations and conclusions often crowded out facts, but the fondness for plain speaking and penchant for aphorism continued. In the first of the new pieces, Kilgore wrote:

> *New paper currency could be printed by the bale, but if it didn't change hands, it wouldn't have any immediate effect on prices. New credit could be made available in the banking system, but if nobody uses it—what difference would it make? . . .*
> *The dollar's value now depends on what people think of it.*

On page one, Kilgore also now occasionally branched out to write of international politics as well as economics. It was not an entirely wise move. He did not bring to foreign policy anywhere near the same sophistication he routinely displayed on matters of finance and business. Kilgore greeted a relatively standard message from FDR to a now-forgotten peace conference as perhaps the most "spectacular and stirring appeal for peace" in "the world's history." An encouraging response from Hitler he accepted nearly at face value.

"Reading the News" continued, initially on a weekly basis, then sporadically for a bit more than four more months; the decline in frequency made it unnecessary to pad the column with "Footnotes," and these ceased. By midsummer of 1933, the column was running on the *Journal*'s editorial page without its title; Kilgore's byline may have been enough to signal the content to readers. Throughout the summer, continuing the daily competition with Woodlock, Kilgore alternated venues between the front page and the editorial page, keeping up an enormous output. Other than headline styles, the two offerings, one ostensibly "news," the other "editorial," differed not at all; both were distinguished from the rest of the newspaper by the distinctive voice of their young author.

In the late summer of 1933 Barney Kilgore took his work in another direction. Having sat largely at a desk in New York for more than eight months, observing and opining on events, he now moved on to the most basic of newspaper work—as a reporter of the news. He began with two weeks in Washington that culminated not in any published report, but in a 21-page private memo to Hogate. It concluded with optimism about the New Deal; "my inclination at the start was strongly skeptical and now is less so."

FDR's big gamble, the National Industrial Recovery Act, and his instrument, the National Recovery Administration, were bidding to transform the economy and break the back of the Depression. Kilgore, Hogate, and his editors wanted to know whether Roosevelt's plan was working, and it had become clear to them that the answer could not be found on Wall Street, at least not yet.

Instead, following the unpublished memo setting the scene in Washington, Kilgore decided to look first, closely, and this time for publication at how the NRA was faring in upstate New York. For three weeks, he canvassed the state, beginning in Albany, but ranging over Syracuse, Rochester, Buffalo, and Binghamton. In just over three weeks, Kilgore filed fourteen stories.

Out among ordinary people, Kilgore found a sense of nuance that was impossible to gauge sitting in Manhattan. His first article noted that it "might be safer to describe [Albany's] people as interested and hopeful so far as the NRA is concerned rather than notably enthusiastic." The second story turned to the real-life mechanics of how wage complaints under the NRA's "Blue Eagle" system were adjudicated. The result, rather than focusing on mandated increases in wages, also described how overtime hours were also being cut, and how many, if not most, small employers were formally or informally seeking exemptions from the NRA's codes.

Moreover, Kilgore took his first chance to do reporting for the *Journal*'s New York edition to experiment with writing forms. He began the first installment of the series by setting a scene:

> *The Blue Eagle graces the doors and windows of practically every establishment in the capital city of New York. A parade that required between two and three hours to pass the reviewing stand took place on the half holiday set aside by the Governor to do honor to the NRA and its noble bird. The local NRA chairman described it as a "corker."*

The third article was cast as what modern readers would immediately recognize as a "reporter's notebook" of vignettes. And Kilgore himself began to appear in his own stories, albeit in passing first-person references. The fourth story began by reminding his readers just what Kilgore was up to:

> *One way to get some first-hand information on the credit-supply and demand questions that are the topic of many recent dispatches from*

Washington is to go out and ask a lot of people a lot of questions. This writer has been doing that very thing in the central New York section.

He also discovered the virtue of whimsy as a way to shed new light on familiar phenomena; eventually he would place such a story on the front page of each day's *Journal.* For now, an article from Rochester led off this way:

> *Your correspondent is a trifle dizzy. He has just concluded a whirlwind interview with one Milton D. Crandall, "parade expert," ballyhoo artist and promoter extraordinary, who has been touring the country for more than a year now leaving a trail of bigger and better prosperity celebrations behind him.*

Today these forms seem unremarkable; in 1933 they were all nearly unprecedented.

Like all good reporters, Kilgore was guided by what he found, rather than seeking to prove a set of preconceptions. As a consequence, his views of the NRA shifted in the course of his work on the series. In his columns, he had been somewhat skeptical, because of the enormity of the task faced by the NRA, but generally supportive; now he became more dubious. In Geneva, New York, he learned that the NRA had enabled taxi drivers to fix higher prices, but at a cost (and not only to taxi riders). One driver explained:

> *We charge 25 cents for one person and 50 cents for two and so on up. It used to be 25 cents for one, 35 cents for two and 50 cents for three. . . .*
>
> *There are seven cab operators here in Geneva and we all have to charge the same now. There was one fellow, of course, that wanted to keep a low rate but even he's cooperating now. You bet he is! He found out it was cheaper in the long run to cooperate after he bought a couple of new windshields and a new set of tires.*

Nearly everyone seemed to want Roosevelt's plan to succeed. But the reporter in Kilgore also noticed that "the NRA is more a matter of psychology than economics. Perhaps that explains why most of the skepticism . . . is to be found at or near the top of the business structure." And Kilgore realized that one corollary of the notion that the NRA was a psychological rather than economic fix was his early realization that it would likely fail if it was politicized, that is, if the still substantial number of Republicans were thrown into opposition to it, or even if the "ballyhoo" couldn't be maintained. By the end of his reporting trip, the summer economic boomlet was fading, and the NRA proposed a "Buy Now" campaign to reignite activity. But Kilgore's doubts were building, and so, he reported, were those of people he was meeting.

The NRA was not happy with Kilgore's reporting, and especially not with his increasing disaffection. Three days after the last—and most critical—article in the series had been published, NRA chief General Hugh Johnson, addressing the Washington convention of the American Federation of Labor to call for an end to strikes, also lashed out at others. He refused to dignify Kilgore or even his newspaper by calling them out by name, but there was no doubt what he was talking about:

> *There are enemies of the NRA. Yesterday I heard that a prominent Wall Street journal was going to conduct a survey of small employers for the purpose of demonstrating that the President's Re-employment Agreement was a failure. I know something about Wall Street. I used to work there. It has been much maligned and also properly criticized. But the idea of a Wall Street journal going out to demonstrate through the little fellow the fallacy of a great social regeneration is one of the grimmest, ghastliest pieces of humor of all the queer flotsam of our daily work.*

Not yet twenty-five years old, Barney Kilgore was under withering attack by someone who, right then, was almost certainly the second most powerful man in the United States.

Johnson spoke on Tuesday night. On Wednesday the *Journal* editorial page leapt to Kilgore's defense with a piece published Thursday. The editorial, entitled "Blue Eagle—and Blue Pencil?" said, "*The Wall Street Journal* reiterates its faith in the accuracy of Mr. Kilgore's observations." Kilgore reported to his father that Hogate had written the piece personally. The editorial emphasized the separation of the news and editorial pages—a distinction, of course, that Kilgore's work throughout the year had been blurring. More generally, in words that would echo two decades later when Kilgore's *Journal* confronted the nation's largest company rather than its most powerful bureaucrat, the newspaper declared that "it conceives itself as under an obligation to its readers to report, accurately and without bias, the operations of all measures which have an effect upon the business structure of the country."

Beyond this, it saw through Johnson's attack: "Can it be that his remarks are in reality a blanket warning to newspapers to refrain from publishing facts unpalatable to the National Recovery Administration?" If any such effect was intended, the *Journal* wanted no misunderstanding. In a most unusual move, the editorial announced that Kilgore would soon follow his reporting trip through New York with one to the Pacific Coast. Within days, Barney Kilgore was on his way; one week after the editorial, the first article of his new series, datelined Atlanta, appeared in the *Journal*.

This second, national series on the NRA began, perhaps in light of Johnson's attacks, on a decidedly more skeptical note than had Kilgore's New York tour. The South, he declared in his first story, was looking at the NRA with "mixed feelings." His article honed in on one of the unintended effects of regulations capping wages—the widespread replacement of black labor in many parts of the South with white, "because the belief that white labor is superior to colored labor, if both must be bought at the same price, is fixed firmly in mind of the average southern employer."

From Atlanta, Kilgore's 1933 reporting trip continued on to New Orleans, where he spent a day on the floor of the Cotton Exchange. He then boarded a train for California, apparently not stopping anywhere along the way. He referred to the trip as a "vacation," noting that he was only writing half the time and had received a month's pay in advance.

From Los Angeles it was north to San Francisco, a return to Kilgore's early posting for the *Journal*. Kilgore's arrival followed close on Roosevelt's fourth fireside chat on October 22, announcing FDR's decision to have the government devalue the dollar and buy gold in an effort to "manage the currency."

By the end of nearly two weeks in San Francisco, Kilgore was reaching a conclusion about the NRA, crystallizing the doubts that he had begun to harbor in upstate New York two months earlier. Roosevelt, he decided, had overreached. The plan

> *was scheduled to go too far and too fast. While the theory of industrial planning may have been sound to begin with—and may still be sound for that matter—it never was something that could be put into practice overnight and it never should have been billed as a depression-ending device.*

In the fall of 1933 he returned to New York via Chicago after a tour that had taken a month since his departure for Atlanta and had included a stop at home in South Bend. Kilgore summed up what he had found: confusion, especially about the gold policy, possible early stirrings of a Republican revival, a degree of fatalism mixed with widespread continuing popular faith in the president personally, but with this faith much less prevalent among businessmen. In short, the boost in confidence which had spurred economic activity in the spring of 1933 had faded somewhat by fall, and Kilgore recognized that his optimism in that early season now needed to be tempered. It was a sober judgment, but a wise one; the Depression was far from over.

By the following spring, the shortcomings of the NRA would be widely recognized. Kilgore, somewhat uncharacteristically, took a moment to gloat in his column:

> *It isn't the habit of the writer of these paragraphs to go about chanting, "I told you so." But he does find it interesting to recall that a short swing across New York state last September, when he was hunting for first-hand information on the operation of the NRA, disclosed, on a small scale, the very same difficulties which are becoming increasingly apparent now on a large scale.*

As 1933 turned into 1934, Kilgore continued to write his "noncolumns" for the *Journal*. From mid-December 1933 they ceased to alternate between the editorial page and page one and found a fixed place, roughly five days a week, on page two. His output continued to be prodigious. When he made a brief trip to Indiana at Easter, he filed a full week's worth of stories from Chicago and environs; when he lectured at the University of Virginia, he used the peroration of his speech to fill his space one day, and filed a story from a conference in Charlottesville two days later.

As the Depression deepened for most Americans, and even for most of his colleagues, Kilgore was increasingly flush. He received an unsolicited $10 per week raise in early March 1934, bringing his pay to $95 per week, or about $72,000 annually today. He sent money to his father again in December 1933 and yet again in February 1934. He visited a dentist, for work costing the current equivalent of nearly $900, had his apartment repainted, and began living without a roommate.

Many of his columns continued to follow the daily ins and outs of the debate on monetary policy, especially surrounding gold. (The Gold Reserve Act passed the Congress on January 30, 1934, and the next day FDR put the country back on the gold standard, repegging the dollar at $35 per ounce of gold.) But Kilgore was increasingly aware of the centrality of fiscal policy to economic outcomes. One implication of this was that the financial action, in the second year of the New Deal, was continuing to shift away from markets in New York. As he advised a reader in a "Dear George"–like column written mostly in the form of a letter, "You, and thousands of small investors like you, will simply have to pin a good deal of faith on the foresight, integrity and ability of the men you have sent to Washington."

Washington, in other words, was where the story was.

And as Kilgore turned his attention increasingly to Washington, that attention was returned. On March 14, 1934, a Kilgore article explained the difference between the government issuing currency as opposed to selling bonds. The two practices, Kilgore emphasized, "have no logical connection whatever." Issuing currency to meet obligations would be in the way of a forced loan, rather than one on consensual terms, he wrote, and would undermine the dollar. Moreover, he noted, there was an important psychological difference, even between "fiat currency" and "fiat credit." The difference might leave

> *the threat of wild inflation hanging by a slender thread—but still hanging nevertheless. That might be important. After all, while Damocles undoubtedly would have felt better if the sword over his head had been suspended by an iron chain instead of a hair, so long as he had no choice in the matter, he must have been terribly interested in the tensile strength of hairs.*

One of the contexts in which the issuance of currency to pay debts had been suggested was that of the World War veterans, strapped for cash by the Depression and thus seeking immediate payment of their bonuses, otherwise due in 1945. At his press conference on the same day Kilgore's article was published, with newsmen crowded around his desk in the Oval Office of the White House, President Roosevelt was asked to comment on House action on the bonus. He declined, but quickly added:

> *There is an article in this morning's* Wall Street Journal *by Bernard Kilgore that really anybody who writes about finances and bonuses and currency issues and so forth ought to read, because it is pretty good. I don't agree with the story all the way through; but it is a good story. It is an analytical story on an exceedingly difficult subject—on the question of issuing currency to meet Government obligations. I think that Kilgore could have gone just a bit further than he did.*

"Of course," FDR immediately noted, "this is all background." That is, he was not to be quoted, but he could be cited. And he was, including on the front page of the next day's *New York Herald Tribune*.

The presidential praise quickly grew into a *Journal* legend, enhancing the position in Washington of both newspaper and reporter. The paper's Washington bureau manager wired Kilgore,

> YOU ARE FAMOUS, THAT IS STILL MORE FAMOUS. FOR YOUR INFORMATION ROOSEVELT IN THE PRESS CONFERENCE THIS MORNING CALLED ATTENTION TO YOUR STORY IN THIS MORNING'S PAPER, SAID IT WAS VERY WELL DONE, THAT ALL INTERESTED PEOPLE SHOULD READ IT.

He concluded, "WE MADE IT THE TEXT FOR A LECTURE AGAINST THE BONUS." Within six weeks, Kilgore was dispatched to begin his first significant in-person coverage of the capital.

Kilgore reported for his page-two noncolumn from the capital—on the NRA, the Federal Reserve Board, an ill-advised speech on savings and investment by an official of the Public Works Administration, more from FDR on silver and gold, the Treasury Department's efforts to influence the money supply, and new legislation regulating margin trading—for all of two weeks before he began writing a four-part series, published on consecutive days, on his impressions of government in the city. Privately, even on a brief earlier trip, he had told his parents that he considered Washington "a better place to work than New York in many respects. More air and sun, and no subways. Perhaps I will be able to arrange to get down here again from time to time."

Publicly, the new series sought to make a virtue of Kilgore's status as a "comparative stranger" in Washington, to adopt the point of view of "one who is none too sure of anybody's ability to tell what is really going on in the national capital today." The confusion, Kilgore had almost instantly recognized, ran all the way to the top: "The New Dealers," he wrote,

> *considered as a group, have had, since March 4, 1933, a definite political philosophy. . . . They have had, too, a vague social philosophy. . . . But they have lacked and continue to lack any economic philosophy whatever.*

Instead of the administration moving right politically, Kilgore saw it slowing the breakneck pace of change.

The consequences, the series noted, were becoming clear. The NRA, Kilgore concluded, summing up more than six months of reporting, was left with a "salvage job":

> *because of its haste in pursuing the objective of a code for everyone and everyone under a code, and the degree to which it succeeded in attaining that objective, it now finds itself with an enforcement problem on its hands which staggers the imagination.*

General Johnson, Kilgore's old adversary, was described as a man "who can back down more aggressively than anyone else in Washington, [and who] speaks less of 'cracking down' these days and more of voluntary cooperation."

But if the New Deal was faltering, Kilgore was under no illusions that it was in any meaningful political danger. "The opposition," he noted, "lacks leadership, it lacks organization, it lacks an economic philosophy even as, not so long ago, it lacked a voice."

It was a masterly performance of what we have, in later years, come to call "parachuting" into unfamiliar journalistic territory and making sense of it for busy readers even less familiar with the terrain. A *Journal* editorial touted Kilgore's series as "a refreshing and clarifying breeze." Praised by the president, promoted by his colleagues, Kilgore had become the *Journal*'s star performer.

And he was beginning to assemble allies in his emerging quest to reshape the newspaper.

On his earlier trip to Washington, in late August and early September 1933, Kilgore had attended his first FDR press conference and had first spent time with William F. Kerby, who would become his closest associate over more than a quarter of a century. Now, in late April 1934, Kilgore stayed with Kerby, in Kerby's parents' home in Chevy Chase, Maryland.

Kerby, just three months older than Kilgore and also a Hogate recruit, nevertheless presented a striking contrast to the young man from Indiana. Kerby's family had come to America in 1654, had been close to Lord Baltimore, and traced its lineage to President James Monroe. Kerby's favorite aunt kept on her own former slaves as domestic servants. Vice President John Nance Garner was "something of a longtime family acquaintance," and poet Carl Sandburg was a visitor to the family home. That home in Chevy Chase boasted a maid who came in to cook breakfast each day for the visiting young reporters.

But Kerby's father, while sporting "Monroe" as his middle name and playing to a six handicap at the elite Congressional Country Club, was a lapsed Episcopalian, an anti-Communist Marxist, and devoted follower of Socialist Eugene Debs. He was also a reporter, mostly for the Scripps newspapers, whose work took his young family from Washington to New York to Cleveland and back to Washington during the years of Bill's upbringing.

After flirting with an academic career (Bill had attended the University of Michigan in preference to the University of Virginia at his father's suggestion, had been admitted to Phi Beta Kappa, and was offered a teaching job on graduation), young Kerby followed his father into journalism. In fact, his father sponsored his newspaper career early and often. Bill got his first job in journalism at the age of eighteen, working for the Washington *Daily News,* a paper owned by the same Scripps chain that employed his father, as a summer fill-in police reporter. In 1928, William Henry Grimes, then the *Journal's* Washington bureau chief and a "friend and golfing partner" of the senior Kerby, offered the young man another summer posting.

Grimes liked Kerby's work, although he did bestow on him a parting present of a pocket dictionary. "You have a job here next summer, but it would be nice if you would just learn to spell." Kerby returned to the *Journal* for the summer of 1929, just as Kilgore was arriving in New York, and then being shipped off to San Francisco. Kerby did well enough to be offered a job for 1930, following his graduation from Michigan.

When the market crashed, the job offer, like so many others across the country, was rescinded. Kerby managed to secure a substitute offer from a small Washington outfit called Federated Press, although he was unaware for years that this came only because his father had secretly arranged with yet another friend to pay his $15 per week salary. After a short stint at Federated, Kerby moved on to the United Press wire service (another Scripps property), the office in which Grimes had worked before coming to the *Journal*. It was his fourth job in journalism, and the first that he had secured on his own.

By 1933 the *Journal*, while no better off economically than it had been when his job offer had been rescinded, had seen enough of Kerby's work with United Press covering the Congress to want him back. Hogate invited Kerby to lunch in the House members' restaurant. After consuming two orders of the establishment's seafood pie—recalled by Kerby as "an enormous dish composed of creamed lobster, crab, oysters, shrimp, and filet of sole, topped with a baked mashed potato cover and embellished with a full two ounces of beluga caviar"—Hogate turned to business.

> *"Bill, where were you born?"*
> *I replied the District of Columbia.*
> *"That's terrible," said Hogate. "Where were you brought up?"*
> *I replied, mostly in and around Washington.*
> *"That's even worse! Where were you educated?"*
> *The University of Michigan.*
> *"Well," said he with a broad grin, "there may be some hope for you yet. The salary is $55 a week to start, and when can you start?"*

Bill Kerby was not a visionary, but he did bring important skills to a partnership with Barney Kilgore. He was another practical man, a believer in what he called the appeal of the "greatest common denominator news story" that "the most successful articles are those which directly affect the personal lives of readers." He acknowledged that such stories would often be about the weather. Beyond this, Kerby could turn a phrase, had a prodigious appetite for work, and loved newspapers. Most important, he was content to play second fiddle while Kilgore led.

5

"What's News"

The Great Depression, of course, was first evident on Wall Street and rippled out from there across the nation and the world. *The Wall Street Journal* was hardly immune to the problems sweeping through finance and business. But for nearly five years after the Crash of 1929, the *Journal,* as a business itself, hardly reacted.

Kilgore experimented journalistically and rose within the organization and in the esteem of readers. But the paper was not fundamentally different from what it had been before he joined in the heady summer of '29. It was just smaller and poorer—like most of the firms it covered. Circulation had fallen from a 1930 peak of 56,000 to just half that level in 1932. (Total U.S. newspaper circulation was actually much stronger, dropping just 12 percent from 1930 to 1933, and then recovering, even as many papers were merged out of existence.)

At first, like many American businesses, the *Journal* and Dow Jones seemed almost willfully ignorant of the changes swirling around them—and being recounted in the newspaper's pages. In 1931, Dow Jones filed plans for the partial demolition of the headquarters building it had occupied since 1893 and the reconstruction of the building. The site, at 44 Broad Street in Manhattan, was just down the block from the New York Stock Exchange, and still just a few hundred yards from where the company and the newspaper had been founded. Cost: $400,000 (roughly $5.7 million today).

The *Journal* proudly reported that

news and editorial rooms, occupying all of the third floor, ventilated with conditioned air and equipped with improved lighting system and fixtures and Fenestra windows are simply and pleasantly decorated with buff walls, white ceiling and brown trim. The walls, moreover, are lined with sound-deadening celotex. Partitions, all of steel, also are done with brown trim, with sound-insulated panels. In the matter of interior design and decoration, a feature of the building is the reception room, on the fifth floor: furniture, fixtures, fireplace, walls and ceiling are early American in style.

Dividends in 1929 were $770,000, or nearly $8.8 million in today's dollars. By 1931 annual parent company profits came to $1.33 million, or roughly $17 million today. (By contrast, *Fortune* estimated in 1930 that the *Chicago Tribune* and *The New York Times* each earned perhaps $7 million in 1929, or about $82 million today.) The *Journal* moved to temporary facilities in August 1931, and the new offices were ready and open for business by April 1932, by which time the profits had all but evaporated, and salaries were being slashed. (By 1938, the company would make just $23,000 for the year, net of taxes.) On June 27, 1932 the *Journal* published a special issue marking the fiftieth anniversary of Dow Jones & Company. The edition, running 80 pages, was said to be "the largest issue of any newspaper ever published in New York City in one press run." It nevertheless sold for the regular seven cents. Triumphs over the fifty years, an introductory note stated, "vitalize confidence that the natural difficulties of the present will surely fade."

The executive team that had been installed at the time of the death of Clarence Barron in 1928 remained in place: Barron's principal heir was his stepdaughter Jane; her sister, Martha, had died in 1916, two years earlier than their mother. Jane's husband, Hugh Bancroft, was president of the company, Casey Hogate vice president and general manager (a role he had assumed in 1926). After the death of William Peter Hamilton in 1929, Thomas Woodlock, who returned to the *Journal* in 1930, dominated the editorial pages.

Cyril Kissane, installed by Hogate in 1929, was managing editor. Hogate was a strong figure, but, in Bancroft and Kissane, he was sandwiched between lesser men. In cases such as Kilgore's "Reading the News" column, Hogate did not hesitate to manage around Kissane. Kilgore noted shortly after the column began that "I had anticipated a little trouble with the managing editor on the way it was to be handled—his ideas differing from Mr. Hogate's somewhat—but all he had were a couple of suggestions and said the stuff was interesting."

Sometime in 1932, the strains of business and personal life overcame Hugh Bancroft. He suffered some sort of breakdown and largely retired to the blacksmith shop on his estate in Cohasset, Massachusetts. The masthead of the *Journal* continued to list him as president of Dow Jones, but he was that in name only. As is often the case in such circumstances, however, Hogate hardly had a free hand to make sweeping changes; the fact that he was only thirty-five years old probably did not help. Indeed, with business suffering, the company was not only bleeding, but also somewhat paralyzed.

Hogate's opening came as a result of tragedy. Mary Bancroft, Hugh's daughter, later recalled: "During my father's life, he had had several nervous breakdowns, as they were called, when he wouldn't speak to anyone for days on end and had to have someone constantly with him so that he wouldn't, I was told, 'harm himself.'" One afternoon in the summer of 1933, Bancroft was chopping wood with Mary looking on, when he set his hatchet down and collapsed on a stump. He told his daughter, "'I'm afraid I'm going to have another breakdown.'" She sought to reassure him, but the blackness was closing in. On October 17, less than a week after the *Journal* editorial defending Kilgore against the attack of the NRA's General Hugh Johnson, Hugh Bancroft could bear his pain no longer. He escaped once more into his blacksmith shed; drawing on instructions in a book he had recently taken out of the Boston Public Library, he mixed the ingredients he had purchased for poison gas. Both the *Journal* and *The New York Times* reported the cause of death as a heart attack.

Jane Bancroft, newly widowed, never wavered. At the reception at her home after her husband's funeral on October 19, she took Casey Hogate aside and told him, "I want you to do what's best for the company. Don't you and the boys worry about dividends." That same afternoon, at a formal conference of the directors of Dow Jones's parent company, she nominated Hogate for president, indicated confidence in his leadership, and quickly concluded the meeting. Family ownership of Dow Jones and *The Wall Street Journal* would continue; family management of the enterprises was at an end. In fact, as Edward Scharff wrote in 1986,

> The Wall Street Journal *would be almost the only major American newspaper owned by a family that did not feel compelled to install its heirs as publishers and editors, which may be the most succinct explanation as to how the* Journal *came to be the most successful newspaper in the country.*

Hogate, his wife later recalled, felt pressure from the Bancrofts to "maintain . . . their horses and their yachts and so forth," but he was always given a free hand, both commercially and editorially.

Perhaps because he had already been general manager for seven years, perhaps because it was simply hard to fathom the Depression's depths, perhaps because the downturn had seemingly crushed his earlier dreams of the first national newspaper and of refocusing the *Journal* beyond finance to include business, it was some months before Hogate moved to exercise his newfound freedom of action.

He used the occasion of a staff dinner four weeks after Bancroft's funeral to deliver something of an inaugural address. Hogate told the troops that, as Kilgore put it in a letter home, "everything would go along just about as in the past." He said that "no radical staff changes are contemplated" and praised twenty-one colleagues by name in the course of his speech; Kilgore was not among them.

But Hogate was quite candid on the difficulties ahead. He said that the company's cash reserves "have shrunk most drastically. They were chiefly in what appeared to be high-grade common stocks, and little more need be said." He added that "if this is only a severe depression our reserves are such as to lead us to believe that we ought to get through it. If it is an economic revolution, no one can foresee the end or the consequences." The company as a whole was in the black, as was the recently struggling Pacific Coast edition. Nevertheless, further salary cuts of 10 percent were instituted.

But Hogate clung fast to his vision. "I am a news man," he declared, "and I always intend to remain one." He posed a question for his audience of comrades in arms:

> *How many of you news men have dreamed, as I have dreamed, of being able to produce some day a newspaper free from all "sacred cows" and from all restraints from the top—but a newspaper dedicated in idealism to the presenting of the truth? Well,* The Wall Street Journal *is that kind of a newspaper—if you'll make it so.*

What sort of newspaper would it be? Hogate saw, first, "the financial and business paper of record," but then, *also,* "a journal of opinion and interpretation." In all of this, he explained, "We are not the paper of management. We are the paper of the ultimate investor."

With this in mind, during the summer of 1934 Hogate finally moved ahead. On Tuesday, September 4, the day after Labor Day, Hogate's changes were unveiled. Kissane—whom Hogate had praised in his dinner speech ten months earlier, but who had become ill, and whose parochial and plodding style had earned him the nickname "Stupid" with the Washington bureau staff—was out as managing editor, to be replaced by Washington bureau chief William Henry Grimes. The afternoon edition of the *Journal* was discontinued, effective immediately. The afternoon edition was the newspaper's original incarnation—the morning *Journal* did not appear until 1898, nine years later—but it had long been slumping under the irrelevancy caused by a 3:00 P.M. deadline, and the morning paper was outselling it by a ratio of nine to one when Hogate finally shut it down.

Most important, and most notable by readers, the *Journal*'s front page began to be transformed. In the waning days of Kissane's editorship, a fairly typical front page might contain fifteen or even twenty articles, some of them quite brief, all of them displayed helter-skelter. On the first day of Hogate and Grimes's new paper the count fell to eleven articles. Small advertisements, nearly all of them for securities brokerage services of one kind or another, continued to run down the left- and right-hand columns of the page to a point "below the fold." But an entirely new sort of newspaper feature filled the page's second column. It remains on the page, its headline and basic typography essentially unchanged, to this day. And Barney Kilgore was its first writer.

It was (and is) entitled simply "What's News." It was apparently Hogate's idea, and he enlisted Kilgore to write at least the first column. As it appeared that Tuesday in the late summer of 1934, "What's News" ran from the top of the page all the way to the bottom. It contained thirteen different items, beginning with this: "The first day of the long advertised textile strike brought the usual claims and counter claims from the contending forces." Four more crisp sentences summarized the textile industry labor situation before the column moved on to another four-sentence item, this one about relief for the unemployed. Other subjects that first day included the level of Irving Fisher's commodity price index, a change in leadership at the Salvation Army, summaries of Labor Day speeches in Chicago (by New York mayor Fiorello La Guardia), Idaho, Kansas, and Alabama, the political prospects of the French government, items about the outlook for railroad legislation, oil regulation, and milk price guidelines, news from the tennis tournament at Forest Hills, a preview of that day's Democratic primary for the Senate in Nevada, and the view from London on exchange rate fluctuations.

In just a few minutes, a reader of "What News" could feel informed— actually be informed—about the high points of the full range of the day's news. It may have been Hogate's idea, but he was wise to ask the author of "Reading the News of the Day" to execute it. Kilgore's experience with that vehicle had taught him to reduce items to their essence, and even to compress important fragments of analysis into just a few words or sentences. The first item, on the textile strike, ended, "Future union operations in the South may increase the apparent effectiveness of the tie up there, but at the present reading the labor leaders give the appearance of men who have over-reached themselves." The outlook, in thirty-three words.

Most significantly, "What's News" sketched what Kilgore saw as the scope of the *Journal,* ranging across business news from regulatory issues to labor concerns, and across finance from commodity prices to exchange rates (with news limited, of course, by the long weekend)—but also including news outside of business, from a leading charity to a sports championship. And, of course, in all of this, ranging across the country with the recognition that the community for which the newspaper was being written was a community of interest rather than geography.

"What's News" is, today, somewhat standard fare for newspapers; many have similar summaries, at least in form (if not in editorial elegance), placed prominently on their front pages. But in 1934 the column was revolutionary. The New York *Sun* had only introduced a summary of the *week's* news in 1931; *The New York Times* and *Washington Post* would not follow with a weekly recap until 1935. The *Journal's* daily summary, produced on the fly, was unprecedented, at least for American newspapers. *The Richmond News Leader* would add a page-one, column-one daily digest in April 1935, and *The Buffalo Times* would place a daily summary, "This Day: The News of the World in 15 Minutes," on the front page of its second section in 1937. Hogate and Kilgore were the pioneers.

But "What's News," for all of its prominence and importance to the *Journal,* was hardly Kilgore's sole occupation in the new *Journal.* On the same day "What's News" made its debut, Kilgore wrote a column entitled "Thinking It Over" on the editorial page. The title was dropped after one day, but soon reappeared as the name of Thomas Woodlock's editorial column, written in succeeding years under the slightly spruced-up title "Thinking Things Over" by Grimes, Vermont Royster, and Robert Bartley.

Kilgore reverted to the "noncolumn" approach, with no title, but a regular format (four or five items, each introduced with a bold sub-hed placed in a small bit of square white space inset into the text). After the first day, the column moved to the news pages, most often page three, and appeared roughly five times a week.

Simply judging by the volume of these "noncolumns," it seems likely that Kilgore on his own only wrote the first one or two installments of "What's News" before being succeeded in that role by fellow DePauw alumnus Buren McCormack. Indeed, the tone of the second day's column was notably more flippant than the first, and much heavier on the sorts of adjectives in which Kilgore rarely indulged. Kilgore wrote his mother, ten days into the new regime, that "McCormack is supposed to be learning to write it but for the time being I have to give considerable time and attention to it." By the fourth day, each item in the summary contained its own one- or two-word sub-hed, including "Der Fuehrer" for an item on the Nazis' Nuremberg Party Rally. But the key elements had been established literally from the first day: pithiness, breadth, heavy on facts, but not devoid of analysis, designed to be read or just scanned, as the reader's time permitted. And Kilgore kept his hand in the column, acting as vacation relief for McCormack as the column's author during at least one period a year later.

William Henry Grimes, Hogate's new choice as managing editor, did not confine himself to executing the boss's vision. He grabbed the newspaper and shook it out of its torpor. He not only presided over the demise of the afternoon edition, he created three versions of the morning paper, extending the final editorial deadline from a relaxed 6:00 P.M. to an aggressive midnight, with the earliest edition closing at eight o'clock, a standard to which the *Journal* would roughly adhere for the rest of the twentieth century. A front-page note in the first issue under Grimes's leadership said the changes in deadlines "will result in an enlarged and improved newspaper."

Grimes established the first copy desk at the *Journal,* bringing professional editing where previously there had been a lone proofreader. This step also enabled him to upgrade headline quality, taking the writing of headlines—which really is a distinct art—away from reporters. In small steps at first, and later more systematically, he also opened up headline styles; under the *Journal's* previous approach, as Bill Kerby later recalled, "The most talented headline writer was hard pressed to give more than a vague general impression of the story's subject matter." Finally, Grimes hired the paper's first makeup editor, someone to lay out articles on pages in a thoughtful and reader-friendly rather than haphazard manner. Grimes placed news judgment for readers ahead of printers' composing room priorities, and brought an editorial outlook to the placement of stories on inside pages for the first time. The September 4 note observed that "Some of the betterments are apparent in today's issue; others will follow at an early date."

More broadly, and ultimately more significantly, Grimes also firmly and conclusively separated the news and advertising functions at the *Journal.* He banned his company's own advertising salesmen from the newsroom, ended the practice of reporters occasionally selling advertising, and forbade journalists trading in stocks about which they were writing. Nor were Grimes's moral qualms confined to the advertising side of the business. As Bill Kerby later recalled,

> *Grimes reserved his most profound loathing for public relations men. He regarded them as some sort of subspecies of humanity and the natural enemies of honest newsmen. When one of his longtime friends left newspaper work to accept a position as public relations man for a government agency, Grimes was deeply upset. "There must be some flaw in his character which I didn't detect all these years."*

All of these steps were essential to establishing not only the newspaper's integrity, but its reputation for independence, on which any effort to broaden its appeal would need to be premised. If Barney Kilgore would later revolutionize *The Wall Street Journal,* and he would, William Henry Grimes laid the necessary groundwork for such a revolution.

The man behind these changes was another of Hogate's preferred Midwesterners. Grimes was six years older than Hogate, forty-two at the time he became managing editor. He had attended what was then Western Reserve University, but had not graduated, and had gone from there to work on a number of the daily papers in Cleveland before moving to the Washington bureau of the United Press wire service, ultimately as editor of a wire covering market news.

Hogate hired him in 1923 into the *Journal*'s Washington bureau, and had made him bureau manager in 1926, replacing John Boyle, seventy-one years old, who had led the office since 1901, the days of Dow and Bergstresser. (When Boyle died, in 1936, Kilgore noted that Boyle "drank about a quart of whiskey every day for several decades.") At the time of Grimes's appointment, Hogate agreed to expand the bureau's size at that time from three men to five. By the time Grimes moved to New York to become managing editor eight years later, and especially with the advent of the New Deal, the size of the bureau had grown to thirteen.

Grimes was a consummate reporter, both a graceful stylist (he would, much later, win the *Journal*'s first Pulitzer Prize) and remarkably well sourced. His key contacts in the twenties and early thirties included Andrew Mellon, secretary of the treasury, and Eugene Meyer, chairman of the Federal Reserve. Meyer actually attempted to recruit Grimes to *The Washington Post* shortly after he purchased it in 1933. It seems possible that this overture may have played some role in Hogate's decision to elevate Grimes to managing editor, offering him a role and challenge even greater than Meyer was prepared to dangle before him.

But if Grimes was another of the Midwestern men, he hardly shared the stereotypical equanimity of that region. Tales of his explosive temper were legend. He threw clubs in golf, and cards in bridge. Frustrated after a telephone interview with a secretary of the treasury (presumably not Mellon), he was said to have yanked the pay phone at the National Press Club out of the wall. Kerby recalled Grimes's frustration with orders from Kissane to chase a wild rumor in a Walter Winchell column that President Roosevelt was about to resign (Grimes may well have been the originator of Kissane's "Stupid" nickname):

> *Purple-faced, Grimes rose and leveled a kick at his typewriter stand. It flew across the office, banged the wall, and the typewriter wound up on the floor, a mangled mass of wreckage.*
>
> *To [the messenger]: "Tell Stupid to go to Hell."*
>
> *To me: "Bill, please call the typewriter people and tell them I need a new machine immediately." Then, "And tell them to bill me personally."*

With his ire almost never aimed at them, talented reporters could not help but love the man. His *Journal* obituary many years later recalled him as "a shy man who spoke so softly he could barely be heard across the width of a desk."

Kilgore, Grimes, and Hogate did not innovate in a vacuum, of course. But to the extent they were inspired by other publications, those were magazines, not newspapers. In particular, the most exciting publications of the period were Henry Luce's *Time* (which began publication in 1923) and *Fortune* (1930) and Harold Ross's *New Yorker* (1925).

Writing in 1934 in his book *City Editor* (the position he occupied at the *New York Herald Tribune*), Stanley Walker concluded that the weeklies *Time* and *The New Yorker,* "although different in appeal, nevertheless have demonstrated what some people suspected all along—that facts, marshaled in smart, orderly fashion, can be charming." Newspapers, he urged, should strive for more focus "on what is happening and what is about to happen, for even more cold realism, and for a broadening of interests. It may be that tomorrow newspapers will discover that there are types of news somewhere in the clash of people and ideas, which will be . . . revolutionary . . . and . . . profitable."

While there is no record of Kilgore (or Grimes or Hogate) consciously patterning his work after *Time, The New Yorker, Fortune,* or any other magazine, Bill Kerby did later write that he, Kerby, was a "charter subscriber and intense admirer" of Luce's business publication. In *Fortune,* "here was a formula which, adapted to daily business news reporting, could be even more successful because of the timeliness of a daily as compared with a monthly publication."

But if the notion of summarizing the news drew on *Time,* and if attention to the quality of prose was inspired by *The New Yorker,* and if the sense that business reporting did not have to be dull drew inspiration from *Fortune*—and all of these are likely—the changes that began to be made to *The Wall Street Journal* in 1934 were still crucially innovative. First, eleven years after the first appearance of *Time,* nine years after the start of *The New Yorker,* even four years after *Fortune,* no one with the opportunity to put ideas into practice had seen how these lessons might be applied to newspapers.

Next, both the style and substance of the changes in the *Journal* were highly original. *Time* used summarization to completely blur the distinction between reporting and editorializing; the *Journal* used the same device to sharpen the distinction—"What's News" never opined. *The New Yorker* was written for a self-consciously narrow audience, a self-regarding elite; the changes in the *Jour-*

nal were, from the first, all designed to broaden its audience, to make its offerings more accessible to more readers. The *Fortune* of the 1930s was a work of art, a beautiful publication, with words by the likes of James Agee and Archibald MacLeish and photographs by Margaret Bourke White and Walker Evans, while Kilgore and others increasingly sought to transform the *Journal* into a businessman's tool. *Fortune* invented the modern corporate profile, to be sure, but its monthly schedule forced it to almost systematically avoid the news.

Kilgore continued his torrid productivity in the months after the debut of "What's News." He had actually taken a two-week holiday in July 1934, including a visit home to South Bend, apparently the only significant break since he had come east eighteen months earlier. In his first piece on returning he confessed:

> *It is extremely difficult, even when one is vacationing in a spot far removed from both Wall Street and Washington where current issues of metropolitan newspapers are few and far between, to keep from thinking about the state of the nation or to avoid wondering what will be the final outcome of that curious mixture of economics and politics called the New Deal.*

Kilgore's skepticism about FDR's program was hardening. The Agricultural Adjustment Administration, in particular, troubled him as a student of economics:

> *The very fact that any government deems it necessary to fix the price of anything usually indicates that it is unwilling to admit the utility and the power of general supply and demand factor. Hence governments almost invariably fix prices at uneconomic levels.*

Kilgore remained impressed with Roosevelt's political appeal and his ability to inspire confidence. But the president had not changed Kilgore's views of the economic capabilities of government:

> *No government ever really creates purchasing power. It merely has the power to redistribute it. Hence, despite all claims that the New Deal has*

no intention of robbing Peter to pay Paul, the fact is slowly emerging that
it must either tax Peter to pay Paul (which amounts to about the same
thing) or it must tax Paul to pay Paul (which is even more patently a ring-
around-the-rosey game).

In late September 1934, just weeks after the first appearance of "What's News," Kilgore set off on a four-week reporting tour of the country. Each of the resulting articles ran on the *Journal*'s front page; the series was called "Viewing America." Again, as in his series a year earlier, he began in Albany, going back to the president's old baliwick.

Now, however, Kilgore had one of his conclusions not at the end of his series, but in its first sentence: "Business men, if sentiment here could be considered representative, are fast becoming more and more certain they don't like the New Deal." But that was not the end of the first sentence; it concluded that businessmen were "less and less certain why they don't like it." Albany, as a center of government, actually saw business picking up. But at Kilgore's third stop, Cleveland, the gains since the dark days of March 1933 had largely been surrendered.

Regulation continued to strike Kilgore as the problem. Leaving Cleveland, he wrote: "As one shrewd observer remarked to me the other day, 'If the Administration really wants to plan a recovery all it has to do is to quit planning.' "

But beyond his policy conclusions, Kilgore's determination to go out and test them in the country was remarkable. From Cleveland, he stopped at home in South Bend, then went on a whirlwind trip to Chicago, Des Moines, Kansas City, Dallas, Houston, New Orleans, and Atlanta before returning to New York. He wrote nearly every day, accomplishing this feat by reporting during the day and writing aboard trains in the evening.

When he found that most voters didn't share his own views, he did not hesitate to say so, noting that FDR was more popular in Iowa than he had been in 1932, and that while the president was disliked in business circles in Dallas, the average citizens at the nearby Texas State Fair had a different view. "Go out through this country," he quoted a salesman in Texas, "and see how many farm houses have Roosevelt's picture up on the wall. You'd be surprised."

Returning home, Kilgore wisely discerned a pattern:

a definite stratification of opinion—a sort of "class" feeling—with re-
gard to the New Deal program. Whether the New Deal is responsible for

this class feeling or whether the rise of this class feeling is responsible for the New Deal might be a good subject for long philosophical discussions next winter.

He was also more confident of his own range as a journalist. Back from a reporting trip, he would effortlessly return to explanatory columns. A four-part series on "job insurance," for instance, disposed of much of the debate this way:

It is probably no exaggeration to say that a good deal of the popularity of unemployment insurance proposals here today is due to the mistaken idea that some magic formula can be found to cure the present relief problem. Obviously, this has nothing to do with "insurance" in any sense of the word.

One who searches for greater security in this frame of mind is exactly like a man hunting for a fire insurance policy that will pay for the rebuilding of a city that has already been partially destroyed by fire. He simply hasn't the ghost of a chance to find what he is looking for, although he may be able to fool himself and some of his fellow men with complicated devices and high-sounding phrases.

Just weeks after the "job insurance" series came another four-article offering, this one on "credit inflation." Kilgore's explanations had become so popular with *Journal* readers that editor's notes and then advertisements began to offer reprints of the series to any reader sending in three cents for return postage.

Kilgore's skepticism about the New Deal had by now overcome his optimism about the timing of economic recovery. Progress on unemployment in 1934 had been "next to nothing." And the stimulus from federal spending he believed to be temporary—and thus illusory. His first 1935 column declared that "the foundation has been laid for a boom, not lasting prosperity." The signs of incipient recovery he had detected in 1932, 1933, and 1934 he now dismissed as "boomlets."

Taxes, he felt, were hardly an answer to the nation's problems. One column pointed out that confiscatory taxation of *all* corporate profits and *all* individual incomes over $5,000 per year would have yielded revenues sufficient to fund only half of what the Roosevelt administration had spent in 1933.

Kilgore's sense of humor was intact. He ridiculed an attempt to rationalize payment of a veterans' bonus by simply printing money as "very much like saying that Mr. X would make a qualified engineer for the Twentieth Century Limited because he only runs through red signal lights when his brother-in-law asks him to, which doesn't happen more than once every two or three years."

But his economic conservatism was hardening.

6

WASHINGTON

G RIMES'S APPOINTMENT AS MANAGING editor left a vacancy in the key position of Washington bureau manager. Grimes named Thomas Phelps to the post, but it was soon clear that this was not a permanent solution; Bill Kerby recalled Phelps as "a lost man in Washington," always seeking a purely rational explanation in the often emotional world of politics. The urgency of filling the Washington job with someone strong became particularly acute when, less than two months after the debut of Grimes's reforms, Kerby, newly engaged, was refused a raise and left the paper for an increase from $60 a week at the *Journal* to $105 as a publicist for the archconservative Liberty League, Al Smith's vehicle for attacking the New Deal.

Kilgore, only twenty-six years old, was probably being groomed by Hogate for the bureau manager role even before he recognized it. In mid-January 1935, Hogate invited Kilgore to be a guest for a ski weekend at his farm near Pawling, New York, less than thirty miles from the estate of Hogate's friend, Franklin Roosevelt. Jane Bancroft, a widow now for fifteen months, was there along with young Jane, one of her two daughters. It was the first time Kilgore had ever socialized with the family that owned Dow Jones. Hogate's wife and one of his daughters later recalled that Casey had in mind matching Kilgore up romantically with young Jane, who was four years Kilgore's junior, but nothing ever came of it.

The weekend, in addition to providing the Bancroft women with a chance to look the young man over, may have been intended as a reward for Kilgore's latest coup. On January 7, the Supreme Court, in what came to be known as the *Hot Oil* case, had struck down as unconstitutional a provision of the National Industrial Recovery Act. Kilgore's column on the case, published on January 9, had emphasized how unusual it was for the Court to invalidate an act of Congress, and had expressed doubt that the Court would continue to nullify New Deal legislation, such as the balance of the NIRA, or the Agricultural Adjustment Act.

In this prediction, which turned out to be off the mark—the Court and the president were soon on a collision course, culminating in Roosevelt's 1937 proposal to "pack" the Court—Kilgore proved less adept at charting the course of legal events than he usually was with economic matters. But he did again capture the attention of the nation's chief executive. At his afternoon press conference in the Oval Office on the day the column appeared, Roosevelt, the *Journal* reported, was asked to comment. He "at first declined, then added that if the newspapermen really wanted to understand the situation, they should look up Mr. Kilgore's article. . . . It was a good job, the President declared."

Hogate was so happy he quickly raised Kilgore's salary another ten dollars a week, to $105, although this may also have been intended to partially offset a payroll deduction for a new program that had Kilgore contributing $25 per week—a large sum at the time—to purchase Dow Jones shares.

Tecumseh was at once delighted and wary.

> *We were proud to know the President mentioned you in the press conference. This sure means a lot to have the President point you out as a man able to tell the real story of things of national import and I am glad you are able to do it. I too thought your article on the Court [d]ecision was about all right. I may be mistaken but I thought I could detect in your article [two days later] on the budget the faint fragrance of a bunch of violets in a boutonniere for the President in return for the bouquet he handed you in the Press Conference.*

Barney was quick to defend himself, however. The second article, he pointed out, "was written before Mr. Roosevelt said anything."

Kilgore did move, though, to parlay Roosevelt's compliment into additional journalistic advantage. He wrote the president a letter seeking an interview, and one was arranged for "a couple minutes" late on Wednesday afternoon,

January 23, just two weeks after the *Hot Oil* column. A memo in the *Journal*'s files recorded that Kilgore found FDR

> *in a serious but friendly mood and he talked very frankly. He even said I could write about his ideas as long as I didn't tie anything so closely to the White House that it would make trouble among the regular Washington correspondents. After I left, my head was buzzing with ideas and I sat down and wrote a piece about gold and silver money.*

Kilgore's account in a letter to his parents goes much farther. FDR gave him nearly an hour:

> *He didn't act like I expected him to. There was none of this grinning and wisecracking. He was quite serious all the time and didn't ask me very many questions. Part of the time I was in his office this English portrait painter was at work over in one corner. He was having quite a time of it, because the President doesn't stay very still much of the time.*
> * All in all, I think just about what I always thought about the President. He is pleasant, has a lot of things to contend with that most people don't know much about and still has very vague ideas about money. Of course, I didn't undertake to argue with him on any points. He did the talking and I listened.*

FDR invited Kilgore to return on his next Washington visit. "I think he probably meant it. At least, I intend to try to see him again."

In mid-March, his status in Washington greatly elevated, Kilgore briefly revived his "Dear George" column, absent from the *Journal*'s pages for more than twenty-six months. The first seven of these columns were a diary of a new man's first days in the capital at the dawn of what historians would come to call the Second New Deal. They represented Kilgore at his best.

Instead of the usual Washington reporter's approach of masking ignorance and affecting the tone of omniscience common to those who frequent the capital, Kilgore made a virtue of his naïveté. The first paragraph of his first column included the following:

> *If you happen to have a good newspaper on your desk at this very minute you undoubtedly know a whole lot more about what went on today in*

Washington than I do. The set-up is much too complicated for one man to follow except in a very general sort of way. I haven't been here long enough for that and the only broad impression I could offer you right now is that it is likely to rain before dinnertime.

The letter to "George," now signed "B.K." in place of the "J.W." of 1932, described a visit to Capitol Hill. Watching a committee hearing featuring testimony by Federal Reserve chairman Marriner Eccles, Kilgore noted that Eccles "has been explaining for days and days and days what the proposed banking act of 1935 is all about" but that "perhaps it isn't exactly right to say" that Eccles and the congressman questioning him "exchanged views" as they were, as usual at such hearings, talking past each other.

A floor debate in the House prompted these observations:

It is frightfully difficult to hear anything that is said in the House unless the speaker happens to have a loud voice and is all fired up about his subject. You can, however, amuse yourself by looking at the stained glass panels in the ceiling skylight.

The next day, four years before Frank Capra's *Mr. Smith Goes to Washington,* the young man from Indiana continued in the same vein, beginning his second letter,

Well, it has cleared up a lot here since last evening. The weather, I mean. So far as the political atmosphere is concerned, visibility is just about as low as ever. This has not been what you would call a particularly exciting day. Or perhaps it would be more accurate for me to say that if there was any excitement around here today I managed to miss it. Funny thing about prowling around this city—it gives you a curious feeling of being almost completely out of touch with things.

Perhaps in a dig at Phelps, who had been posted to Washington since 1932 and had been writing a quite dry column on goings-on in the capital, Kilgore continued,

There are about a hundred and one different places a man would have to be at the same time in order to be able to sit down of an evening and

write intelligently on what is commonly described as the Washington scene. There are a few people down here who can do it, of course, but they all have a lot of experience in the first place and a lot of help in the second.

A visit to another congressional committee hearing, this one featuring Clarence Darrow testifying about the NRA, drew the observation that "I don't think Darrow knows much more about the NRA than Will Rogers or Clark Gable does." Checking in on the United States Senate, Kilgore saw for what it was a ritual other reporters had long since come to ignore:

> *Along about 1 o'clock, one of the Senators got up and suggested the absence of a quorum. Anybody with half an eye could see there weren't more than twenty members in the chamber, but they went through a roll-call and enough others showed up long enough to answer "here" when their names were called to make a majority. Then the session went on as before—except that just after a quorum had been officially registered as present, there were only twelve or fifteen Senators in their chairs, instead of twenty. Curious.*

This was Washington coverage written for and from the perspective not of insiders but of *readers*. Once again, Kilgore was using an unconventional form of narrative to bring himself closer to his audience, writing not so much for those making the news as for the many more affected by it.

The third of the new "Dear George" letters continued to make a virtue out of the confusion of the new kid on the block:

> *You remind me of that old story about the young lady who married the rich old gentleman who promptly fell very ill and threatened to die. The bride called the doctor and paced up and down by the bedside, wringing her hands and moaning, with a great show of emotion, "Is there any hope?" Is there any hope?' The doctor turned to her with a knowing look and gravely replied, "That depends, madame, on what you are hoping for."*
>
> *So it is with Washington. Everything depends on what you are hoping for. Just at present, anyone who tries to tell you exactly what is going to happen down here and when is either kidding himself or kidding you. Paste that in your hat.*

After a week in Washington writing his column every day, Kilgore claimed to be just as confused as he had been on arrival, although perhaps more definitively so:

> *The New Deal doesn't seem to head up anywhere—that is, there is no single source or authoritative information on what it is or where it is going. To mention a couple other words that you are no doubt sick and tired of hearing, there is still no way of telling the proportions of "recovery" and "reform" in its basic formula.*

Kilgore's fortunes, in the sixth year of the Depression, were increasingly diverging from those of his parents, emphasizing for him both his own good fortune and the privation still widespread in the country. His latest raise brought his salary to the equivalent of nearly $78,000 today, and he was writing also for *Barron's,* and freelancing for Vincent Astor and Raymond Moley's *Today* magazine (which was eventually merged into *Newsweek*). One of the early pieces for *Today* brought notice from his hometown *South Bend Tribune,* which declared, "Watch that boy. He isn't through yet."

Kilgore and his parents could speak fairly often by telephone for the first time, but he encouraged them to call him collect. Barney sent money home at least four times in 1935. At one point that fall, his father acknowledged his desperate need, noting that "your check came in pretty handy. I had three dollars in my pocket and $1.20 in the bank when it came."

Kilgore continued writing "Dear George" after his return to New York. The column now reverted to something close to the approach taken in San Francisco, explaining complex matters in relatively simple terms. But the focus had shifted from principles of economics and business largely to regulatory, legislative, and policy matters. One of the best of the columns unpacked the then-popular idea of mandating a thirty-hour work week, pointing out that such a proposal, if it was not to cut the pay of those already employed, would require a 33 percent increase in wage rates—and thus in prices of manufactured goods. Farmers, Kilgore noted, would have no way to recoup these costs.

The column continued even on a train trip to Texas by way of a stop at home at South Bend in the late Spring. Kilgore shared a practical reporting tip with "George": "I always talk with brakemen whenever I travel. This is not hard to do because the brakeman has to stand on the rear platform part of the time to wave at the signal-tower men as the train rushes past. He can't get away." And the reporter continued not to let his preferences cloud his observations: Roosevelt, he found, remained strong in Texas.

Kilgore or a colleague also took to publishing letters to the editor of the *Journal* about the column under the pseudonym "Simeon S. Snuffkins" of Westerly, Rhode Island, one of a group of characters who were said to gather "daily at Zeke Tulliver's General Store to get the mail and talk over the affairs of the nation," and, apparently, to admire the journalism of Barney Kilgore. The origins and meaning of this inside joke appear to be lost, but the letters do serve as a reminder of what a small world the *Journal* continued to inhabit in 1935.

Just days before resuming "Dear George," Kilgore started yet another column as well. On its first appearance, it was called simply "New Publications," but it then became "Financial Bookshelf."

The column did not yield anything near Kilgore's best work, but it did serve to underline his incredible pace of production. From mid-March through early October 1935 (and even with taking August off from book reviewing, or at least from publishing book reviews), Kilgore wrote twenty such columns over a period of twenty-nine weeks, writing short but fairly comprehensive reviews of forty-one books—an average of better than one book read and reviewed every five days. This came while he was also writing his nearly daily regular "noncolumn."

Kilgore took his task as book reviewer quite literally in most cases, briefly summarizing a book's argument, and quickly and simply passing judgment on whether it was worth reading and, if so, by what audience. But on one occasion, his reporting intruded. Reviewing a book called *Handout* by one George Michael, devoted to unmasking the "propaganda" efforts of the Roosevelt administration, the reviewer had this to say:

> *Part of it may be true. I don't know. I stopped reading when I got as far as page 28 [of 242 pages] and encountered a statement which I know, from personal experience, to be false. That spoiled the rest of the book.*

The statement follows:

"It is the unwritten law that any White House scribe who wishes to ask the President a question at the coming [press] conference, must tip off [Steve] Early, the President's press secretary, to that question at least one day in advance of the conference."

This is pure bunk. I have attended several of the President's press conferences and asked questions—and received answers—without tipping off anybody. Furthermore, I have listened to questions and answers about events in Washington which had just occurred and which, obviously, couldn't have been tipped off to Mr. Early a day in advance.

Mr. Michael may have a good subject, but he has let his enthusiasm or something run away with him.

The second run of "Dear George" ended in early June 1935, although "Financial Bookshelf" continued. Kilgore, ever restless, had a new column idea, but it ran only once, under the heading "Footnotes on the News" under the pseudonym "Jonathan Wright" and then in only one edition of one day's paper, an edition which seems to have been lost—and, along with it, any idea of what the column was about—before being put aside so that Kilgore could fill in for Buren McCormack in writing "What's News" during McCormack's summer vacation.

After McCormack returned, Kilgore was invited on a Labor Day outing to the Bancroft family estate in Cohasset, Massachusetts, his first visit to the family compound. Writing to his mother, he pronounced it

> *good fun. Cohasset is a suburb of Boston, a little south of the city and close to the ocean. The Bancrofts have a very swell house there, of course. It has a swimming pool and garden off to one side, a tennis court across the road and a very elaborate barn where horses are kept. I did some riding and some swimming and some tennis-playing—besides a lot of very fine eating. They are nice people in spite of the fact that they are rich.*

During or shortly after the weekend in Cohasset, Hogate made clear that he wanted Kilgore to move to Washington and run the *Journal* bureau, and Kilgore soon agreed to do so, having secured Hogate's agreement to upgrade the quality of the *Journal*'s offices; Phelps was brought to New York as the editor of *Barron's,* "special work at which he is probably better than running a bureau."

Kilgore turned down an offer to work for William Randolph Hearst after giving it serious consideration. The offer must have been tempting, as Hearst, at seventy-two, was still the nation's leading media owner. His holdings, as reviewed in a *Fortune* article at just this time, included twenty newspapers, including the *Journal, American,* and *Mirror* in New York, the *Herald* and *Times* in Washington, and the *Examiner* in Los Angeles. The newspapers, in eighteen cities, had an aggregate circulation of 5.5 million daily and 7 million on Sunday. Hearst also owned thirteen magazines, led by *Good Housekeeping,* with an aggregate circulation of 4.5 million, the dominant King Features Syndicate, and eight radio stations, including New York's WINS.

Kilgore got another raise in connection with either the promotion, or the spurning of the Hearst offer or both, to the equivalent of more than $95,000 today before the mandatory company stock purchase. But it was likely far less than Hearst would have paid. The *Fortune* piece noted that nearly a hundred Hearst employees earned $25,000 or more per year (more than $350,000 today). His father warned that "it looks like Hogate might be thinking of making an executive out of you instead of a writer."

Kilgore looked forward to the move to Washington, repeating earlier observations that it would be a more enjoyable place to live than New York. "I doubt," he noted, "I would want to remain there forever. However, I don't think I would want to remain in New York forever either."

In Washington, Kilgore took on his first assignment as a manager, but he also continued to write, and to do so prolifically. He continued to write his "non-column," and also to cover the news. Some of his work was prescient, some of it not; much of it was insightful.

Looking at the recently enacted Social Security program, Kilgore warned against counting revenues from payroll taxes to offset current deficits, while also supposedly counting on the same money to pay future retirement claims. He rejected the then-prevalent notion of "permanent" unemployment, noting that:

> *The secret is this: If one thinks in terms of permanent unemployment,*
> *one thinks in terms of just a certain limited amount of work to be done in*
> *the national economy. If, on the other hand, one thinks of unemployment*

*as a problem that can really be solved, one thinks in terms of expanding
production of both goods and services.*

And he clearly saw the centrality of this issue.

*Unemployment is the depression. The lack of official and exact figures
doesn't detract from the importance of the problem a bit. Upon the trend of
unemployment, in the last analysis, depends the trend of governmental relief expenditures and upon relief expenditures depends the Treasury's bud-
getary position.*

He continued to be at his best when doing on-the-ground reporting, taking
advantage, for instance, of a trip home to South Bend for Christmas 1935 to
report and write a column out of Chicago in which he reminded readers (and
himself) that

*$100 is still a whole lot of money to most of the citizenry hereabouts.
They can understand what $100 is, and what it means in terms of work or
groceries—whereas billions of dollars spent by the Government are just in-
comprehensible figures.*

The same visit to Indiana enabled him to place in context the Townsend
Plan to cure the Depression by miraculously sending checks for $200 per
month to every senior citizen and then requiring them to spend the money.
Kilgore noted momentary popular enthusiasm for the plan, but likened that
phenomenon to the previous year's chain letter craze, and concluded, "The
Townsendites, generally speaking, don't know anything at all about economics. Probably they wouldn't be Townsendites if they did."

His powers of prognostication—especially outside the context of the financial markets—continued to be mixed at best, to reflect either the con-
ventional wisdom or, even more often, his own preferences. He incorrectly
predicted that the Supreme Court would overturn the Wagner Act governing labor relations. He consistently overestimated Alf Landon's strength in
1936, especially after spending time with Landon, even suggesting privately
to his father, just a week before the election, that Landon might carry Ohio;
Roosevelt's margin in the state exceeded 20 percent. He was insufficiently
skeptical of Roosevelt's repeated hints that he was not interested in a third

term. On the other hand, he was close to the mark in forecasting the large Republican gains in the 1938 congressional campaigns. And he was one of the first reporters to note the groundswell of interest, particularly in the Midwest, in the 1940 presidential candidacy of Wendell Willkie, although he was quite surprised by Willkie's nomination. In addition to analytic pieces, Kilgore, as bureau manager, also occasionally assigned himself to cover breaking news, especially out of the Supreme Court, as he developed substantial expertise in the constitutional questions governing the validity of New Deal legislation. He first suggested that Roosevelt might seek to tilt the balance on these matters by enlarging the membership of the Court in July 1936, more than seven months before FDR proposed what came to be known as his "Court-packing" scheme.

Beyond all of this, Kilgore actually stepped up his freelancing. After writing four pieces for *Today* in late 1935 and the spring of 1936, he wrote one long feature a week nearly every week from August 1936 through February 1937. One of these was about Margaret Rohwedder's father's sliced-bread machine. Kilgore noted that sliced-bread had been a novelty in 1928, had "caught on like a whirlwind in 1929," and had progressed to nearly universal usage eight years later, with new model machines slicing twenty to twenty-seven loaves per minute. His story indicated that "I happened to be in Davenport [Iowa] when the first slicing machine, hand made, was completed." He did not say why he had been there, and never mentioned his relationship with "the fair Margaret" in the story.

Beginning in 1936, Kilgore also began, for the first time, to cover politics, attending both parties' national political conventions. The 1940 Democratic Convention was perhaps the most unusual of those Kilgore witnessed. As he noted in his first article from Chicago, he could find no news at the convention—could not, amid FDR's efforts not to be seen to be actively seeking a third nomination, find anyone who was "ostensibly . . . running for President. While several gentlemen are actively seeking the Vice Presidential nomination, on the record at least no one wants to head the ticket."

Kilgore joined a number of colleagues in a parade down Michigan Boulevard promoting the mock vice presidential candidacy of Bascom Timmons, the Washington correspondent for a number of leading newspapers (including the *Houston Chronicle, Chicago Sun, Fort Worth Star-Telegram,* Raleigh *News and Observer* and Nashville *Tennessean*). Timmons rode in a 1906 Maxwell touring car. A photograph later published in *The Saturday Evening*

Post shows Kilgore standing nearby, holding a sign that declares, "WIN WITH TIM!"

Possibly disoriented by the situation, or even just hung over from his role in the Timmons "campaign," Kilgore ignored an early tip from Labor Secretary Frances Perkins that the vice presidential nomination would go to Agriculture Secretary Henry Wallace because he considered it so highly improbable, and thus missed an important scoop. Timmons ended up with one delegate vote, and told Wallace, "There was one man for me, and one man [FDR] for you."

His place in the Timmons "campaign" marked Barney Kilgore as a member in good standing of the Washington political reporting establishment. The badge of this status Kilgore wore most proudly was his membership in the Gridiron Club. He had been disappointed when he was not even invited to the Club's December 1937 dinner, and was delighted to be proposed for one of the fifty Washington-based memberships in April 1938. He was the first person from the *Journal* to be selected for the honor since Casey Hogate.

Once a member, Kilgore threw himself into the Gridiron's trademark skits and songs. At his first dinner as a member, in December 1938, Kilgore joined four other new members in a skit lampooning FDR's "Good Neighbor" diplomacy in Latin America, with the journalists impersonating Secretary of State Cordell Hull and recent Republican presidential candidate Alf Landon, among others. Practice for the spring and December 1939 dinners took place three evenings each week as the big evenings approached. Kilgore proudly took both Hogate and Grimes to the December dinner as his guests, and reveled in Gridiron events for the rest of his life, taking special pride in being able to take his father as his guest to the 1949 dinner—the first time Tecumseh had ever worn a tuxedo.

Kilgore's personal finances continued to improve sharply during his early years in Washington. He received a raise to $130 per week from Hogate in November 1935, and another to $140 per week (or about $103,000 per year today) in February 1936. A further raise followed in November 1936, and yet another in February 1937. He was also writing freelance articles for Raymond Moley's *Today*, *The American Mercury* (which had been founded by H. L. Mencken) and *Nation's Business*. Under an arrangement he made with Hogate, Dow Jones kept one-third of his freelance fees. With the proceeds from all of this, Kilgore took on a maid for his Washington apartment, bought his first new car, and eventually moved to a new and larger apartment at the Woodley Park Towers near the National Zoo.

The stock in Dow Jones that he had been compelled to buy began paying dividends, and he "put it in a savings account because it is money that I didn't earn by working. It is 'investment income' and perhaps someday I will want to live off of it." Some months later a letter to his parents included the news that

> *I bought some peanuts today. There was nothing remarkable about the peanuts except that they were compound interest peanuts. They were paid for by the interest on my savings account which, in turn, consists solely of dividends received from* Wall Street Journal *stock. They were paid for with money earned by money which I earned. I thought it was interesting.*

He continued sending money home, and did so at least five times in 1936, before beginning, in November of that year, to have the *Journal* send a regular weekly check to his father for $20. He urged his parents to consider the regular payments "a kind of dividend on your past investments in the bothersome brat who always hated (and still does) to get up early mornings." He added, "I am just awfully thankful that I am able to do something like this with so little trouble. I don't think I could even take credit for generousity [*sic*] because I won't really have to do without anything."

With these checks, in 1937 Kilgore's parents received more from him ($1,480, or just under $21,000 today) than they earned ($1,208.47), and so could be listed on his tax return as his dependents. By 1938, Tecumseh was again earning more than he was receiving from his son; the weekly checks kept arriving, but Tecumseh began returning those he could do without.

Barney's social life during these years was active. Through the spring of 1936, he was dating a woman from New York named Skippy who worked for U.S. Steel, but also began seeing a woman in Washington named Rosamond. (His letters never reveal their surnames.) As late as 1936, Barney was also in touch with both Margaret Rohwedder Steinhaur, his college girlfriend, and Vera Westerfield, his San Francisco girlfriend, both of whom sent him birthday greetings that year. The relationship with Rosamond was likely fairly serious, as she supervised Barney's birthday celebrations in both 1936 and 1937 and seems to have met his parents. But she moved to Maine for a new job in January 1938, and that apparently concluded the relationship, although Kilgore's letters shed no light on which was cause and which effect in this sequence of events.

At the end of August 1938, Barney noted in a letter to his father that "this DePauw girl from Greencastle" had been present for a weekend at the beach near Washington. Sometime between two and three weeks later—the letter is, unfortunately, lost—Barney sat down to tell his parents that he was seriously involved with the "DePauw girl." On September 23, just a day after that letter arrived in South Bend, he wrote again to say that he and the woman were going to be married on October 1. He had tried to arrange the wedding for "sooner than that, but she thought she ought to have another week at home to finish up her job and arrange things." He had met her parents briefly; she had never met his. Barney never explained what the rush was about; there is no reason to believe the bride was pregnant.

Her name was Mary Louise Throop, and she was twenty-six years old, although Barney told his parents that she was twenty-seven. (Even after they had been married more than three years, he was unsure of her birthdate.) Her father, James Throop, was a dentist in Greencastle, and she had taught English and public speaking at Greencastle High School after her graduation from DePauw. They had met on a visit by Kilgore back to DePauw for the college's centennial in 1937. Her new fiancée described Mary Lou as "the nicest girl I ever met. . . . a brunette. She is smart and she can cook. My friends here [in Washington] all think she is a swell girl too." Within a year, and forever after, Barney called her Lulu.

Barney secured the license on September 28, and engaged the chaplain of the House of Representatives, another Indiana native, to perform the ceremony. Barney's sister, Martha, drove to Greencastle and called on the Throops. The small wedding was held at the home of friends who lived in Bethesda, Maryland. Late in the afternoon of October 1, Tecumseh and Lavina received a telegram at their home in South Bend: "JUST MARRIED. HAPPIEST COUPLE IN THE WORLD. THINKING OF YOU. MARY LOU AND BARNEY."

The couple honeymooned for five days at a place called Skyland in Virginia's Shenandoah National Park, about ninety miles from Washington, where, according to Barney's report, they "had a cabin with fireplace and everything—about four rooms." Soon after that, Mary Lou joined Barney on his preelection political reporting swing, covering the 1938 congressional campaign.

In Kilgore's political reporting, he was consistently fascinated by the then-emerging science of public opinion research, and was immediately drawn to the work of Dr. George Gallup. For his own part, Kilgore set out to sample the opinions of voters anecdotally, but also with a fair degree of rigor.

During July and August 1936 he published a twenty-five-part series in the *Journal* reflecting travels through the Midwest recording the views of voters. Getting out of Washington (or New York), as usual, seemed to sharpen Kilgore's eye. A sampler:

> *The average fellow in the street declines to believe that a political crisis is in the offing. It is, to him, just another election and he is rather more interested in whether he will have a job next Winter than he is in whether Mr. Roosevelt will have one.*

> *The casual visitor viewing Plymouth [Indiana]'s four blocks of business section first thinks he sees three banks. Two of them have big clocks out in front, in typical bank style. . . .*
>
> *On closer examination, it appears that both the bank clocks have stopped. One forever points the hour of 12:40 and the other ceaselessly claims it is half past three. On even closer examination, it turns out that the two banks have also stopped.*

> *Interviewing farmers, by the way, is an interesting business. It takes a lot of time, but it's worth it. The average farmer, if you ask him point-blank, won't tell you whom he intends to vote for. He says he doesn't know for sure, and that's that. However, if you begin by asking him about the weather or any one of a dozen other things, and then drift casually into politics with questions as to how his township or county will vote, nine times out of ten he'll dodge the question as to the county or township but wind up expressing his own personal views.*

The *Journal* increasingly saw Kilgore as a marketable commodity, a marquee name. Of the twenty-five articles in the series, eleven included his name in the headline, another ten in the subhead. References by name to Kilgore also became much more frequent in the *Journal*'s editorials. By the spring of 1938 a sixteen-part series on "Washington Now" was trumpeted in advance with a full-page house advertisement that included Kilgore's photograph. At this, one of the low points of the Depression, Kilgore wrote his parents that "our business is lousy, of course, but I don't think the *WSJ* will fold up for a long time. They tell me they sold a good many subscriptions with the Washington series as bait." Similar promotional treatment was accorded another series, devoted to "business recovery" and marking ten years of Depression, in June and July 1939.

The 1938 series was introduced with a note explaining that, in Washington, "the waves often run one way and the tide another. It is with the tide, rather than the waves, that this series of articles primarily will be concerned. Is the tide changing in Washington today?" While Kilgore's analysis was clouded by an excessive view of the threat that New Deal regulation posed to the capitalist system, he did correctly sense that the New Deal itself, just ahead of Roosevelt's futile attempt to "purge" his own party, had largely run its course.

Today we often forget that Roosevelt and the New Deal were in deep political trouble in 1937 and 1938, with Depression lingering after recovery had seemed at hand in 1936 and with the President defeated first on Court-packing, then in his party's 1938 primaries and finally with Republicans resurgent in the 1938 congressional elections. FDR and his policies were almost certainly rescued by the economic and political consequences of the advent of the Second World War in 1939. Kilgore, living in the moment, saw the story clearly:

> *Mr. Roosevelt's strength, during his first term, largely was the result of his ability to grasp and express in effective language the hopes and aspirations of a whole people. His weakness, as his second term got under way, would appear to have been the result of an unwillingness or inability to resolve the inevitable conflicts among those hopes and aspirations and to carry forward the enormous task of administering economic and social reform projects.*

Later in 1938, Kilgore was one of the first to see the potential in defense spending for finally breaking the back of the Depression.

During the summer and fall of 1938, Kilgore set off on additional political reporting tours of the Midwest and central Atlantic states and occasionally experimented along the way with new forms of reporting. One day, from Kokomo, Indiana, he filed (and the *Journal* published) unadorned notes from a diary recorded during a hundred-mile slow drive along the old Dixie Highway.

Another day, he stood on a street corner in Erie, Pennsylvania, and conducted a poll of his own, questioning more than one hundred voters on their plans for voting in the forthcoming elections for governor and United States senator. But having learned an important trick of the trade from Dr. Gallup, Kilgore went one key step further. He added a third question, inquiring who each voter had voted for in the most recent presidential election, the 1936 contest between Roosevelt and Landon. Before analyzing the answers to the first two questions, Kilgore then checked the answers from his sample to the third question against the actual 1936 results from the city and county of Erie. When his sample's answers for 1936 came out in the narrow range between the actual city and county results, he concluded that it was fairly reliable. The next day, he repeated the experiment in Pittsburgh, dubbing his own poll "the Buttonhole Institute of Public Opinion." And two days after that, he analyzed *The Columbus Dispatch* straw poll on the same basis. Kilgore almost instinctively recognized the potential polling had for revolutionizing political journalism. As he concluded his report from Columbus,

> *Your correspondent has no apologies to make for devoting an entire article in this series to a discussion of another newspaper's straw vote. After all, Ohio is normally the best sample state for political purposes in the whole country. And since straws in the wind are about all that would be political writers have to go on anyway, more than 50,000 straws—even if they have been collected at random—are not to be sneezed at.*

For 1938, this was an incredibly sophisticated approach to sampling public opinion; moreover, it took some of courage, given the famous fiasco in which the 1936 *Literary Digest* poll, based on the return of 2.3 million postcards, had forecast a 57–43 percent Landon victory, instead of the 61–37 percent Roosevelt landslide that actually occurred. Gallup had taught Kilgore well.

In 1940, Kilgore also began to see how polling was changing not just political journalism, but politics itself. The viability of the 1940 presidential nomination campaign of Thomas E. Dewey, a man who had been defeated for the governorship of New York just two years earlier and had not yet attained any office higher than that of New York County district attorney, he saw as a creature of such surveys. "The Gallup polls and others like them," Kilgore wrote, "provide for the first time a widely accepted measuring stick to gauge the results of a campaign that is aimed at the general public over the heads, as it were, of the Republican organization leaders." And Kilgore saw early, too, that candidates who live by polls can die by them. Polling was crucial, he noted, in the preconvention rise of Willkie, and it helped deny Dewey the nomination. "Dr. Gallup may have as much influence on the GOP convention this year as all the Presidential preference primaries put together."

Kilgore's professional reputation in Washington had been boosted enormously by favorable mentions of his coverage by President Roosevelt, first in 1933 with respect to the Bonus Bill, then in 1935 regarding the *Hot Oil* case. The *Journal* itself played up the incidents, although other papers did as well. The president granted Kilgore another private interview in January 1938. Kilgore reported to his parents that FDR was "quite nice and said the big business people were treating him like they treated Teddy Roosevelt." In early 1939, however, perhaps stung by his own political reverses, as well as Kilgore's unsparing coverage of them, Roosevelt seems to have subjected Kilgore to a less pleasant sort of attention.

What happened was this: FDR had nominated left-winger Thomas Amlie, former Progressive Party congressman from Wisconsin, to a vacancy on the Interstate Commerce Commission, and the nomination instantly became a source of controversy. At the president's news conference on January 24, an exchange on the subject began in a lighthearted vein:

> Q: *Can you tell us anything about the background of the Amlie appointment, who is for him or anything of that sort?*
> FDR: *I suppose I might put it this way: I have to pick a non-Democrat. [At this point, the official transcript records "Laughter"]*
> Q: *And were Republicans naturally barred?*
> FDR: *Oh, no; what was he?*
> Q: *A Progressive.*
> FDR: *All I wanted to know was, "Is he a non-Democrat?" And they said "Yes," and that was all right.*
> Q: *With whom did you have this conversation? [Laughter]*

The transcript does not reveal the identity of the reporter who asked the next question. In any event, the president's mood instantly darkened:

Q: *What about his qualifications for the post. Did you take cog-*
     nizance of that?

FDR: *Do you suppose I would have sent his name in if I thought he was*
      not qualified?

Q: *I am asking what the qualifications are, I assure you.*

FDR: *Have I ever been asked a question like that in all our Press Con-*
      ferences? Do you want me to give you a list of the qualifications of
      people whose names I submit to the Senate? Do you want me to
      give you his life history, a list of the things he said or that he did
      for last twenty years? That is silly.

And, with that, the subject was awkwardly and abruptly dropped.

The next day's *Journal* fully recounted the exchange in one paragraph, call-ing Roosevelt's response a "stern[] rebuke."

But three days later Kilgore returned to the scene of the crime with a column headed "Washington Nightmare." Written in the tone and manner of a fable, it tells of a "young reporter" who "bolt[s] down a bowl of Chili and a slab of mince pie" and then quickly heads home to "a deep troubled sleep." Very soon, the reporter faces a slew of angry questions from his managing editor, with the list of questions turning into a snake and wriggling under his bed.

In the nightmare, dials fly off telephones, which then melt. When the young reporter runs out, barefoot, to gets answers to his questions, a series of old men refer him, rudely, from the State Department to the Treasury Department to the Federal Reserve Board to the Securities and Exchange Commission to the Com-merce Department and back to the State Department. Finally, he is sent to the Interstate Commerce Commission, where one last old man instructs him that,

"Nobody here knows anything about railroads[.] Haven't you heard the
news?"

Amo. Amat. Amamus. Amatus. Amlie.

"Amlie, Amlie, Amlie," he added, his voice rising to a shriek.

The locomotive bell rang, then rang again; then faster, faster, faster. Un-
til it sounded just like an alarm clock.

The young reporter awoke with a start and cold feet. He shut off the
bell.

And to this day, he hasn't been able to make up his mind whether it was
all—quite all—a bad dream.

Kilgore was just thirty years old. It seems inconceivable that he would have published the "nightmare" had the "young reporter" been anyone but himself. The *Journal* never again referred to the incident, and never identified the reporter involved.

Perhaps reflecting some greater animus after the White House press conference exchange, the 1939 series on the outlook after ten years of Depression reflected Kilgore's increasingly harsh view of the New Deal. The second article of the series, for instance, blamed the Roosevelt administration "for a scatterbrained approach to the recovery effort and a punitive rather than constructive approach to the major problems of economic and social reform." The next article concluded: "The federal budget is simply out of control."

But none of this seems to have affected Kilgore's marketability. In October 1939, he received a visit in Washington from James McGraw Jr. of McGraw-Hill who "wanted to talk some about the possibilities" of Kilgore working for them. McGraw told Kilgore that newspapers were failing, while magazines, such as those published by McGraw-Hill (including *Business Week*) had more of a future. Kilgore did not entirely disagree at this point. He noted that extreme cost pressures at local general-interest newspapers had created a trend toward cutting business coverage, which was only accelerating the newspapers' downward spiral—although it was benefiting the *Journal,* and especially its Pacific Coast edition.

Kilgore told his father that he "wouldn't be interested at all unless they talk in terms of large sums of money," well above the $10,000 (about $140,000 today) that McGraw-Hill was offering as its opening bid, and perhaps not even then. In the end, the McGraw-Hill offer moved him no more than had that from Hearst. "I think," he wrote Tecumseh, "I have got hold of a form of journalism in which I can make a pretty good showing and naturally the time to make the money is while I can get some fun out of it." Mr. McGraw had told Kilgore from the outset that he intended to discuss his approach with Hogate; within a month, the discussion had turned to the possibility of the *Journal's* Washington bureau, under Kilgore's leadership, "taking over [McGraw-Hill's] Washington work," although nothing ever came of this idea. Kilgore did, however, get another $25 per week raise.

With Mary Lou's help, Kilgore was also raising his social profile in Washington. George Gallup accompanied him to a Gridiron dinner. He and Mary

Lou were invited to the White House for Sunday lunch with Mrs. Roosevelt. Supreme Court Justice William O. Douglas and later Senator Robert Taft came to the Kilgore home for dinner. The latter occasion prompted the observation that "Bro[ther] Taft is a very good egg when he is among people he thinks are his friends and when nobody is trying to impress him. He talked a lot—which is rather unusual for him—and seemed to have a good time." Casey Hogate had been slated to be the Kilgores' guest at their beach house at Plum Point, Maryland, for Labor Day 1939 before the outbreak of war in Europe aborted the weekend. The Kilgores did host twenty-five *Journal* staffers for breakfast the morning after the 1940 White House Correspondents Association dinner.

Kilgore also stepped up his appearances on the radio, including joining a panel for a national hookup on "America's Railroad Problem" as part of The American Forum of the Air that reacted to a speech by Senator Harry S. Truman of Missouri, and discussing Social Security on NBC's Red Network.

Kilgore believed from the start of the 1940 campaign that Roosevelt's reelection was unlikely. That belief was substantially strengthened by his travels with Willkie during the last weeks of the campaign. An article he wrote on the Friday before the general election placed Willkie's chances at "better than 50-50 to win." In the event, FDR won a third term handily.

But Kilgore then did something unusual for national political reporters—he wrote and published an article on why he had gotten it so wrong. His conclusion:

> *I don't know why a lot of other people made mistakes. Some of them, of course, were thinking wishfully. Some of them may have had their orders, as the saying goes.*
>
> *In my own case, frankly, I was fooled by the noise.*

What he meant was that he'd been misled by the enthusiasm of the crowds greeting Willkie. From this, however, he took a valuable lesson about the difference between the *intensity* of political beliefs and their *prevalence*—a lesson many reporters continue to miss today. As always, Kilgore could explain clearly. He noted that the rough 55–45 margin for Roosevelt was the same as an 11–9 division in a group of 20, and he went on:

If you went into a room full of 20 people and one less than half the
group were talking rather emphatically in favor of one presidential candi-
date and one more than half were discussing the other one rather quietly
you might get the impression that the majority was the minority and vice
versa.

But you would be wrong, as he had been.

Kilgore's contributions to the *Journal* as Washington bureau manager extended
beyond his work as reporter and editor. He was also engaged in continuing the
remaking of the newspaper as a whole that Grimes had begun in 1934. Early in
1940 he wrote his father that Grimes "is a good guy and a fine feller to work
for and with. I think sometimes his judgment of men is better than Bro[ther]
Hogate's." Together, he indicated, "we are trying to make our Washington stuff
more interesting to average businessmen."

Soon he had developed a new vehicle for doing this. On Friday, September
20, 1940, Kilgore engineered the publication of a new column, a "Special Report from *The Wall Street Journal*'s Capital Bureau." It ran the full length of column five on the newspaper's front page, the column one removed from the
right-hand margin. The new entry comprised a series of brief items, ending
with even shorter points headed "Minor Memos." The first item began in near-
telegraphic style: "Forty-five days 'till election. After that, adjust your safety
belt." Additional subjects, each covered in no more than three paragraphs, included the constitutionality of the draft bill, the likely timing of congressional
adjournment, the outlook for antitrust action against the oil industry and for
changes in corporate income taxes. Among the "minor memos": " 'No brass
bands' is Secretary of War Stimson's decision on handling conscription of men
and Secretary of the Treasury Morgenthau's policy on selling 'defense bonds.' "

The column was introduced by an editor's note that ran at the bottom of
the column:

The Wall Street Journal believes that a staff of newswriters ordinarily as-
signed to specific segments of the Capital's news-making machinery might
pool their information about once a week in a more informal, more inti-
mate report. This may assist in a more accurate size-up of the Washington
scene.

The column was headed "Washington Wire."

Reader reaction was quick, strong, and favorable. Kerby later recalled that Grimes had agreed to place only the initial column on page one, and that Kerby "suffered a convenient loss of memory" and placed the second column in the same position the following Friday. In any event, by the third installment the subhed called it a "Special *Weekly* Report." Kilgore was pleased, noting in a letter home that "Washington Wire is getting a lot of good comment" and soliciting his parents' reactions "because it is supposed to be written to be interesting to folks outside Wall Street and the banks." This was crucial, he knew, because, "We have a lot more readers outside New York than inside."

"Washington Wire" ran in the *Journal* every Friday from its first appearance until December 2007, and ran in its column-five position until 2002. It soon became the model for much more substantial changes in the *Journal,* all of them driven by Barney Kilgore.

7

Managing Editor

BY THE CLOSE OF 1940, Kilgore had headed the *Journal*'s Washington bureau for more than five years, by far the longest he had ever held a single job. He had led the coverage of three congressional and two presidential campaigns and done much of the on-the-ground political reporting himself, had pioneered a new sort of column for the *Journal*'s front page with the "Washington Wire," and had established a comfortable life for himself in the nation's capital, a young married man of rising income and strong prospects, a delighted member of the Gridiron. The *Journal* bureau in Washington was the second-largest of any newspaper.

But while Barney Kilgore was well fixed, the same could not be said either of his country or his newspaper. The Depression lingered, now in its twelfth year, while Europe was engulfed in war, with Britain holding out almost alone against the Nazis. The war, however, seemed to him far away. Kilgore, still a lieutenant in the Army Reserve, was asked, in January 1941, to join the War Department, "as an economic expert or something if I want to go on active duty for a year." It "would be interesting as Army work goes and a good place to be, but not as interesting and I doubt whether as important as newspaper work." So, he told his mother plainly, "I am going to turn it down. Army pay is not very good as compared with newspaper salaries and I don't think there's that kind of an emergency." When war did eventually come, Kilgore worried briefly about the draft, but never seems to have considered enlisting.

The *Journal,* meanwhile, seemed stuck in a business rut. There was no question that Grimes, in his more than six years as managing editor, had vastly improved the paper, due in no small measure to Kilgore's "What's News" column, and the strong coverage of Washington, now highlighted by "Washington Wire." Yet total paid copies were 32,000, not far from the 30,000 level to which they had fallen in 1932. Competitor *Wall Street News* had been acquired, but its circulation soon bled away. The circulation of the *Journal* seemed to rise and fall not more than 10 percent, largely in concert with the markets, hitting a low of 28,400 in the economic decline of 1938. Profits had bottomed (very near to zero) in 1938 as well; they remained extremely anemic.

On the third night of 1941, Kilgore and Mary Lou hosted Casey Hogate for a Friday night dinner at their apartment in Washington. Hogate was in town for a radio appearance the following evening. Among the subjects the two men discussed was Hogate's desire for more front-page columns along the lines of "Washington Wire."

Less than three weeks later, Kilgore made a trip to New York to help pursue this notion. Grimes seems to have agreed on the necessary direction, but also to have concluded that Kilgore was essential to driving it forward. On the evening of January 21–22, the two men sat around the *Journal*'s Broad Street offices until two o'clock in the morning discussing how the paper might be improved.

The next day, Kilgore worked in the office on

> *the possibility of using the Washington Wire form and style for New York news too. They had gotten together some material but they wanted somebody to show two or three men in New York how to handle it. I worked on it all day and also did some work on the What's News column, which they are trying to improve. They've taken some reader surveys which show that readers like summaries and they are going to try to do more summarizing.*

A bit less than two weeks later, Kilgore was back in New York, ostensibly continuing the same mission. But Hogate and Grimes had reached a dramatic conclusion. It seems likely that Grimes actually led the way, perhaps resolving himself after the late-night discussion during Kilgore's earlier visit. Sometime on February 3 or 4, Hogate and Grimes jointly asked Kilgore if he would like to be managing editor of the *Journal,* with Grimes moving to chief of the editorial page, with the title of "editor." "Mary Lou and I talked it over," he later wrote, "and decided it would be a good idea."

It was an extraordinary move, especially for Grimes. Kilgore was his direct subordinate, and, at thirty-two, sixteen years Grimes's junior. But the older man had clearly concluded that he had taken the *Journal* as far as he could, and believed that Kilgore could take the paper farther. There was true selflessness but no false modesty in this—Grimes was temperamentally modest, but hardly lacking in self-esteem—and the decision was taken without a hint of bitterness. If anything, the personal bond between Kilgore and Grimes was strengthening. On his second New York trip to discuss the front page, Kilgore ended up bringing Mary Lou along, but he had indicated to his parents that, had he come alone, he would have been staying with Grimes overnight in Brooklyn. In the years to come, the two men would grow even closer, as Kilgore surpassed Grimes, but also justified the confidence the older man had placed in him.

For now, Kilgore sent a telegram to his parents at midday on February 5:

IT IS STILL A SECRET AROUND HERE BUT I AM SUPPOSED TO MOVE TO NEW YORK AND BECOME MANAGING EDITOR SOUNDS LIKE A GOOD IDEA TO ME. WE ARE GOING BACK TO WASHINGTON TONIGHT AND MOVE IN A COUPLE OF WEEKS LOVE, BERNARD

As always, Kilgore was moving to New York with personal reluctance, but he saw the career imperative. It was past time to transition out of the bureau manager role:

I don't think New York will be as pleasant a place to live as Washington, but Mary Lou and I are too young to settle down permanently if there is opportunity elsewhere. A good many Washington newspapermen go to seed around here and probably it is a better place to come back to on the way to retirement. I've done about all I can do here now and it's pretty much a routine proposition.

As for the newspaper of which he was about to take the helm, Kilgore was optimistic, quietly confident in his own vision. "I think a lot of things can be done with the paper. It is a much better paper than it was and, I think, a fairly successful paper, but it has much room for future development."

———

Kilgore's page-one story of February 1, 1941, on defense labor policy was the last of his more than 1,300 articles in the *Journal* in the eight and a half years since "Dear George" began. With the exception of a single story filed from Albany on the strategy of Governor Thomas Dewey's 1944 presidential campaign, Barney Kilgore's byline would never again appear in *The Wall Street Journal.* But he had only really begun to change the newspaper.

Precisely what happened in Kilgore's first days and weeks on the job as managing editor is difficult to reconstruct. The Kilgore letters provide some reliable detail, and it is reflected in the account that follows here. The memoirs of Bill Kerby, who had left the Liberty League and rejoined the *Journal* as a news editor in 1936, and had been promoted to assistant managing editor in 1938, provide a more thorough account, and have largely been accepted by historians. But Kerby's details, written down forty or more years after the fact, are often demonstrably inaccurate; here as elsewhere, I have relied on them only to the extent they seem not inconsistent with established facts.

Before leaving New York on the day he telegrammed his parents, Kilgore agreed with Hogate and Grimes on other key personnel changes in the *Journal's* news operation. Gene Duffield, a reporter Kilgore had hired in Washington after a stint at the *Chicago Tribune,* would succeed Kilgore as bureau manager in Washington, while Kerby, with whom Grimes had previously discussed a transfer back home to Washington, would take the lead role in developing the new columns modeled on "Washington Wire." Kerby lost his assistant managing editor title for a time, but it was restored within a year. Hogate announced all the new assignments (beginning with those of Grimes and Kilgore) on Friday, February 14. His note acknowledged that "while this seems a sizable change, all the personalities are well and favorably known to the entire staff, and everyone affected, including even those more remotely affected, is in hearty approval." He thus expected the "usual hearty cooperation."

Kilgore spent two weeks in Washington preparing to move north. He returned to the office in New York on February 20, and was officially listed as the *Journal's* managing editor for the first time in the newspaper of February 21, 1941.

Barney and Mary Lou took up residence in New York at the Barclay Hotel on East 48th Street, living there in a barter arrangement off a *Journal* advertising due bill. They moved in the spring to an apartment on East 35th Street, and again in late summer to another apartment in Brooklyn Heights, all the while looking for a home outside the city, for weekend use if not as a permanent residence. After a nearly year-long search, they purchased Snowden, an estate in Princeton, New Jersey, whose main house was sixty years old and greatly in need of refurbishment. It cost them $10,000, or about $124,000 today, of which they put 10 percent down in cash.

With Kilgore installed as managing editor, changes at the *Journal* came quickly. Hogate largely gave him a free hand, and Grimes confined himself to the editorial page. The first of the projected new front-page columns to emerge was called "Commodity Letter," billed as "A Special Staff Report on Price and Production Trends Affecting Industry." It made its first appearance on March 8, in Kilgore's thirteenth edition as managing editor, on the *Journal*'s commodity markets page. "Commodity Letter" followed the format of "Washington Wire" closely, with nine fairly short items, ranging over commodities from rubber to silk to grain to cotton, and a collection of briefs filling almost an entire column.

On Monday, March 17, Kilgore and Grimes moved "Progress of the Week," a weekly page-one "editorial review" written by Frederick Kossmeyer, who had been the *Journal*'s chief editorial writer since the death of William Peter Hamilton in 1929, to the same column-five slot as "Washington Wire," and revised its format into a series of short items, although it later evolved into an essay. The column, begun in 1935, had moved to the top of the Monday "What's News" column later in the same year. It has continued to change over the years, but still runs in the Monday *Journal* to this day under the heading "The Outlook."

The next week, Kilgore turned his attention to "What's News" proper. On March 26, the column's display was revised a bit to point up its separate sections on business and finance on the one hand and general news on the other. A week later the general news was given its own column, beginning at the top of the page, widening "What's News" to three columns—and thus covering nearly half the paper's front page. The general news was also given the new title of "World-Wide," which it retains to this day. The three-column display was used until near the end of 1941, when a set of embedded charts and indexes was removed and the current two-column format adopted.

In April, not yet two months into his new job, Kilgore nearly completed his basic remake of the newspaper's first page. As he noted in a letter to his father, "We are trying awfully hard to get out a front page which will be interesting to a wide assortment of people, some of which are not much intrigued by the stuff we carry inside the paper."

"Commodity Letter" was moved to the same page one, column five slot as "Washington Wire" and "Progress of the Week" on April 1. It would run on the front page each week in the Tuesday *Journal* for nearly twenty-four years; in early 1965, it was shifted to an inside page and Monday publication. It was discontinued in 1966.

The next day brought the debut, in the same full-column slot, of "Tax Report," a Wednesday "Special Summary and Forecast of Federal and State Tax Developments." Again, "Washington Wire" supplied the format. "Tax Report" continues to run in the *Journal* each Wednesday, although since 2002 it has appeared in the Personal Journal section rather than on page one.

The Thursday column slot, using the now-familiar format, was given over to "Business Bulletin," a "Special Report on Trends in Industry and Finance," beginning the next week. The column ran each week through the year 2000. With that, seven weeks into the job, Kilgore had completed a weekday lineup of column-five features, with "Progress of the Week" on Monday, "Commodity Letter" on Tuesday, "Tax Report" on Wednesday, "Business Bulletin" on Thursday, and "Washington Wire" on Friday.

This tour de force is all the more remarkable because, in the midst of it, Barney Kilgore lost his mother. Lavina had been suffering throughout the last months of 1940, a victim of what her husband referred to as "hardening of the arteries" and nearly monthly "attacks" with serious gastrointestinal symptoms. Her eyesight was failing, and she had become hypersensitive to light. On occasion she would rally, but the trend of her health was clearly adverse.

On Sunday evening, March 16, 1941, just as the *Journal*'s presses were churning out the first copies of the issue with the new placement of the "Progress of the Week" column, Lavina suffered her final attack. In South Bend, Tecumseh scribbled on a letter he had just received from his son, "I called him from the dinner table on account of Mother's change for worse. She passed away Sunday at about 7 pm. He arrived [in South Bend] at around 3 pm [Monday]."

Barney and Mary Lou remained in South Bend for Lavina's funeral. The weeklong stay likely delayed the changes in the *Journal* by a similar period. En route to New York by train on Saturday night, March 22, son wrote father that "I wish we could have stayed in South Bend longer but my job now is in New York and I want to make good at it. I want you to be proud of me because I have always been proud of my parents."

It is tempting to think that on his eighth week on his new job Kilgore rested. But, of course, he did not. On May 16 the *Journal* published a special "defense edition," marking a year since President Roosevelt's request to Congress for significantly increased defense appropriations. The special issue ran sixty-four pages—four times the usual length of a *Journal* issue at that time—and further, albeit more modest, special issues followed on the chemical and utilities industries.

Most important, having reinvented the center of the *Journal*'s display page with forward-focused analytic columns on specialized subjects, Kilgore and Kerby now turned their attention to the front-page feature stories, the "leders" (journalistic shorthand for "leading article") that ran on the page's outside columns. Here the shift came not on any one day, but more gradually, with traditional news articles increasingly replaced by narratives of a new sort in a daily newspaper.

The changes were comprehensive. Grimes in 1939 had changed the look of the stories with the introduction of "flashlines," brief, boldface headlines-above-the-headlines, usually of one or two words, but the focus now was on content. Substance was broadened; style was revolutionized and then sharpened.

Substance: Reporters were told that they should no longer write stories about banking with an audience of bankers in mind—better to aim for the almost infinitely more numerous bank depositors. As a later article summarizing the changes would put it, the new view was that "business news embraces everything that relates to making a living." Kilgore bluntly acknowledged that "financial people are nice people and all that, but there aren't enough of them to make this paper go."

Articles no longer needed to be pegged to news that had occurred, or could be made to have appeared to occur the previous day. Indeed, the use of the words "today" and "yesterday" in leders was strongly discouraged. Trends were what was important. As Kilgore had noted in his key "Dear George" column nine years earlier, readers were more interested in tomorrow anyway. And thoughts of readers' geography were to be discouraged. The audience was a national community of interest, uniting businessmen, in a phrase they later developed, "from Portland, Maine, to Portland, Oregon."

Above all, *Journal* leders needed to be distinctive. The newspaper was designed to be a second read, a complement to a metropolitan paper. Accordingly, it need not write about everything ("What's News" would cover reader's basic needs in that regard); it needed to hold reader's attention on those subjects on which it did choose to engage. They were sufficiently successful in this regard that Kerby recalls an offer from a Scripps-Howard syndicate for "second-day rights" to leders. Kilgore and he rejected the offer, despite Dow Jones's need for revenues, because they concluded it could limit their ambitions for the *Journal.*

Style: The old "inverted pyramid" newspaper story Charles Dow had learned from Samuel Bowles—"Put it all in the first line"—and that had evolved into a formulaic "who, what, when, where, and why" was, Kilgore noted, simply boring. Its decree that the information in a story become less important the farther the reader got into the story certainly helped editors in the composing room cut stories to fit the available space, but it also implicitly encouraged readers to stop reading. This was precisely the opposite of what Kilgore understood an editor should be seeking. "The easiest thing in the world for any reader to do," he reminded Kerby, "is to stop reading." Even worse, the inverted pyramid formula implicitly discouraged analysis. Many articles would be more effective if they began, as had many that Kilgore had written in his trips around the country these last eight years, with a telling anecdote or a provocative quote.

Articles beginning with "anecdotal leads," however, also required a new element, a straightforward explanation, before a story got too far along, about what the article was actually *about.* In time, this statement, placed in a short paragraph of its own, became known as the "nut graf." It is very difficult to determine the extent to which Barney Kilgore and Bill Kerby invented anecdotal leads and nut grafs in the newspaper context, but there is no question that both concepts became closely identified with, and typified by, *Wall Street Journal* leders.

Not every story, of course, could or should begin with an anecdotal lead. Some news stories were so urgent that such an approach would be counterproductive. And the emphasis on national scope soon gave rise to a new sort of story, the "roundup," where reporters in *Journal* bureaus all across the country quickly and simultaneously tracked the impact of a new development in their local communities, with Kerby's team in New York pulling all the threads together into an instant national tapestry.

The scope of their ambition, particularly in extending their revolution to the writing of leders, meant that Kilgore and Kerby needed help. Almost from the first, when offered his pick of the paper's entire New York staff, Kerby found that help in Buren McCormack, who, in effect, became "Kerby's Kerby."

McCormack, another Indiana native and Rector Scholar, was a year behind Kilgore at DePauw, although only three months younger. He and Kilgore were fraternity brothers in college, although their friendship seems to have begun in earnest only when Kilgore came to New York in 1933. McCormack roomed with Kilgore and fellow DePauw alumnus Perry TeWalt in Brooklyn before McCormack's 1933 marriage. Kilgore spent New Year's Eve 1934 and New Year's Day 1935 with the McCormacks. He stayed with them in New York at least twice during his years in Washington.

McCormack delivered newspapers as a boy and founded a paper at his high school. He was a frugal and responsible young man, establishing his first checking account when he was ten, and accumulating $1,000 in a savings account before he went off to college. (Kilgore did not save that much until he had been out of college for seven years.) McCormack had worked all four years in college on *The DePauw,* and joined the *Journal* as a reporter in September 1930 or 1931 (the records disagree). He had quickly moved through New York postings on the copy desk and various editing jobs before being named to lead the paper's banking and financial coverage. During Kilgore's managing editorship, Kerby and McCormack now undertook to write or edit nearly every leder on the *Journal's* front page.

Kilgore knew he had made progress with the paper, but he was far from satisfied. "Some days I think it is pretty interesting as a paper and other days it falls a little flat."

The key test of the new regime came on a Sunday, less than ten months into Kilgore's tenure as managing editor. Until that weekend, it had been the *Journal's* practice to largely lock up the Monday paper on Saturday, with only half staff in the production group working Sunday. Kilgore decided to change the system, simply "on the theory a newspaper ought to have its shop force on the day it goes to press." Early in the afternoon of the new system's first Sunday, Kilgore came to the office "to see how the new system was working." Shortly after 3:00 P.M. the wire services flashed a bulletin. It was December 7, 1941. The Japanese had attacked Pearl Harbor.

As many staff members as could be summoned were called in to the office, and the *Journal* was produced on schedule, with an additional fourth edition added, on which the final deadline was one o'clock in the morning. (The opening installment of a planned series on how workers would be able to afford the new, higher income tax rates was hastily moved to page 8 from page 1, with Kilgore sending a note of apology to its author.)

The Sunday staffing plan was not the *Journal*'s only stroke of luck that day. Kerby, in place as Sunday editor since early in the year, had been the author of two page-one stories on the defense buildup back in March and April. He had also written the lead piece for the special "defense issue" in May, although, it was suddenly and appallingly clear, that piece had been wildly optimistic in celebrating the ability of a U.S. fleet that "proudly keeps the peace in the Pacific" and "is now more powerful than that of any other nation."

More recently, Kerby and Duffield had collaborated on an extensive series of articles to be published under the rubric "Defense Economy." A number of the articles had been completed, and were simply awaiting publication. Drawing on them, and with the first edition deadline looming, Kerby now banged out the paper's lead story, with Kilgore serving as copy editor as each paragraph, most of them consisting of a single sentence, emerged from Kerby's typewriter as a separate "take." Hogate, having rushed to the office, stood reading over the two men's shoulders.

Monday's *Journal* was published under a rare banner headline: "U.S. Industry's Sole Objective: Arms Production Speedup; / Congress Prepares to Act; Tax Bill Will Be Rushed; / N.Y. Stock Exchange to Open As Usual Today, Says Schram."

Kerby's story was a masterpiece, the perfect embodiment of the new *Journal*'s reach and aspirations. Above all, on a day when people would pick up the next day's paper expecting to hear about "yesterday"—the very word with which Roosevelt would begin his famous speech—*The Wall Street Journal* was helping its readers focus on "tomorrow." "War with Japan," Kerby's story began, "means industrial revolution in the United States." Its prescience continued:

The American productive machine will be reshaped with but one purpose—to produce the maximum of things needed to defeat the enemy.

It will be a brutal process.

It implies intense, almost fantastic stimulation for some industries; strict rationing for others; inevitable, complete liquidation for a few.

War with Japan will be a war of great distances.

Thus, certainly in its preliminary stages and probably for the duration, it will be a war of the sea and the air.

This means unlimited quantities of ships and shells, bombers and bombs, oil, gasoline.

Eventually, it also means an army dwarfing the present military establishment—5 million, 8 million. It's a guess. But that will come later.

Duffield, meanwhile, wrote the day's other leader, a military analysis of war "on 2 Oceans and 3 Continents." Kerby later called Pearl Harbor the key "turning point in acceptance of the *Journal* after it changed from a stock market–oriented publication to a national business newspaper."

Duffield and Kerby's series, now restyled "War Economy" rather than "Defense Economy," was rewritten, completed, and published in eleven installments between December 23, 1941, and February 9, 1942. Apart from three articles on advertising in wartime that were published the following August, Kerby, too, had now had his last byline in the *Journal*.

War did not stop Kilgore from continuing to remake the newspaper, nor did it deprive him of his sense of humor. In November 1941, he and Grimes had added a daily cartoon on the editorial page to the long-running snippets that ran under the heading of "Pepper and Salt." The first such cartoon showed a car coming off an assembly line with a tank turret emerging from its roof. In the caption, one observer says to another, "That one went through on the switch to defense orders." The cartoon continues in the *Journal* to this day.

More significantly, as Kilgore resolved the "What's News" package into two columns toward the end of 1941, one hole remained in the format of his new front page. Columns 1 (on the far left) and 6 (on the far right) were for leders; columns 2 and 3 were devoted, respectively, to the "Business & Finance" and "World-Wide" columns of "What's News"; column 5 hosted the new weekly features; but that left the fourth column. Particularly for a nation at war, Kilgore had the sense that some relief was necessary to what was likely to be a dark and heavy diet of news and analysis.

Thus was born, on December 17, 1941, what would come to be known in later years as the "A-hed," so named because the widening-as-it-descended typography of its headline style was said to resemble a capital A. A-heds were intended to be quirky stories, sometimes funny, sometimes simply diverting— slices of life, if you will. They have remained a distinctive feature of the newspaper's front page ever since, treating everything from carrots to camel wrestling; the best of them have been collected in numerous anthologies.

Kilgore said little over the years about the column's origins, but such stories fit squarely into his own sense of humor, and he had been groping toward such a form himself occasionally over the years. Indeed, a story Kilgore wrote in 1936 can be said to have been the first *Journal* A-hed in style, if not in placement.

The article was datelined Grand Rapids, Michigan, and was written in the middle of Kilgore's preelection political tour of the Midwest just ahead of the Roosevelt-Landon presidential contest. The roving star reporter happened upon the factory of the American Seating Co., and beheld a machine he simply could not resist writing about. It was a seat tester.

The *Journal*'s editors seem not to have known what to make of Kilgore's report, but they did agree to place it on page four under the straightforward, if unlikely, headline, "Kilgore Makes Non-Political Detour into American Seat Co.'s Plant and Sees Wooden Seat-Testing Machine at Work." The story began, "America has stood a lot, they say, during the last five or six years. But, today it seems to be sitting down a good deal, also." Then, in fourteen un-self-conscious paragraphs Kilgore described the ways and means of seat manufacturing, culminating in this description of the seat tester itself:

> *The research experts have to know how fabrics, springs and other construction items hold up under wear. Instead of a crew of sitters to report on how many ups and downs such and such a product will stand they have a machine to do the trick. With mechanical precision, this machine rams a suitably carved chunk of hardwood against the most important part of any chair and by and by the engineers read the counter and know how many years the thing would last, say, in Radio City Music Hall.*

Four years later, while on another political trip, Kilgore took time out to write another story, similar in its light slice-of-life tone. It recounted his drive along the full 160-mile length of the new Pennsylvania Turnpike, from Harrisburg to Pittsburgh, along the nation's first long-distance rural highway. The road had opened less than two weeks before the article was published, and Kilgore was particularly struck by its lack of a posted speed limit. He also noted, in reference to its tollbooths, that "the road of tomorrow is financed like the road of the day-before-yesterday."

In 1941, with these stories perhaps in his mind as a model, Kilgore found a regular place in his newspaper for such bits of whimsy. The first example he and Kerby actually placed in the paper needed to be sensitive, coming, as it did, just ten days after Pearl Harbor. It reported on prices for American flags, noting that they had risen both with increased demand since the attack and ensuing declaration of war and with scarcities in necessary materials. It bore no dateline or byline. As with the seat-testing story, the distinctive mark of the short tale came in its use of telling details, such as the possibility that rayon might be employed as a substitute material, and in its deployment of choice quotations, including one from an unnamed flag manufacturer who noted that "we have been preparing for this in a quiet way and dealers have good-sized stocks on hand."

Kilgore's remake of page one was essentially completed a month later, with the final addition of a special weekly column for Saturdays. "London Cable" was billed as a "Report at the Week-end from *The Wall Street Journal*'s Staff Correspondent" George Ormsby. It began at a time when Prime Minister Winston Churchill was in residence at the White House, but would run for just over nine years, and, again, followed the format of the "Washington Wire."

As America entered the war, Kilgore's changes were drawing a strong response from readers, and beginning to be noticed in journalistic circles. Ten days after Pearl Harbor, he reported to Tecumseh that new subscriptions were coming in a rate of "over a hundred a day," especially noteworthy in light of a relatively quiet period in the stock market. Circulation continued to rise in the months that followed. The 1941 year-end paper ran eighty pages—the capacity limit of the *Journal*'s presses, making it the largest edition the paper had published since 1932.

The profile of these readers was impressive—and changing. Nearly a fifth earned $25,000 year or more ($300,000 today), with a majority having annual income above $10,000 (nearly $125,000 today). An extensive survey of readers in Ohio found that only about a quarter worked in banking or finance, while the majority were involved in industry or business. Kilgore was succeeding in broadening the audience while maintaining its elite nature.

In mid-January 1942 Kilgore received an offer to join *Time* magazine to run its Business & Finance department. His initial reaction was that he didn't "think this is a good time for me to switch jobs," but he pondered the offer for nearly two months, lunching with *Time*'s publisher, clearly tempted when he learned that *Time*'s offer was for $20,000, or roughly $240,000 today. That was an enormous increase over his *Journal* salary of $12,000 (roughly $144,000 today), although Kilgore repeatedly noted that the very high marginal income tax rates reduced the appeal considerably.

He did not discuss the offer with Hogate, and was unsure whether to do so. He told his father that

> *the only reason I would consider leaving the* WSJ *would be a belief that the times ahead were going to be very bad for it or a belief that I wasn't getting anywhere around here. The* WSJ *carries a good deal of deadwood, as any enterprise this old usually does, but it has made out pretty well thus far.*

At that point in Kilgore's deliberations, fate intervened. One week after he wrote that letter, and with *Time* "still talking to me about [the offer] whenever they get a chance," Casey Hogate, whose health had been in decline for a year, was felled by a stroke. The matter was being kept very quiet, but initial reports reaching Kilgore and Grimes indicated thickening of speech and impairment of Hogate's left arm, with expectations that he would be out of the office at least three months, although his doctors had recommended even before the stroke that he retire completely.

Hogate's absence left a large void at Dow Jones. In the first days, Grimes took charge, acting on behalf of the Bancrofts. Kilgore thoroughly approved, writing that "Mrs. Bancroft regards Grimes as the best man around here— which is true and proves she is a smart old woman—and if he really is allowed to take hold and they don't monkey around too much I think the paper will get along all right."

In line with his own earlier observation about "deadwood," Kilgore noted that Grimes would need to do "some cutting down and some tough management—which Mr. Hogate's health of recent months has not really allowed him to give it—but all newspapers are pretty much in the same fix."

For himself, Kilgore was inclined "to stay and back up Bro[ther] Grimes who will probably need some backing up." That would require rejecting both the *Time* offer and one from Du Pont to work in corporate public relations. "Publicity work I don't want at all," he wrote. If things somehow went awry at the *Journal,* Kilgore thought he would go with *Time,* "but I really think I'm happier on a daily paper, with full charge."

Then something did go awry. Kilgore's letters only hint at what happened, and no reference to it has ever before been published. But it appears that, about three weeks after his stroke, with his mental faculties impaired, Hogate, perhaps in a fit of paranoia, may have moved to dismiss both Kilgore and Grimes. In her greatest service to Dow Jones and the *Journal* since at least the day of her husband's funeral nine years earlier ("Don't you and the boys worry about dividends"), Jane Bancroft seems to have intervened at that point. Kilgore, who had just visited Indiana and discussed the matter in person, wrote his father on March 30:

> *Everything here at the office has been fixed up I think and Mrs. Bancroft's lawyer [Jack Richardson] has taken charge at least temporarily. Mr. Hogate has been ordered by his doctors to have nothing whatever to do with the office for three months or more and that clears up all the hocuspocus. So I feel pretty good about it.*

Tecumseh remained uneasy. He wondered "what [Hogate] will do to Brother Grimes and you if he does get back on the job." But he was not without sympathy for the ailing chief executive: "I can imagine Brother Hogate's feeling when he thinks about being laid on the shelf before he is fifty years old [Hogate was actually only forty-four]. It irks me some times to have to acknowledge that the younger bloods are passing me in the Life Insurance business and I am sixty-seven."

Two days later, Barney reported that Hogate's secretary "is right much worried about Casey's mental condition . . . at least he's in a bad state of nerves anyway." Hogate may also have earlier attempted some inappropriate financial maneuver, but, if so, he had been outflanked on this as well. Kilgore noted, "We are getting along here. . . . and I think they'll be no trouble. Every department head is studying the whole situation; I went over all the books myself this afternoon, although I cannot say that I understand them."

Hogate's recovery was slow. Kilgore received a note from his mentor in late April and concluded that "he doesn't expect to come back for quite a while yet. I think he is still pretty sick." In September, Kilgore heard that Hogate was expected back part-time the following month, but Hogate did not actually appear until November 12, more than eight months after his stroke.

By then any hard feelings on Kilgore's part seem to have dissolved. He described Hogate's return this way:

> *I think he was glad to see the place again. As a matter of fact however he is quite a ways yet from being a well man but I think Mrs. Hogate and the doctors believe that if they let him come into the office occasionally it will speed up his recovery—which as a matter of fact it may. He still likes the paper and I hope he will get back fulltime one of these days soon.*

The complications stemming from Hogate's illness were not concluded, however. Someone, it was clear, needed to run the company, and Hogate, it was equally clear, could no longer do so. The two candidates, all involved seem to have understood, were Kilgore and Joseph Ackell.

Ackell, just a couple of years older than Kilgore, first worked for Dow Jones in 1925 as a stenographer in the advertising department, following a series of odd jobs after quitting Brooklyn's Commercial High School at the age of fourteen. In the 1920s and '30s, as the company's director of manufacturing, Ackell and colleagues had developed a new news ticker for the Dow Jones News Service that could spit out copy at the then-amazing rate of sixty words per minute, and an automated mailing machine for the folding and wrapping of copies of the *Journal* and *Barron's*.

But he was not a newsroom favorite. Edward Scharff described Ackell this way:

> *[He] was something of a school superintendent in appearance. Stiff in bearing and stern in countenance, he favored dark clothing that accentuated his sallow complexion. He had thinning hair and silver-rimmed spectacles, and if you came on him abruptly, some said, he could seem almost sinister. Ackell spoke in a low, rigidly controlled monotone, and he often seemed to have something cynical to say. Nor did it help that many on the news side felt Ackell distrusted them.*

On his second or third day back in the office, Hogate appeared to make his choice. He asked Kilgore if he wanted to "take over a new job as his assistant," that is, move from managing editor of the *Journal* to become, in effect, the head of the business operations of all of Dow Jones. Kilgore laid out his thinking, and what he took to be Hogate's, as follows:

> *I think he really hated to do it in a way because he figures it was taking over business responsibilities that ruined his health, but on the other hand he wanted to give me a chance to turn it down before he offered it to anybody else. I think I will take it. In many ways it will be a tough proposition, but on the other hand . . . I don't want to work for a guy who was brought up in the business office of a newspaper. That's the bad part—you come to a point where you either have to take on a lot of management worries in a newspaper or you have to let nonnewspaper people run the shop—and that's very bad indeed. So I guess at least for the time being I will shove along. Only I think I will take Bro[ther] Hogate's very earnest and heartfelt advice and watch out for my health.*

The matter was not so easily resolved. Hogate asked Kilgore to consider the matter for a week, but three weeks later, he had still not reopened the discussion. Kilgore wrote his father that he guessed that Hogate "has changed his mind about the matter probably because he believes he is getting stronger himself and can handle all the details again. If he does that, he'll get sick again I am sure."

In fact, however, Hogate may have changed his mind not about himself, but about his choice of Kilgore over Ackell. One night in December 1942, Kerby later recalled, he was at home in Brooklyn Heights when Grimes, a neighbor, telephoned to say that Hogate intended to name Ackell as general manager of Dow Jones. Grimes, according to this account, said that, in such an event, both he and Kilgore would resign. Kerby noted that he would as well.

With that, Grimes said he would call Jack Richardson, Jane Bancroft's Boston lawyer, and propose Kilgore's appointment instead. Later the same evening, Grimes called Kerby back and asked him to come over. When Kerby arrived, he found Kilgore, who still also had his apartment in the Heights, already there: "Said Grimes, Barney's in as general manager. I stay as editor and keep an eye on all news operations, and you are the new managing editor of *The Wall*

Street Journal." Kerby immediately chose Buren McCormack as assistant managing editor.

Whether this account is strictly accurate (neither Kilgore, Grimes, nor Richardson seems ever to have written of the events), there is no question that Grimes, once again, and for the second time in as many years, played a key role in advancing Kilgore, this time to a position as his superior. Previous historical accounts have reflected Kerby's report that there were tensions between the two men, but Kilgore's letters home belie this. In fact, during this period, the Grimeses seem almost certainly to have been the Kilgores' closest friends. The older couple hosted the younger for no fewer than fourteen weekends at their Hopewell Junction, New York, farm in the year after Kilgore became managing editor. The visits declined in frequency only when the Kilgores acquired a weekend place of their own in Princeton in the spring of 1942.

Kilgore almost matter-of-factly noted his promotion ("you may be interested to know") in a New Year's Eve 1943 letter to his father. As he described the job, "I will operate for [Hogate] a good bit of the time until he gets able to spend more time in the office—which he hopes to do gradually but it will be a period of some months." Kilgore probably knew that Hogate's return to work was unlikely. In fact, Barney Kilgore, just three weeks past his thirty-fourth birthday, was now the top executive at Dow Jones and *The Wall Street Journal.* It was a job he would hold for the rest of his life.

8

OVER THE HUMP

KILGORE'S INSTALLATION AS GENERAL manager of Dow Jones and, in effect, acting publisher of *The Wall Street Journal* still did not really give him a free hand during the war years. In a sense, he was left to re-live the role Hogate had played during the last years of Hugh Bancroft's unhappy life—in theory he had the power, and in fact the responsibility. But his predecessor remained something of a presence, and respect alone dictated that changes, if any, be modest, or at least undertaken with modesty.

Hogate came in to the office on January 6, 1943, Kilgore's third official day on the job, and indicated that he expected to "come in about once a week and take it easy." He treated Kilgore generously, giving his protégé what Kilgore described as "a fine big office next to his—it is much too fancy for a newspaperman, however."

But just a month later, Hogate had what Kilgore at first termed "something of a set-back." Hogate's wife indicated that he might be up and around in two or three weeks, but Kilgore was skeptical, noting that Hogate's eyesight was now impaired "and I don't think that is a very good sign." In fact, Kilgore would not see his boss again for four months, and then only when he went to the Hogate farm for a daughter's wedding. After that, it was another fifteen months, until September 1944, before Kilgore seems to have seen Hogate again, and this came only with a Kilgore visit to Hogate's farm. On that visit Kilgore found Hogate able to read a bit, but "he still has trouble in talking however and he gets tired out quickly." The illness was clearly psychological as well as physical; Kilgore referred to "the damage to his nervous system." Hogate now just "push[ed] business out of his mind somehow and avoided even worrying about it." In all, the Kilgore letters give no indication that Hogate came in to the office at all after January 1943, and substantial indication that he did not.

In addition to this factor in limiting Kilgore's ability to innovate, the Second World War had the effect of putting a good deal of the newspaper business—like many other businesses—on hold. In the case of newspapers especially, two key ingredients were in short supply: newsprint and men. Newsprint, like many other commodities, was rationed in wartime, and hard to find even under the ration caps. Manpower, of course, was being drained off by the military, with many of those Kilgore and Kerby had begun to train in their new methods called into national service.

At the end of a first, abbreviated New Year's week in his new job, Kilgore observed that "our first big problem is to get enough paper to print the *Journal*." Prewar papers had often comprised as many as eighteen or twenty pages per issue. For the duration of the war, the average issue would shrink to twelve.

In trimming, of course, there were two types of content that could be cut back: news and advertising. First, Kilgore set Kerby to the task of getting control over the volume of news content. Kerby later recalled his approach:

> *I reviewed some 30 issues of the Journal and reedited every story of any substantial length. I then proceeded to my mathematical calculations and arrived at the average number of columns per day needed to present tightly edited news in adequate fashion. I issued a ukase to the copy desk. From now on, the* Journal *would contain no more than 54 columns (nine pages) of news content. This included complete market quotations and a half (three-column) editorial page.*

Only Kerby himself would have the power to make an exception, and these would be rare.

As Kerby and Kilgore quickly realized, however, this was another case of a necessity actually constituting a virtue. Kerby concluded that the paper became "much better edited, more concise, meatier. . . . Filler stories, which our readers didn't really want, or need, were completely eliminated. Our composing rooms knew exactly how much type they had to set each night, and weren't forced to staff for the occasional 'big' papers."

But cutting news space (the "news hole") solved only half the question for a wartime publisher. The next issue concerned advertising. Even as the supply of newsprint was contracting, the demand for it from advertisers was being driven up by two important factors: first, an economy that finally, after more than ten years of depression, began to boom, largely on the back of defense spending; and, second, tax policy that inadvertently promoted advertising spending. The tax side of this equation was driven by a wartime excess profits tax and by very high regular marginal corporate tax rates. Both provisions of the tax code left businessmen thinking that it made more sense to spend on ads—today we would say to "build brands"—than to remit nearly all of the same funds to the government.

So, despite Kerby's strict controls on news output, Kilgore was left with a choice: Did he ask Kerby to make further cuts when enough advertising was available to fill more than the available space, or did he refuse or postpone advertising in order to deliver to readers a full news report?

Different publishers during the Second World War reached different conclusions on this question, and the postwar history of many papers hung in the balance on the answers. At the high end of the New York broadsheet market, for instance, the *Herald Tribune* opted, at the margins, to accept the advertising, while the *Times* gave preference to news. The *Herald Tribune* profited during the war from the advertising but went into decline soon after. The *Times* gained readers during the conflict and advertisers after, and only then achieved its modern status as the nation's dominant general-interest newspaper.

Kilgore noted this later, when called in to consult for the *Herald Tribune* in 1958. But he had seen it in 1942. He had long since decided that a relentless focus on the desires of *readers* was the key to newspaper publishing. Kerby recalled Kilgore's saying that war was "the time to build"; that is, clearly, to build readership. "There'll be lots of time later to get advertising."

The manpower challenges hit even closer to home, and many could not be avoided. Kilgore worried about the draft as early as May 1942, and finally heard from his draft board in April 1943. He believed his history of childhood tuberculosis (undiagnosed at the time, but later detected by X-rays) would likely shield him. Nevertheless, he sent a Dow Jones official to "an Army man who helps handle draft matters" for reassurance. He was soon reclassified 2-B "as a necessary man in an essential industry. . . . It was very nice of them I thought because it was all done without any fussing or appealing or anything like that." In late June, he was still required to report to an induction center. He described the experience this way to his father:

*I got to go through the Army induction process here by special arrange-
ment with the Colonel who is in charge of the whole thing and the Army
threw me out. It was the regular official examination so I guess if and
when my draft board gets around to me there isn't any chance I would
be accepted. They'd have to change the rules. They took about four extra
X-ray pictures of my chest and announced that I was all right but that there
were too many spots to fit their rules. So that's pretty much that.*

A blood test followed in October 1943, but another chest X-ray in December,
almost exactly two years after Pearl Harbor, yielded the same conclusion. At
no point did Kilgore express any guilt about not serving, nor any reservations
about receiving special treatment during the process. Kerby similarly escaped
service. His childhood illness had been polio, which left him with a slight
limp, and Selective Service had exempted "managing editors of general daily
newspapers." With his first child on the way, Kerby was especially relieved.

Others on the staff were, of course, not spared. One way Kilgore and Kerby
made up for the shortfall in talent was, for the first time, to add women to the
Journal's news staff, recruiting them from leading journalism schools. The eight
reporters were dubbed the "beauty chorus," and none remained past 1949, in
significant measure because Kilgore may have seen newsrooms as a place for
men only. In any event, no significant number of women would again join the
Journal until after Kilgore's death.

Next on Kilgore's list of priorities was more closely aligning his first real home
at the *Journal,* the Pacific Coast Edition ("PCE") out of San Francisco, with
the main paper published in New York. The PCE had gone its own way before
this. It had not, for instance, switched to Kilgore's Sunday production schedule, and had completely missed the Pearl Harbor story. Kilgore summoned
Deac Hendee, still the paper's West Coast news chief, to New York in February 1943 to talk about the PCE, seeking greater cooperation from him, and
from Carl Miller, the paper's publisher, based in Los Angeles. "Otherwise,"
Kilgore wrote his father, "it might as well be closed down, because it loses a
little money every year steadily."

To Miller, he was only a bit less direct. A memo to Hogate outlined the approach Kilgore intended to take with Miller: "Editorially, the PCE is out of gear
with the New York Edition. We are, in effect, publishing two distinct papers

rather than two editions of one newspaper." It was past time for the PCE to adopt "the basic elements which a long process of sweat and trial and error has established as the philosophy formula of the 'new' *Wall Street Journal.* In our opinion, the PCE is making some of the same mistakes we made here and is (as much our fault as anybody's) some years behind the [New York edition]."

By late 1943 the two editions of the paper were much more alike—and nearly indistinguishable on their front pages. Kilgore also renewed his relationship with Bob Bottorff, his deputy from *The DePauw,* who had been named managing editor of the PCE in 1942. Bottorff hosted Kilgore when, in November 1944, the latter made his first visit back to San Francisco since a reporting trip in 1933.

With the immediate challenges of newsprint, the draft, and the Pacific Coast edition under control, Kilgore could turn his principal attention to the *Journal*'s readers—and the question of how to attract more of them. In a tactical move now standard but then highly unusual, Kilgore, in May 1943, commissioned a study of how readers actually read the *Journal.* Subscribers were surveyed in five cities: New York, Chicago, St. Louis, Milwaukee, and Providence. "What's News" was the best-read feature, delivery problems the chief complaint. (Both findings remain hardy perennials.) The news was generally encouraging, especially the high rate of subscribers' intention to renew, and the indications that higher sales levels were possible if early-morning delivery could be expanded.

To a considerable extent, newsprint rationing, in which allocations were based on prior usage, placed a ceiling on the growth of the *Journal*'s wartime circulation, or at least on marketing expenditures to that end. In January 1944, Kilgore wrote his father that "at the moment, we are not in a position to go after new circulation." But he did eke out enough newsprint supply to grow circulation steadily through the war years.

In early 1941, when Kilgore succeeded Grimes as managing editor, the combined circulation of the New York and Pacific Coast editions of the *Journal* had remained under 32,000. That was an improvement from the 1938 low of just over 28,000, but it was essentially flat over the nine years since 1932. In Kilgore's two years as managing editor, 1941 and 1942, circulation had risen about 10 percent, to 35,000. In his three war years as general manager, the growth accelerated, with increases of 20 percent in 1943, 17 percent in 1944 and 19 percent in 1945. When, in 1944, during the usually slow month of August, the field staff selling door-to-door garnered 700 new *Journal* subscriptions,

Kilgore was delighted. Early in 1945, *Wall Street Journal* circulation hit an all-time high, higher for the first time than it had been before the onset of the Great Depression. (By way of contrast, the Dow Jones Industrial Average, as a measure of the financial markets, did not recover to 1929 levels until 1954, nine years later.) By the end of 1945, circulation stood near 59,000.

With rising circulation and advertising—to the extent the latter could be accommodated with Kerby's fixed news hole—profits were again healthy under Kilgore's stewardship. Dividends to Mrs. Bancroft and her fellow shareholders totaled $416,000 (about $4.8 million today) in 1943, $283,000 ($3.2 million today) in 1944, and $166,000 in 1945 ($1.9 million today). When this trend began in 1943, Kilgore was quick to disclaim credit with his father. He noted that the company was making "quite a bit more than it has for a long time"—in fact, 1943 profits were the highest, in constant dollars, since 1930 or 1931—but he added, "Not my fault at all but it does naturally make the job easier—in fact there isn't much to it." Shortly thereafter he summed up the business performance as "mostly luck, but still good to look at."

That sort of modesty was, no doubt, excessive. Kilgore's changes to the *Journal* had unfurled the company's sails sufficiently to catch the wind of wartime expansion. But there is a sense in which Kilgore was clearly operating at less than full speed during the interregnum of the war years and Hogate's illness.

He and Mary Lou took the leftover time to attend to domestic life with much greater attention than they had in the past. They gave up their apartment in Brooklyn Heights early in Barney's tenure as general manager, and moved to Princeton.

There it seems they sought, in Snowden, to create a bit of Indiana in Central New Jersey. Shortly after closing on the house, in the late spring of 1942, Barney had taken his first-ever three-week vacation to spruce up the place. In 1943 they harvested on their own property green beans, yellow beans, currants, peas, cabbages, strawberries, raspberries, cherries, corn, tomatoes, apples, broccoli, grapes, and watermelon, as well as raising (and later killing, plucking, and eating) chickens, ducks, and turkeys. Where earlier they had been frequent weekend guests of the Grimeses, now they played host and hostess, with the editor and his wife overnighting in Princeton at least six times in 1943 alone. (Kilgore also filled in for Grimes at work, writing editorials when Grimes took vacation and again when Grimes injured a knee.) Once he had the new job under control, Kilgore thought nothing of taking a few days off, here and there, to plant trees.

The lifestyle was almost self-consciously Midwestern. Barney and Mary Lou, for the first time in their marriage, joined a church, Princeton's First Presbyterian. At one point Kilgore approvingly quoted Wendell Willkie "when he said the competition was too strong for him in Ohio and he came to New York where he could do better. . . . [Midwesterners] seem to do things the natives [here] never think about doing or don't have the energy to do if they think about it." At Snowden, Kilgore saw himself as something of a modern homesteader.

The next step, of course, was to fill the homestead with offspring. The couple had known since November 1944 that Mary Lou was pregnant, but they only told their parents that "Lulu is looking for the stork to come" in February 1945. The baby was due in June. "Thought you would be interested," Barney deadpanned. By May, they had names selected for both a boy and a girl, James Bernard or Kathryn.

Kathryn Kilgore was born Friday, June 1, 1945, shortly after noon, and was named after Mary Lou's mother. Barney took Mary Lou to the hospital on Thursday night and returned home to await news. He called a few times to check in, and the doctors telephoned him as well. He arrived back at the hospital about fifteen minutes after the birth to find that "Lulu was eating ice cream and enjoying it very much." The baby weighed six and half pounds. By Monday morning, her father was back at work.

Rising profits no doubt eased Kilgore's relationship with Jane Bancroft. And tending that relationship now became an important responsibility. As he noted to his father, Jane Bancroft was "pretty much interested in the business and since Mr. Hogate has been ill she doesn't get much chance to talk things over with anybody." He visited Boston to confer with Dow Jones's principal owner roughly quarterly beginning in late 1943. A formal annual meeting of stockholders was held in Boston each spring. On at least one occasion, at a birthday party for Hugh Bancroft Jr., Kilgore and Mary Lou stayed overnight with Mrs. Bancroft in Cohasset.

By spring 1945, just as the war was ending in Europe, and just ahead of the birth of his first child, Barney Kilgore finally felt sufficiently secure at the helm of Dow Jones to reorganize the company's management and to start talking publicly about what he and his colleagues were accomplishing.

On the day after Franklin Roosevelt's death, Kilgore named an executive committee of four men in addition to himself. Grimes continued as editorial director; Robert Feemster, who had been in charge of advertising sales for the *Journal* and *Barron's,* became head of all sales efforts at the company; Kilgore's former rival for leadership, Joe Ackell, was promoted from production manager to assistant general manager; and J. C. Hoskins continued as treasurer (what would today be termed chief financial officer). Privately, Kilgore told his colleagues that he was only making "official" arrangements that had been "tr[ied] out informally." The article in *Editor & Publisher,* the leading trade journal, announcing these appointments was accompanied by another on Bill Kerby's plans for the postwar *Wall Street Journal.* All five executives were pictured. Neither article mentioned Barney Kilgore.

This was the essence of the changing management style Kilgore brought to the company he now led. Hogate had tried to read—and, when healthy, often actually had read—and frequently correct, every word of copy before it was published in the *Journal.* His management of other functions was said to be similarly detailed. Kilgore, from the first, declined to interpret his job as any "great burden of daily chores. I deliberately try not to take on anything that someone else can do—and I also intend to avoid a lot of outside responsibilities, which is one of the things that made good-natured Brother Hogate sick I fear."

At roughly the same time that David Packard, at General Electric and then Hewlett Packard, was perfecting the technique he later christened "management by walking around," Kilgore noted that "most of my working day is spent in somebody's else's office." Here is Vermont Royster's description of how Kilgore chose to lead:

> [H]e hardly ever had any department head to his office. Instead, he made a daily practice of going to see them.
>
> After the morning's paper work, he would start from his eyrie on the top floor and walk through the building, floor by floor. On the way he would stop in at the office of the advertising director, the circulation manager, the comptroller, the editor, the managing editor and other key people. If they were busy, he might wave and pass on. If not, he would stop and ask them what was going on in their area, what plans they had and so forth. If he had questions, he asked. If he had thoughts, he would express them, more often phrased as suggestions rather than orders.
>
> Along the way he would also stop to chat with secretaries, clerks or

copyboys. These journeys would end in the basement where the printing presses were located. There, too, he would talk not only with the production manager but also with linotype operators and pressmen, many of whom he knew and all of whom knew him. Only the newest employee ever called him Mr. Kilgore. To everyone else he was Barney.

The closest thing to a management committee during most of Kilgore's years running Dow Jones was an informal daily meeting he did not even chair. It was known as the kaffeeklatsch, centered in the *Journal*'s news department, and supposedly chaired by the paper's managing editor.

The kaffeeklatsch was ostensibly a morning editorial meeting, and Kilgore joined it nearly every day, with his copy of the newspaper marked up with suggestions and critiques. Then the agenda would turn to the next day's paper and plans for future news coverage and possible changes in the paper. But because news was at the heart of the entire enterprise, because all the senior news people had worked together for so long and so well (many of them since college at DePauw—which was also the alma mater of the top two members of the ad sales staff), and perhaps most of all because it enabled Kilgore to manage with a light hand, the kaffeeklatsch became a corporate forum as well.

During Kilgore's quarterly visit to Boston in late September 1945 Mrs. Bancroft explained that Hogate was prepared to bow to reality; he had "suggested to her that he become Chairman of the Board of the company and that I be elected president. This is being done." Hogate, Kilgore told his father, "has written me a very nice letter on the subject and wished me luck."

Kilgore acknowledged that "naturally I am pleased with it" and expressed his confidence that "I think I can handle the new job—it won't be much different of course from what I've been doing." He missed writing, but noted, as he had three years earlier when he became general manger, that the only alternatives wouldn't be satisfactory. "Perhaps," he wrote wistfully, "I can bring somebody along in time to do the hard work and get back to the easy chores of writing pieces. But that will be some time off." In fact, he had already published his last article in the *Journal*.

Out of respect for Hogate, and "because I think a good many people would misunderstand about [his] condition, which," Kilgore continued to insist, "is actually getting better slowly," no announcement was made of the changes.

But on Wednesday, November 7, 1945, three names, rather than the previous one, appeared in the *Journal's* masthead. William H. Grimes was editor. Kenneth C. Hogate, now forty-eight years old and having been president of Dow Jones since he was thirty-one, was listed as chairman. Bernard Kilgore, his successor as president, was two days short of his own thirty-seventh birthday.

The immediate postwar years saw Kilgore's *Journal* unleashed.

It had taken the *Journal* forty-five years to first achieve 50,000 copies in circulation, and then seventeen years after the coming of the Depression to regain that level. But the second 50,000 copies—that is, growth to the 100,000 level—took just about two years. Circulation at year-end 1945 had been roughly 59,000. By the close of 1946, it was 76,000, and by the end of 1947, 103,000. As Kilgore observed to his father, "Business is booming." An article in *Kiplinger Magazine* soon noted that the *Journal's* had become "the most readable front page of all U.S. newspapers."

Kilgore was helping the boom along. The *Journal* was now spending $100,000 a year (about $1 million today) on advertisements in other publications promoting new subscriptions and sending out two million pieces of direct mail soliciting subscriptions each year. A study Kilgore commissioned from the Princeton research firm Benson & Benson suggested that circulation could grow to half a million someday, although nearly everyone thought this a pipe dream.

The key, of course, as with any business on such a growth trajectory as the *Journal's*, was how to sustain and manage the growth. Kilgore took some important steps in this direction; the Bancroft family took others. Kilgore's included promoting Kerby from managing editor to broader responsibilities as executive editor and continuing to bring along Buren McCormack behind him.

With advertising growing, Kilgore and Feemster, his advertising chief, in late March 1946 removed advertisements from the front page of the *Journal,* where they had been since the first issue in 1889. Also in the spring of 1946, advertising rates were increased 35 percent, the first price rise since August 1940.

Jane Bancroft's actions were actually, for the first and only time as the owner of Dow Jones, more extensive. She was guided in these moves by Laurence Lombard, a graduate of Harvard College and Harvard Law School in his early fifties, just returned to Boston from service as general counsel of the

War Production Board. Mrs. Bancroft had turned sixty-eight in 1945, and was, no doubt, beginning to consider the future of her stepfather's company. Moreover, she did not know Kilgore well, not nearly as well as she had known Hogate. And, of course, C. W. Barron had not known Kilgore at all, which must have left him with less standing in her eyes than his predecessor.

Lombard met Mrs. Bancroft through her daughter Jessie, now married to William C. Cox. Lombard recommended a number of important changes: Dow Jones and its holding company, Financial Press Companies of America—a Hugh Bancroft creation—would be transformed, with a new board, including, for the first time, outside directors; the form of business organization would eventually be changed from trust to corporation; Clarence Barron's Boston News Bureau would be closed, and consolidated into *The Wall Street Journal* on the print side and the Dow Jones News Service on the newswire side; and, not least, Bancroft attorney and trustee Jack Richardson, who had played a key role during the confusing first months of Hogate's illness and again in Kilgore's being named as general manager in late 1942, would be replaced by Lombard, and his new firm, Hemenway & Barnes.

Mrs. Bancroft accepted Lombard's recommendations, and Lombard undertook to sell them to the still-ailing Hogate. The key to that turned out to be Harold Boeschenstein. Boeschenstein, the founding chief executive officer of Owens-Corning Fiberglas, had roots in the newspaper business. His father had run a daily newspaper in Edwardsville, Illinois, and Harold had studied journalism at the University of Illinois and then worked for the City News Bureau in Chicago, and later for the *Chicago Tribune.* He had left newspapers for the glass industry at the age of twenty-four. When war came, Boeschenstein took a leave from Owens-Corning to join the War Production Board, where, as head of the Forest Products Bureau, he had been the nation's wartime czar of newsprint rationing—and a client of Laurie Lombard. Hogate knew him from this role as well, and perhaps earlier; Kilgore reported that the two men were "old friends." When Lombard proposed that Boeschenstein be the first outside director of the reorganized Dow Jones, Hogate was sold on the plan.

Whether Kilgore learned of the proposals during one of his rare meetings with Hogate, or directly from Mrs. Bancroft (with whom he met more regularly), is unclear. In any event, Hogate did not play a large role in the discussions. As Kilgore described their summer visit in 1946, "He is cheerful and I think stronger but of course he can't do much. His chief handicap is difficulty in speaking."

Lombard's other nominee for outside director was—Lombard himself. Kilgore, he suggested, should not serve on the new board, so as not to undermine the board's control "if they became unhappy with the job Kilgore was doing." Sometime in 1946, Kilgore managed to get this part of the new grand scheme revised. By the time of the first meeting of the new trustees (the change to corporate form had not yet been effected) in Boston on November 15, 1946, the group comprised Hogate, Mrs. Bancroft, Bill Cox, Lombard, Boeschenstein, and Kilgore.

At first, some measure of tension seems to have existed between Boeschenstein and Lombard, on the one hand, and Kilgore on the other. Boeschenstein had told *Time* magazine in 1944, Kilgore's second year as general manager, that it was his conclusion that "most newsmen burn out young." Kilgore, who uncharacteristically persisted in misspelling Boeschenstein's name (dropping the first "s"), referred to him as being "in the glass business at Toledo," although he acknowledged that "I understand that he is a fine fellow and very successful in his own business." Two weeks after the meeting, Boeschenstein came in to the *Journal*'s New York offices "for a visit" and, by all accounts, the two men eventually developed a strong relationship. Boeschenstein would remain a director of Dow Jones for twenty-six years, the rest of his life. Lombard would serve even longer—twenty-eight years on the board—and, with the exception of the addition of Mrs. Bancroft's daughter Jane in 1949 and the 1951 appointment of a Boston business associate of Lombard's, the board would remain unchanged into the 1960s.

The one significant departure from the new board, at least on a symbolic basis, was Hogate. On February 1, 1947, while spending the winter in Palm Springs as had become his habit since he had fallen ill, Hogate suffered a cerebral hemorrhage. The *Journal* of February 5 reported that he was "critically ill"; he died on Sunday, February 11, still five months short of his fiftieth birthday—and during the week when the *Journal* first claimed circulation over 100,000. The *Journal* mourned him in a front-page editorial that included a large photograph. Its conclusion seems to have borne Kilgore's stamp along with that of editor Grimes:

> *There is gone something that cannot be replaced. There is gone this fine lovable man with his great genius for friendship. The sound of his voice through his office door made you want to hurry to be in there with him. The great booming laugh was a tonic for a lagging spirit. The office is there*

*but it is quiet now. The desk is cleared. The big armchair back of it is
empty. The troubled spirits who sought solace no longer pass through the
little anteroom.*

    *There is left to us who worked with him and to the thousands who
knew him a very precious memory.*

Hogate would, no doubt, have been delighted when, just a few months later,
Grimes's editorials from 1946 were awarded the Pulitzer Prize, the first such
award ever to *The Wall Street Journal.*

    Grimes, of course, was free to write because he had been relieved of nearly
all managerial duties; the editorial page staff was small, and the page design
varied not at all (although Kilgore, Kerby, and Grimes's deputy, Vermont
Royster, would redesign the page in 1950 while Grimes was away on holiday).
Kilgore, on the other hand, missed writing. He had ventured out briefly as a
reporter to write about the Dewey campaign of 1944, but the article he wrote
had been unmemorable, and he had mistakenly believed, as late as a day before the election, that Dewey would defeat Roosevelt's fourth-term bid. In any
event, as noted earlier, Kilgore never had another byline in the *Journal.*

    His passion for writing, especially about politics, persisted. He contributed
an unsigned editorial-page analysis of Gallup Poll results to the *Journal* in October 1946, this time correctly—and in print—predicting the Republican return to control of the Congress. His father recognized his prose, and Kilgore
privately acknowledged authorship, noting that "I wish I had more time to
write politics but there are too many other things to do."

Two of Laurie Lombard's business ideas were implemented in 1947 shortly af-
ter the new Dow Jones Board was put in place. In April, *The Boston News
Bureau* newspaper was closed and its subscriptions were taken over by the
Journal; in June, the News Bureau wire service was also consolidated into
Dow Jones.

    More significantly, Lombard had proposed that the *Journal* create a South-
west edition, opening up a third printing plant (in addition to New York and
San Francisco) to accomplish this objective. In the spring of 1947, Kilgore,
happily taking up this suggestion, directed production chief Ackell to scout
locations in Texas. Dallas was soon identified as the optimal location, and the

new edition was announced in October, with publication tentatively slated to begin on March 1, 1948. The *Journal* article explained the move:

> *Subscribers in the Southwestern states have been receiving this newspa-per two and three days after publication. Through the new edition it is hoped to achieve date-of-publication delivery throughout an area extend-ing some 400 miles from Dallas.*

This would extend same-day reach not only to Houston and Austin, but to New Orleans, Memphis, and Wichita as well.

The start-up in Dallas was rocky, as Ackell, for whom establishing a re-gional printing center was a new task (one the *Journal* had not attempted since 1929), made a number of missteps in planning. The announced start date had to be pushed back two months, and Kerby, who became the on-site project manager in the last month before launch, described the operation as initially chaotic. But the revised target date was met, with Stanley Marcus of the Neiman-Marcus department store in Dallas pressing the button to start the presses, and the Southwest edition immediately began to contribute to the growth in *Journal* circulation. At its inception, Kilgore noted, the readership attained by the new Southwest edition matched that of the Pacific Coast edition, now in its eighteenth year. The new plant was "mighty fine. . . . a great big place but it is roomy for us and all strictly modern—about as nice a newspaper plant as I have ever set eye on."

Kilgore did not attend the Dallas plant opening, not because he had dele-gated the matter to Kerby (he sent Grimes "to tend to the social side of it"), but because Mary Lou was expecting their second child. James Bernard Kil-gore was born on Sunday, May 9, 1948 just six days after the Dallas plant opening. He weighed in at eight pounds ten ounces. His first name was se-lected to honor Mary Lou's father; as Barney explained to Tecumseh, "He has your last name so we gave him Doc Throop's first name. Mine went in the mid-dle. I'll try to get him off to as good a start as you gave me." As he had with Kathryn, Kilgore went back to work immediately after the baby was born, and didn't see the child for days; viewing hours for visiting fathers (through a win-dow) came only at 10:00 A.M. and 2:00 P.M.

While Kilgore does not seem, by modern standards, to have been terribly involved in the lives of his children, especially when they were young, he was surely devoting more time to family and working less hard than he had in his early years at the *Journal*, with summer vacations lasting nearly months and extended winter breaks in Florida.

With the rising tide of the postwar economy, unconstrained availability of newsprint, and the expansion of its printing network, *Journal* circulation continued to rise, hitting 130,000 in 1948. Kilgore understood, however, that simply maximizing the number of copies sold was not his objective. Rather, he wanted—and, especially with Lombard now on the scene, needed—to increase profits even as the paper grew. Likely with this in mind, the *Journal*'s newsstand price, fixed at seven cents since 1920, was increased to ten cents at the beginning of 1948, and the annual subscription price was increased from $18 to $20 (nearly $170 today). Profits continued to rise every year, and, despite the price increases—11 percent for subscribers and 42 percent at the newsstand—sales continued to grow as well, hitting 145,000 in 1949 and 153,000 in 1950.

Dow Jones paid a Christmas bonus of two weeks' pay in 1946, the first time it seems to have done so since 1929. And Kilgore began to receive an additional annual bonus tied to profitability. His shareholdings in the company had reached a value he estimated at $6,000 by the end of 1947, or about $55,000 today. Beginning in 1948, a new twist was included in his compensation: Kilgore (or his estate) would receive a share of the company's profits for ten years after he retired or died. The move had two attractive aspects for Kilgore. First, it supplied greater economic security for Mary Lou and their growing family. Second, as he explained to his father,

> the idea of this kind of incentive plan is that I should get and keep the company in such shape as it will continue to prosper in the future as well as the present because I can get some income out of that future. I have never seen a contract just like this one but it is a very attractive thing.

This was a conceptual breakthrough in compensation, and Lombard was likely its originator, reflecting, it would seem, an evolution in his views on Kilgore's value to the company, and a desire to align management's interests even more closely with that of ownership.

The new contract also provided a stark contrast with Hogate's arrangements; his widow had been paid a bonus of sorts on his death of $35,000, or a bit more than $300,000 today—although, to be sure, Hogate had been kept on the payroll through five years of almost total disability before his death.

Meanwhile, the *Journal* continued to cut an ever-wider path through the national consciousness. One milestone of this course came during a late-September morning during the presidential campaign of 1948. Harry Truman, battling from behind against the Republican candidate, again Governor Dewey, was on one of what would come to be known as his whistle-stop tours through the heartland. In McAlester, Oklahoma, Truman turned a defense of his farm program into an attack on Barney Kilgore's newspaper. On that Oklahoma morning, the president of the United States had this to say:

> *Governor [Harold] Stassen [Republican from Minnesota] started the attack on the farm support program on his boss's doorstep in Albany, New York.* The Wall Street Journal—*I don't know that* The Wall Street Journal *ever cared anything much about what happened to the farmers*—The Wall Street Journal, *and there it is, right there [brandishing the paper], for September 4, 1948, said editorially: "Mr. Stassen is in fact proposing a far-reaching reform of the price support policy, or he doesn't make sense."*
>
> *This is in that editorial right there, and that is the Republican propaganda program. They are going to trim the farmers, if they ever get control of the Government. They would have done it this time, if I hadn't been standing there to keep them from doing it.*
>
> *It was that same paper which revealed on August 21st that "Republican Congressmen were considering cutting supports under farm products in 1949." I can think of no greater authority on the Republicans, and what they believe, than this same* Wall Street Journal *which I just now showed you. That is the Republican bible—that is the special interests publication, published in New York City every day. They use half their editorial columns giving me hell, because I am for the people.*

It was a far cry from FDR's kind words about Kilgore and the Bonus Bill or the *Hot Oil* case, but having the *Journal* chided as the bible of one of the two major political parties was indicative of a newfound status for the newspaper—and for its leaders.

Kilgore had just recently again reorganized that leadership. He had traveled widely within the company, visiting bureaus in Chicago, Cleveland,

Dallas, Detroit, Los Angeles, San Francisco, Philadelphia, and Washington during 1948 alone, and was in unquestioned command.

Joe Ackell, who had learned from the rough rollout in Dallas and whose efforts now appeared ever-more central to Kilgore's dreams of national expansion, was promoted to business manager of the company, in effect the number-two position on the business side of the entire enterprise. That Kilgore was willing to elevate the man he had outmaneuvered to win his own job not so many years earlier was yet another testament to the quiet confidence with which he was revolutionizing the business.

At the same time, Bob Feemster was given the new, but completely ceremonial title of chairman of the executive committee. The move reflected Kilgore's understanding of his advertising chief—both his considerable professional strengths and his maddening personal limitations.

Robert Feemster was yet another of the DePauw group surrounding Barney Kilgore, although his freshman year there immediately followed Kilgore's senior year. Feemster was a native of Cambridge City, Indiana; like Kilgore, he was a Rector Scholar at DePauw and a Hogate recruit to the *Journal*. Both men were even married to Greencastle natives named Mary Louise.

There the similarities seemed to end. Where Kilgore was unfailingly modest, Feemster was loud and obnoxious and constantly called attention to himself. A company biographical sketch he approved stated that "the key to his success comes from his ambition combined with promotion-mindedness" and described him as "always an above average student." He joined the *Journal* as an advertising sales representative the same year he graduated from college, after pneumonia had forced him to withdraw from law school at the University of Michigan. Having lived nearly his entire life in Indiana and New York, he nevertheless sported ten-gallon hats. He affected a habit of smoking extra-long cigarettes held by the tips of his fingers. At five feet, six inches and substantially overweight, he believed that women found him irresistible. He was the sort of person who mounted his own desk on a platform, and shortened the legs of the chairs occupied by visitors to his office.

After Kilgore named him chairman of the executive committee of Dow Jones, Feemster frequently left people with the impression that Kilgore worked for him, not the other way around. He sometimes went off half-cocked, as when he told *Editor & Publisher* magazine in 1948 that a Southeast edition might follow the Southwest edition just launched—even though there were no plans for such a thing at that time.

For all of this, Feemster was a truly gifted advertising salesman and sales executive. In college he had formed the Olympic Advertising Company and sold ads on football and basketball programs, hand fans for use in churches, and desk blotters. In his midtwenties, fresh to the financial ad sales group, he qualified the *Journal,* for the first time, as a "daily newspaper of general circulation" for the purposes of bond offerings, and saw sales of ads for those purposes soar. At twenty-seven, when Feemster's boss died of a heart attack at the low point of the *Journal's* mid-Depression fortunes, Hogate named him director of advertising.

Feemster was not the sort of man with whom Kilgore identified, or even felt comfortable. Feemster roomed with Kilgore in Brooklyn shortly after he arrived in New York in 1933, but the two men then saw little of one another outside of the office until Kilgore married his own Mary Lou. From 1938 through 1944, the couples often socialized, with the relationship between Lulu Kilgore and "Toddy" Feemster clearly the nexus.

Then, perhaps around Christmas 1944, the Feemsters' marriage deteriorated, and the social contact ceased. The Feemsters were divorced in 1949, leaving Toddy with a four-year-old girl. Bob remarried the same year; his second wife had previously been his secretary. Feemster's role at Dow Jones was unaffected. He was just too valuable, too important a part of Kilgore's revolution.

While Kilgore led the way on creating the *Journal* as a product and channeled Ackell's efforts in production and distribution, it was Feemster who positioned the *Journal* in marketing terms. For readers—and potential readers—beginning in the postwar years, the pitch was simple, but powerful: "Everywhere, Men Who Get Ahead in Business Read *The Wall Street Journal.*" As Edward Scharff has written,

> *in twelve short words Feemster had captured the essence of Barney Kilgore's newspaper concept: Everywhere [the newspaper was ubiquitous], Men [clearly it was a virile publication] Who Get Ahead [aggressive types, not fat cats with their feet propped on their desks] in Business [the new subject matter of the paper] Read [they don't just use it as a coffee table ornament] The [a unique product] Wall Street Journal.*

For advertisers, the pitch was even simpler: The *Journal*, Feemster's sales force intoned over and over again—even before it was true—was "the only national business daily."

In late 1949, Barney Kilgore's *Journal* was riding high and Laurie Lombard's plan for the reorganization of Jane Bancroft's ownership of Dow Jones finally reached fruition.

Kilgore observed privately that

> *our business is certainly good—best since back in the old days of 1929 and 1930. I think the paper is now pretty well over the hump as a national paper and should make money pretty regularly. I hope so.*

Board and management had returned from a successful—and convivial—trip by private railroad car to California in October to celebrate the twentieth anniversary of the Pacific Coast edition. Kilgore had planned the adventure as what would now be called a "team-building" exercise. As he told his father, "I think this trip will be good fun and probably do the whole organization some good."

The company was soon reincorporated in Delaware, and the trustees were replaced by corporate directors—although the persons filling these roles were largely the same. Kilgore became chairman of the board as well as president. At the same time, a profit-sharing retirement plan was created for all employees; the plan was unusually generous by the standards of the time, and became even more so until its terms were revised, roughly fifty years later.

The first meeting of the new corporate board was held in Boston on December 2, 1949, its location chosen so that the ailing Mrs. Bancroft could attend. Nineteen days later, she died, aged seventy-two. She left her controlling interest in the company to members of her family. These included her three children, Jessie (married to Bill Cox), Jane (married first to Ernest Decker, then to Edwin Steele, later to Benjamin Cochran, and finally to Werk Cook), and Hugh (who was much less active in the company's affairs than his sisters, and who died in 1953), as well as trusts for their benefit with Lombard as trustee.

Lombard issued a statement to employees, describing the board structure in place since 1946 and declaring that "I think Mr. Kilgore will agree that within his experience relations and cooperation between management and stockholders have never been closer than since this Board has been functioning." Lombard also announced that "I am authorized to say that no change whatsoever is contemplated in the policies or in the operations of the Dow Jones enterprises as a result of Mrs. Bancroft's death." The Board resolution mourning Mrs. Bancroft concluded that "she was a very great lady." It said, "We know why this was. Mrs. Bancroft had that great virtue without which other virtues are a sham and in the presence of which other virtues seem so overshadowed as to be well nigh useless. She had integrity of character."

That, of course, didn't stop the buzzards from circling. Joseph Pew of Sun Oil, an associate of Kerby's from his days at the Liberty League, called offering to fund what we would now call a management buyout. Kerby told him that was unnecessary. Some years earlier, Jane Bancroft had rejected a potential acquirer, saying, "They are not fit to own *The Wall Street Journal*." Now former ambassador Joseph Kennedy offered to buy Dow Jones from the Bancrofts, prompting Jessie Cox to respond, "Grandfather's company is not for sale to anybody—at any time, at any price." That resolve would remain firm for another fifty-eight years.

While any change in ownership was ruled out, some tensions did arise. The regard between Kilgore—the almost-certain author of the board resolution calling her a very great lady and the *Journal* obituary using the same words—and Mrs. Bancroft had been mutual. Jane Bancroft Steele, writing Kilgore in her childlike spidery penmanship, thanked Kilgore for a private letter of condolence: "Mother was so fond of you, Barney. And she admired what you are doing and appreciated the difficulties you were in when you first took over for Casey."

But Jane Steele lacked confidence in her own business judgment. She responded to a note enclosing her director's fees by saying, "It really seems absurd that I should be paid anything as I certainly contribute nothing to the meetings." Kilgore demurred, noting that she brought to the board what he called a "basis of understanding," "background and traditions," "intangibles," and insisted that "we must not—any of us—forget about that." Yet Steele asked that her second husband be allowed to join her at board meetings, and Lombard and Kilgore agreed.

Edwin Steele, though seriously ill, immediately proceeded to inject himself at a level of detail previously unknown for Dow Jones directors. He commented on the preliminary financials for 1949 and asked to see the audited version as soon as possible. Then, after being sidelined by illness for a long period, he sent Kilgore a letter with two suggestions:

a quick look at your 8-month figures [for 1951] makes me wonder:

1) If it wouldn't be better to refuse some business. The amount carried down to net income in August was less than that of August 1950 in spite of a very substantial increase in gross.

2) Is it unreasonable to expect 10% of gross to be carried to net?

Kilgore's response was a masterpiece of understatement, and perhaps of controlled anger. He pointed out that the entire falloff in net income, year over year, had come from a new federal excess profits tax and that August was always a slow month for advertising. In sum:

No, I don't think it pays us to refuse some business. If we took in less money we would make less money. We have managed to keep ahead of rising costs thus far only by striving to build up our volume of business. If we gave up that race I think we would be sunk.

On "reasonable" profit margins, Kilgore noted that an after-tax margin of 10 percent in the face of 70 percent taxation would require a pretax profit of 34 percent. "We would be doing better than average in the publishing industry I think at about one-third of that ratio." There is no record that Steele wrote again to Kilgore in this manner. Steele died on the day before Christmas, 1951.

Tecumseh and Lavina Kilgore, around 1900.

Barney Kilgore's DePauw
yearbook *(The Mirage)*
photo, 1929, the year he
edited *The DePauw.*

DEPAUW STAFF

Top row—Harry McGoon, Buren McCormack, Gerald Doty, Will Wade, William Johnson, Thoburn Wiant, Farrington Bridwell.

Second row—Joseph Taylor, Lorene Neese, Margaret Winship, Evangelyn Morgan, Martha Kilgore, Evelyn Goff, Virginia Hudson, Howard Hill.

Third row—Ruth Bonifield, Betty Holt, Frances Cauble, Mary Power, Virginia Grishaw, Sally Robards, Harriet Martin, Jane Isaacson.

Fourth row—Robert Bottorf, Margaret Rohwedder, Mary Rhue, Paul Wade, Kathryn Homan, Margaret Harvey, Guernsey Van Riper.

DEPAUW ADVERTISING STAFF

Top row—Robert McDermond, Henry Marsh, John Biggerstaff, Charles Tyler.

Second row—Kimball Reyher, Lucile Hunt, Edith Fisher, Anne Hayden, Gilbert Tribett.

Third row—Robert Wayland, Leah Colter, Faith Ritz, Josephine Newkirk, Robert Lewis, John Shaw.

Fourth row—Paul Boyer, Edward Van Riper, Theodore Callis, Vernon Noe.

Page from the 1929 DePauw *Mirage* yearbook depicting the staff of *The DePauw,* the school newspaper. Included are Kilgore's future *Journal* colleagues Buren McCormack (top photo, top row, second from left), Robert Bottorff (top photo, bottom row, far left), Theodore Callis (bottom photo, bottom row, second from right), Kilgore's sister Martha (top photo, second row from top, fourth from right), and his college girlfriend Margaret Rohwedder, the "fair Margaret" (top photo, bottom row, second from left).

(COURTESY DEPAUW UNIVERSITY)

Charles Dow. When he died in 1902, the *Journal* called the company "Dow's creation" and "Dow's work."

(Courtesy Dow Jones & Co.)

Edward D. Jones. He left the company in 1899 to trade stocks—and possibly to drink.

(Courtesy Dow Jones & Co.)

Charles M. Bergstresser. The unnamed but essential partner—he supplied the capital and named the *Journal*.

(COURTESY DOW JONES & CO.)

Hugh Bancroft and Clarence W. Barron. Barron's family owned the *Journal* for 105 years beginning in 1902. Bancroft, who married Barron's stepdaughter, took his own life in 1933, ending family management of the company.

(COURTESY DOW JONES & CO.)

Barney Kilgore playing the piano at the Maryland shore. Undated, 1930s.

(COURTESY JAMES B. KILGORE)

Mary Lou Throop and Barney Kilgore on their wedding day,
October 1, 1938, Bethesda, Maryland.

(COURTESY JAMES B. KILGORE)

Barney Kilgore, February 1940 as Washington bureau manager of the *Journal*.
(Courtesy James B. Kilgore)

Tecumseh Kilgore, 1948, nearing his fortieth anniversary with Union Central Life.

(Courtesy James B. Kilgore)

Kilgore and his children on the beach, undated, mid-1950s.
Left to right, Jim, Barney, Jack, and Kathryn

Robert Feemster holding the first edition of *The National Observer,* February 4, 1962. Despite his smirk here, Feemster opposed the *Observer* and "all but washed his hands of the whole project."

An unidentfied printer, Vermont Royster, Barney Kilgore, and
Bill Kerby at a *Journal* printing plant, undated, probably early 1960s.

(Courtesy Dow Jones & Co.)

Barney Kilgore.

(Courtesy Dow Jones & Co.)

9

The Boom Begins

*T*HE WALL STREET JOURNAL was not the only business newspaper in New York City, no less in the entire nation. Business papers had been published in New York since at least 1795, when the *New York Price Current* was founded.

One of the *Journal's* leading local competitors at the time of its founding, and through the date when Kilgore joined the paper, was the *Journal of Commerce,* founded in 1827. It centered on the shipping trade, which was so crucial to New York's early growth. From its earliest days, the *Journal of Commerce* printed the manifest of arriving vessels. In later years, it branched out to become more generally a business and financial newspaper.

The heyday of the *Journal of Commerce* came under H. Parker Willis, who was named the newspaper's editor in chief in 1919. Willis had already been one of the key figures in the creation of the Federal Reserve System; he served as executive director of the National Monetary Commission, which recommended the creation of a U.S. central bank. The notion of a system of regional banks was his, as was the idea that these banks should clear checks for system member banks. When the Federal Reserve Act was passed, Willis became the Federal Reserve Board's first secretary, and then its director of research (equivalent to its chief economist).

All through this period Willis was also the *Journal of Commerce's* chief Washington correspondent. Moving to New York, he became not only editor of the paper, but also a professor of economics at Columbia University. Just as

Kilgore was recognizing that finance and business were inseparable journalistically, so—actually a few years earlier—was Willis. In 1927, he wrote in his newspaper's centennial issue: "Business [and] economic life as a whole is a unit essentially and hence demands a unified treatment, which is impossible where attention is solely concentrated on finance or upon some specialized branch of industry."

While Willis may have come first to Kilgore's first great insight, he is little remembered in journalism circles because he lacked two of Kilgore's two greatest assets: an eloquent pen and committed owners.

The *Journal of Commerce* had been owned since the last day of 1926 by the Ridder family, which at the same time also purchased another competitor, the New York *Commercial* (successor to the *Price Current*), merging the two under Willis's editorship. Offices remained on Park Row, the only New York daily remaining on the street near City Hall where nearly all of the city's newspapers had once resided. Combined purchase price: $2.85 million, or about $31.5 million in today's dollars. The *Journal of Commerce* had a circulation of 30,000, the *Commercial* 10,000, and the unduplicated combination 35,000. This compared with *The Wall Street Journal*'s year-end 1926 circulation of just under 30,000.

The Ridders were experienced in the newspaper business. Patriarch Herman Ridder started in publishing in 1876 and later acquired the German-language *New Yorker Staats-Zeitung*. Having successfully ridden out the wave of anti-German feeling assured by the World War, the Ridders were eager to branch out into English-language newspapers, and had purchased the Long Island *Daily Press* before the *Journal of Commerce*. Herman Ridder had been a director of the Associated Press before his death in 1915, and his sons seem to have been interested in the *Journal of Commerce* in no small part for its Associated Press franchise, an asset which could at this time be traded somewhat in the manner of a New York taxi medallion. *Time* suggested the AP franchise alone might have been worth a quarter of a million dollars. The Ridders almost immediately sold it to purchase the *Minnesota Pioneer* and the *St. Paul Dispatch,* on their way to building what would eventually become Knight Ridder.

By 1931, however, they had pretty thoroughly soured on the *Journal of Commerce.* Editor Willis pressed for greater editorial investment in the face of what he believed would be a relatively short depression, but the Ridders opted to cut back further, and Willis resigned, citing "clashes of opinion" with the owners.

The *Journal of Commerce* limped through the rest of the Depression under Ridder ownership, but reaped a windfall during the Second World War when it printed the full raft of wartime regulations in their entirety. Reprints of some of these regulations numbered in the millions.

Meanwhile, in the nation's second city, an entirely separate *Chicago Journal of Commerce* had been founded in 1920. Casey Hogate was close to buying the paper for Dow Jones around the time of the Pearl Harbor attack, but the transaction was abandoned. In 1947, the Ridders seemed to have second thoughts on their prospects in business publishing. One of Herman's grandsons, Bernard, became editor and publisher of the New York *Journal of Commerce* and the Ridders soon purchased the Chicago paper, which then had a circulation of 35,000, for $1.25 million, or about $11 million today. The two papers would continue to publish separate products, but many business operations were combined. Less than a week later, the New York *Journal of Commerce* also announced plans for a new Manhattan editorial and printing facility, finally vacating Park Row.

But the Ridders now proceeded to duplicate a feat of earlier owners of the star-crossed newspaper, failing to prosper in a postwar boom. Within thirty months, as the *Journal* launched the Southwest edition and saw circulation explode, the Ridders went from acquisitions and expansion at the *Journal of Commerce* to wanting to sell.

The first feeler came in May 1950 to Bill Kerby, who was approached by a broker friend and Brooklyn neighbor representing the Ridders. Did Dow Jones want to buy the two *Journals of Commerce*? Kerby recalled that his instant reaction was yes for the Chicago paper and no for New York. Kilgore, reached by telephone at home in Princeton, concurred. A key conversation soon took place between Kilgore and Eric Ridder at the May 13 Gridiron Club dinner in Washington.

Here was an opportunity to truly pursue Kilgore's vision of a national newspaper. *Wall Street Journal* circulation in the Midwest was only 25,000, not much larger than the circulation of the Pacific Coast edition. The Ridders had failed to grow *Chicago Journal of Commerce* circulation; in fact, it had declined a bit, to 34,000. Kilgore had discussed using the presses of Knight Newspapers' *Chicago Daily News* to print an edition of *The Wall Street Journal* there, but hadn't yet made a deal.

A somewhat reluctant Dow Jones board, led by Bancroft trustee Lombard, feared the commitment of what they considered a lot of capital—about $12 million today for the purchase, plus more to upgrade the Chicago paper. Lombard's conservatism in this regard was particularly surprising given that the previous regional expansion—into Texas—had been his idea. But after months of discussions, Kilgore got the go-ahead to pursue his deal. By early October he was confident enough to alert his father to the possibility of the purchase.

Newsprint contracts became a sticking point in the negotiations with the Ridders after rationing took hold with the outbreak of the Korean War in June 1950, but Dow Jones eventually offered a small return over the effects of postwar inflation, and Bernard Ridder, less than a year later, recalled the price as "more than it was worth." (Kilgore publicly rejoined, "We wouldn't sell it today for twice what we paid for it.")

News of the negotiations broke in newspapers in Chicago and New York in early November. Kilgore thought the leak had come from inside the *Chicago Journal of Commerce*. The leak was awkward, because the negotiations were not yet complete, although Kilgore had sufficiently persuaded the Dow Jones board of the merits of the move that his fallback plan was to enter the Chicago market with a new start-up regional edition of the *Journal* "as quickly as we can get it organized." Perhaps sensing this—or threatened with it—the sellers soon came to final terms.

The Ridder family used the proceeds to help finance their purchase of two more papers, the evening *News* and morning *Mercury* in San Jose, California. In New York, they permanently abandoned competition with *The Wall Street Journal,* taking the *Journal of Commerce* back to its roots as a paper of shipping and related trades. As the retreating paper's official history puts it, the *Journal of Commerce* "dropped areas of coverage where there was significant competition, such as food, financial market coverage, and stock and bond tables." *Time* magazine observed that the *Journal* had been transformed by Kilgore from "a worthy but dull financial sheet" to "one of the most readable of U.S. newspapers." In the city where the battle had begun, and in the nation's second city as well, Kilgore and *The Wall Street Journal* had swept the field.

Kilgore signed the $1.5 million check for the Chicago acquisition himself; Kerby recalled it as "the only company check he signed in his entire career." But he left the negotiations, the board presentation and the closing of the transaction to Kerby. Vermont Royster later recalled that Kilgore had even gone on vacation while Kerby completed the deal. "That was his way of show-ing trust in and putting a challenge to Kerby. When that challenge was met, Kerby was thereafter marked" as Kilgore's principal deputy, and potentially as his successor.

It was likely around this time that Kilgore privately—although not publicly—designated Kerby as such, and as, at a minimum, *primus inter pares* among his subordinates.

The two men and their families had grown close socially during the Second World War. The Kilgores often visited the Kerby vacation home at Buck Hill Falls, Pennsylvania, and the Kerbys later visited the Kilgores in Princeton, of-ten with children in tow. The relationship was generally easy, but not without its occasional tensions. Kilgore was the sort of person who expressed his con-fidence in Kerby most often by silence, and Kerby was the sort who could ac-cept this—but not without noticing.

Many years later, when, in Kerby's presence, Kilgore told a seminar at Co-lumbia University that Kerby was "the best business reporter and business editor" he had ever known, Kerby noted that, "In all the years of our associa-tion, that is the only word of commendation I ever heard from the man who was my closest friend, my immediate superior for 26 years, the man who gave me promotion after promotion."

At some point, likely around the time of the Chicago deal, Kilgore handed Kerby a note that said, "Use the enclosed only if you can't manage any other way." The enclosure read, "While I am away, Bill Kerby is in charge. B.K."

This was particularly important because not everyone at Dow Jones thought Kilgore's course was the right one—although Kerby never had to resort to us-ing the note. In addition to the reservations of the board and the Bancroft's trustee, Kerby especially recalled that Grimes, the man who had first hired him at the *Journal,* was terrified that the *Journal's* growth was out of control. As Kerby left for the closing, Grimes accosted him:

> *"Bill," he said, "I want you to stop by the newsroom on your way out. Those people are all your friends. Many you hired. You know their wives and children. Then think to yourself, "I'm on my way to ruin Dow Jones and put all these people out of work." '*

As 1950 gave way to 1951, Kerby led the senior Dow Jones executive team to Chicago. Bob Bottorff was transferred from San Francisco to run the new

"Chicago Journal of Commerce Edition of *The Wall Street Journal*" (soon mercifully shortened to the *Journal*'s Midwest Edition). But also on hand in person for a shakedown period were Kerby, Feemster, Ackell, and Buren McCormack to supervise the daily news operations. They partied on New Year's Eve at the Drake Hotel but adjourned at the stroke of midnight. There was work to do.

Overnight, *Journal* circulation was now more than 190,000. The total employee count for Dow Jones topped one thousand for the first time, with 250 of these in news. Within weeks, with Kilgore having joined them during the first two weeks of February 1951, they had significantly pruned the news staff and then given the survivors large raises, negotiated a new union contract, changed the front-page format from eight columns to the *Journal*'s standard six, purchased and installed new presses and other equipment and overhauled the production and distribution processes. The *Journal*'s Midwest edition was soon the first regional edition of the newspaper to rise fully to the standards of the parent paper, and to adopt its complete look and feel.

Ray Vicker, a *Chicago Journal of Commerce* reporter who was kept on and later had great success at *The Wall Street Journal*, remembered that

> for weeks the top brass of D.J. remained in Chicago working from about 8 am to midnight. I can still see Kilgore in his shirt sleeves studying a galley proof, Kerby running up the stairs like a copyboy from the print shop to the news room, McCormack trying to convince a pressman he knew all about presses. For weeks these guys were getting out the paper, having themselves a ball as they were doing fundamental things that hadn't occupied their attention in years.

John McWethy, the *Journal*'s Chicago bureau manager, recalled many years later that "I will never forget those four guys sitting down on the rim of the desk and how astonished the *Chicago Journal of Commerce* people were that the president of the company could write a headline."

One thing which these men were determined not to change, of course, was their approach to the newspaper's content, not only on the news side, but on the editorial pages as well. On January 2, 1951, perhaps in part by way of expressing his continuing loyalty to Kilgore and Kerby, Grimes overcame his reservations about the acquisition to write the lead editorial in the new Chicago edition. Kerby later recalled that Kilgore had rejected a first draft that Grimes had casually tossed off.

The editorial, now carefully crafted, was simultaneously published in the New York edition as well, and appeared under the headline "A Newspaper's Philosophy." Grimes's piece summed up the *Journal*'s news and editorial approach—the approach Charles Dow, William Peter Hamilton, Thomas Woodlock, Casey Hogate, Barney Kilgore, and he had crafted over more than sixty years—so comprehensively, and with such force, that chunks of it were still being reprinted more than a half century later. Some key excerpts:

> *A business newspaper must be two things at one and the same time. It must be specialized. Yet the interests and activities of its editors must be as diverse as the American landscape.*

> *If the news is good, we are glad. If it is otherwise, we feel our obligation to report it otherwise.*

> *We think that in so far as its information wants are concerned business is universal. The information on which a great automobile manufacturer acts is the same information which influences the man who buys his trucks. If retail trade in New York booms or slumps, there is a man in San Francisco who wants to know the whys and wherefores.*

> *[B]usiness is a national community. We publish* The Wall Street Journal *in New York and we publish it also in San Francisco and in Dallas. Each of those editions is essentially the same newspaper. The readers seem to like it that way. The reason we think they like it is because their number steadily increases. To finish with legends. It was said that a national newspaper was impractical in the United States because the country was too vast, that the mere problem of distribution would be insuperable. We do have a national circulation. We have been printing in three key cities. Now there is added a fourth and that is something to which we have long looked forward. We can now deliver to most parts of the country on the date of publication.*

> *On our editorial page we make no pretense of walking down the middle of the road. Our comments and interpretations are made from a definite point of view. We believe in the individual, in his wisdom and his decency. We oppose all infringements on individual rights whether they stem from*

attempts at private monopoly, labor union monopoly or from an overgrow-
ing government. People will say we are conservative or even reactionary.
We are not much interested in labels but if we were to choose one, we
would say we are radical. Just as radical as the Christian doctrine.

With the acquisition in Chicago, Kilgore, for the first time, had truly realized Hogate's dream—and his own plan—for a national newspaper. Feemster capitalized by creating four advertising regions to coincide with the *Journal*'s four printing plants and four editions for news purposes. Most of the *Journal*'s advertising would be national, and the paper would be positioned for most advertisers as a national buy, but for smaller companies, or those not operating nationally—who perhaps thought of themselves as not *yet* operating on that scale—ads in the newspaper could now be purchased for the Eastern (New York), Midwest (Chicago), Southwest (Dallas), or Pacific Coast (San Francisco) editions. Such local sales had been possible since the Pacific Coast edition had begun in 1929, of course, and some such sales had been made. But having a complete set of such editions comprising a national whole gave all of Feemster's efforts considerable new momentum, and a suite of offerings no other newspaper could match. In time, the flexibility and customization permitted by this suite of offerings also increased Feemster and Kilgore's freedom to raise rates and to attract new advertisers.

In order to pursue the imperative of continued growth, Kilgore and his colleagues now looked to a few key tactics. With the news formula largely in place since his own tenure as managing editor, most of these tactics focused on innovations in distribution, Ackell's province. The two most important of these during the remainder of Barney Kilgore's time at the helm of *The Wall Street Journal* were new means to speed the physical production of the newspaper and new locations at which to print it.

Speeding up production had all sorts of advantages. First, and most directly, it would likely lower costs, at least by holding out the promise of expending less labor, and perhaps by requiring fewer laborers—fewer highly paid printers. More important, as Kilgore and Ackell well understood, faster production meant the presses for the early edition could be started earlier in the evening. That, in turn, meant that early-morning delivery was possible for areas farther from the printing plant. And increasing the number of readers who could be offered early-morning delivery, as the move in Dallas had proven and the Chicago acquisition now confirmed, was the best means the *Journal* had found for gaining additional subscribers.

In 1951, Ackell and his team, working in their lab on lower Sixth Avenue in Manhattan, developed a machine they code-named "Mary Ann," but would later dub the "Electro-Typesetter." Here is how Kerby described it from his first impression:

> *A maze of electronic tubes and other gadgetry was mounted on a series of long tables. From them ran an electrical connection to another Rube Goldberg-ish contraption, which in turn was connected with a standard linecasting [typesetting] machine.*
>
> *The whole apparatus occupied a room some 20 feet square. But it worked. Perforated tape was fed into the first maze, and the line caster, without aid of human hands, was producing errorless lines of type as fast as [the Linotype] could be induced to operate.*

In short order, Ackell had a commercial model. It was compact and portable. Hooking one up to a Linotype machine, Ackell said, "is about as complicated as changing a couple of electric light bulbs." The next step would be placing the machine into use, which meant overcoming the inevitable opposition of the printers' unions.

The payoff, it was clear from the start, could be huge. The Electro-Typesetter set type at twice the speed of a Linotype machine, which had to be manually operated in much the same manner as a typewriter—except that it produced lines of characters cast in an alloy of lead, antimony, and tin, ready to have ink applied to them when arrayed in pages on a printing press. But the critical phrase in Kerby's brief account was "without aid of human hands." Indeed, an existing technology, the "Tele-Typesetter," had similar functionality (albeit at slower speeds), with one key difference: The tape had to be fed into the Linotype machine at the "receiving" location by hand. Ackell's development of the Electro-Typesetter thus meant two things: one was cost reduction in any "receiving" (remote) plant; but much more important was that the Electro-Typesetter actually made it easier for the various regional editions to be identical editorially. Using the new machine to produce two identical editions meant setting type only once, while every difference from one edition to another required that new type be set. Thus, Ackell's technological breakthrough—he quickly applied for, and eventually received, patents on the device—reinforced Kilgore's agenda for Kerby's news package, and for Feemster's national ad sales as well.

Kilgore and Ackell's approach to convincing the printers to let them use the Electro-Typesetter was both ingenious and tough. The initial prong of the attack was to use the new machines first to typeset stock quotations fed from the Associated Press. This reinforced Dow Jones's insistence that the matter was one to be negotiated with the International Typographers Union at the national level, rather than with the recalcitrant New York local.

Ackell then explained to the International officers that Dow Jones's future depended on using the Electro-Typesetter, that it was therefore determined to do so with or without union cooperation, that is, by setting up nonunion plants if necessary, and that, if the machine's use were permitted, *Journal* circulation would almost inevitably grow, creating jobs running printing presses around the country, more than offsetting any job losses in typesetting. When Dow Jones agreed that any individual typesetters actually displaced by an Electro-Typesetter would be permitted to remain in featherbedded jobs until retirement (but would then not have to be replaced), the deal was struck.

Kilgore had publicly announced the development of the Electro-Typesetter in December 1952, even before the negotiations were concluded. He stated that the new device would be brought online first in the New York and Chicago plants early in 1953, and later in Dallas and San Francisco. He said he had "every expectation" of a deal with the ITU, but announcing the rollout before a deal had been struck was presumably intended to underscore the point Ackell had made about going forward with or without the union. An agreement was soon reached, and ratified in both New York and Chicago at the end of April 1953. The *Journal*'s Eastern edition first made use of the new technology to set its stock tables, transmitted directly from the Associated Press and composed into type without further human intervention just two months later. By May 1954, just three years after it had existed only in prototype, the Electro-Typesetter was in full use in all four *Journal* plants; all four were automatically generating identical pages of news, with only one human being involved in the typesetting of any given piece of copy.

The Electro-Typesetter would be the last great innovation over which Ackell would preside at the *Journal*. As much of a breakthrough as it was, Kilgore understood instinctively that, when it came to technology, resting on laurels could be fatal. While Ackell continued to perfect the Electro-Typesetter—RCA would commercialize the Dow Jones patents under license and begin selling versions to other newspapers in 1958—Kilgore wanted his own paper to remain at the forefront of emerging technologies such as offset printing and facsimile reproduction. Kilgore learned of the promise of such ideas from announcements by other companies and at industry conferences. When, by the end of 1955, Ackell, always something of a loner, had not made sufficient progress, Kilgore assigned the further work on such matters to the well-organized Buren McCormack, whom he moved from executive editor to business manager.

The shift proved fortuitous, on two scores. McCormack kept up the pressure for innovation and found himself a home again within the organization, after five fitful years. McCormack, who had been one of Kilgore's closest friends (and at one point his roommate) before the move to Washington in 1935, had succeeded Kerby as assistant managing editor (1943), managing editor (1946), and executive editor (1951). But he was not quite up to Kerby's standard in each job, and, in 1950, an abortive move by Kilgore to place him under Grimes, who was in charge of editorials, had almost caused the resignation of Vermont Connecticut Royster, a former Washington bureau chief and Grimes's heir apparent on the editorial page staff. Kilgore had spotted Royster's talent early, noting in 1946, not long after Royster returned from five years in the navy, that he was "a good man and a fast mover." The *Journal* team was growing sufficiently large—and disparate—that just keeping the group moving forward together was an increasingly important—and difficult—task for Kilgore.

Yet it was crucial that he do so. The imperative was underscored when Royster's work was awarded the Pulitzer Prize in 1953, only the second Pulitzer the *Journal* had received, following that in 1947 to Grimes. Both were for editorials.

With the improvements in production, and thus delivery, *Journal* circulation continued to build. In 1950, before the *Chicago Journal of Commerce* acquisition, it had reached 153,000; with the Chicago circulation added, it was 190,000. But growth continued elsewhere as well, and by the end of 1951, the newspaper that had taken fifty-eight years to attain its first 100,000 readers had doubled that number in just over four years more. By the close of 1954, with the rollout of the Electro-Typesetter complete, circulation was nearing 300,000. The postwar study indicating that it might be possible to sell a half-million copies a day no longer seemed ludicrous. Kilgore told his father,

"Business is still good with us. In fact our big problem these days is getting enough papers printed in time to keep the customers happy."

Most of the new subscriptions continued to roll in as a result of the *Journal's* aggressive direct mail campaign, but door-to-door sales also remained an important source of new readers, with more than 8,000 such sales in 1953. Most important, the rates at which subscribers were renewing their subscriptions or "converting" from trial offers to regular subscriptions were rising even as total circulation grew. By 1953, renewal rates for existing subscribers hit 88 percent, an astounding figure.

But the real explosion was actually coming on the advertising side. Feemster was taking advantage not only of the growth in circulation, but also of increasingly creative—and aggressive—sales practices. To highlight the advantages of national circulation—"the nation's only business daily"—he created a map comparing industrial employment and *Journal* circulation in each of the forty-eight states. *Voila!* The patterns were roughly similar. Recognizing that the *Journal* should not be compared to other newspapers—either general or specialized—Feemster invented a new "field group" of what he asserted were rival publications, despite the fact that all were magazines, and dwarfed the *Journal* in circulation. The list included *Time, Fortune, Business Week, Newsweek,* and *U.S. News.* In time, the *Journal* would overtake most of them in circulation, and, with its greater frequency of publication, all of them in advertising revenue. Finally, Feemster and Ted Callis, another DePauw man and Feemster's deputy, created new arrangements for classified advertising, grouping together the "Real Estate Corner," "Florida Beckons," and, most successfully, "The Mart," the first national classified advertising vehicle for executive job openings.

The results were dramatic. Advertising volume in newspapers was traditionally measured in "lines," literally the number of line of agate type displaced by the advertising involved. Ad "linage" had peaked in 1930, at 5.7 million lines for the year, or very roughly an average of ten pages of advertising per issue. It had bottomed out in 1938—not coincidentally the trough year for Dow Jones earnings—at 1.7 million lines, a decline of about 70 percent in eight years, and yielding a rough average of three pages of ads in each paper.

Of course, it is doubly challenging to grow advertising volume when circulation volume is increasing, because higher circulation almost invariably translates into higher prices for a given volume of advertising, a page, for instance. That said, advertisers are attracted to publications with growing circulation, as this is likely indicative of increasing reader interest. (One exception would be if the circulation growth was the result of a circulation price decrease, but, as we have seen, the *Journal* was actually increasing circulation prices.)

By 1942, Kilgore's last year as managing editor, advertising volume had recovered to two million lines. Feemster then more than met the challenge. In the next nine years, as circulation grew by a multiple of six times, from 35,000 to 210,000, advertising volume *also* grew five times. The overall size of the *Journal* increased from 18 pages on an average day in 1953 to 22 to 24 pages on an average day the following year.

Part of the difference came from another display of strength, another case of addition by subtraction. Just as Kilgore and Feemster had made a statement by dropping front-page advertising in 1946, now, in June 1953, the Saturday edition of the paper, the weakest day from an advertising perspective, was discontinued.

Part of the public rationale came from the end of Saturday sessions of the New York Stock Exchange, but another major factor was Feemster's realization that nearly all of the demand for Saturday advertising could be transferred to weekdays. He was quickly and decisively proved right. Over the seven years from 1951 until 1958, even as circulation tripled, *Journal* advertising volume doubled—and this, absent Saturday publication, with 14 percent fewer issues.

For Barney Kilgore personally, these were good years as well. In 1950, he and Lulu bought a couple of cottages on Little Twin Lake in Milford, Pennsylvania, and combined them, creating a summer home for themselves and their growing family. In 1951, Kilgore received an honorary doctorate of laws from DePauw.

The next month he attended the exclusive Bohemian Grove retreat in California. Talks given during that year's Grove retreat included Senator Robert Taft on "Whither America?" and former President Herbert Hoover on "World Conditions," as well as a leading army general on strategy (with General Dwight Eisenhower in attendance) and the president of Standard Oil on the current situation in his industry. Then-governor Earl Warren recalled in his memoirs that Eisenhower asked other attendees if there was any possibility of his obtaining both major party presidential nominations in 1952. Unfortunately,

Kilgore left no record of his impressions of the retreat, although he returned to the Grove year after year.

On May 1, 1952, the Kilgores had their third and last child, John Harvey, known from birth as Jack. With their family now complete and their fortunes rising, Barney and Mary Lou decided they wanted a more modern house, in what they considered a better part of Princeton. They put Snowden on the market in 1952, sold it in 1953, and moved into the new house they had built on Pretty Brook Road in the spring of 1954. They would remain there the rest of Barney's life.

10

"A Classic in the History of Newspapering"

THE SPRING OF 1954 was a challenging time for the American automobile industry. Business had been booming in the postwar years, and 1953 had seen some of the best sales months ever. But competition was cutthroat, fear was widespread that the postwar boom might be ending, and an auto shakeout was well under way, with smaller firms folding into each other (American Motors had just been created out of such weakness, with the merger of Nash and Hudson; Packard and Studebaker would hold on for a few more months before joining forces). Government scrutiny of the practices, in particular, of industry giants General Motors and Ford was intensifying. The leaders of GM, including chief executive Harlow Curtice, were under substantial pressure.

On April 15, the *Journal* reported that the U.S. Justice Department had launched an antitrust investigation of the industry, focused on "the hammer and tongs struggle for supremacy" between GM and Ford and whether the two companies were trying to create a duopoly. GM's market share had reached more than 45 percent in 1954, its high point since before the Second World War; Ford's share was nearly 32 percent, its highest since Alfred P. Sloan had driven GM to overtake Ford for market leadership; the six-going-on-four remaining automakers were left to divvy up the remaining 23 percent. Each of GM's five brands—Chevrolet, Buick, Oldsmobile, Pontiac, and Cadillac—vastly outsold the entire outputs of each of the smaller manufacturers. Chevrolet, the market-leading brand, sold more cars than

Chrysler, American Motors, Packard, and Studebaker combined. The antitrust investigation was spurred, in part, by pressure from Rep. Shepard Crumpacker of Indiana, who represented the South Bend district in which Kilgore had grown up, and which included the headquarters of Studebaker. It seems likely that Chrysler was also egging on the prosecutors.

General Motors chief Curtice was sixty years old, a Michigan native and GM lifer, having joined the company's AC Spark Plug division as a bookkeeper in 1914. He had become president and chief executive officer in 1953, when his predecessor was named secretary of defense in the Eisenhower administration. Sloan, aged seventy-eight, remained the corporation's chairman. Curtice, an avid *Journal* reader known to friends and associates as "Red," had recently placed a large bet—a billion dollars to expand production. The company he led had larger revenues than any other private concern in the world and employed more than 550,000 people. Two million Americans in 1954 were expected to attend GM's Motorama, a traveling show which the *Journal* described as aiming "to promote the company's cars with much fanfare, music and beautiful models." Only the government, Curtice may well have believed, could stop him from making good on his big bet.

Curtice's world was a sheltered one. He made more money than any other salaried employee in the country. He lived, as he had since 1914, in Flint, a city where nearly two-thirds of the workforce was employed by the company he ran, and flew back and forth on corporate aircraft each week to work in Detroit. As *Time* magazine would soon describe Curtice's existence:

> *In many ways he lives a life that is beyond the comprehension of most of his car owners. Platoons of subordinates jump when he twitches. Garages filled with gleaming limousines and beaming chauffeurs stand ready to transport him wherever he desires. A private 18-plane air force of multi-engined, red-white-and-blue airplanes is at his disposal. Private secretaries and public-relations men take care of bothersome detail, see to it that Cadillacs, hotel suites, restaurant tables and theater seats are there when and where he wants them. High-salaried assistants smooth his path, greet him wherever he arrives, order his drinks, fetch his newspapers.*

On May 3, 1954, Harlow Curtice can hardly have been pleased by what he found in one of the newspapers they fetched. The *Journal* had written two editorials the previous month attacking the government's antitrust investigation and defending GM and Ford's competition with smaller rivals and each other as pro-consumer. But on May 3, a *Journal* "Roundup" article laid bare a tactic the auto manufacturers had recently been deploying to great effect.

The tactic revolved around the practice of "bootlegging" cars—sales by smaller, independent dealers of excess new-car inventories at cut-rate prices. The independents would take the cars off the hands of authorized franchise dealers and unload them at prices the authorized dealers feared could undercut future sales. "Bootlegging" was thus something of a safety valve for the industry, from a dealer perspective, but not necessarily in the interest of manufacturers. A *Journal* story a week earlier had reported that the Justice Department had rejected a GM proposal that it be allowed to ban bootlegging through a new provision in the standard franchise agreement with dealers.

Now the *Journal* revealed that GM and the other manufacturers had apparently tried another means to limit bootlegging. GM, Ford, and Chrysler were the nation's three largest newspaper advertisers. In 1953, GM had spent nearly $33 million on newspaper advertising; Ford and Chrysler combined for nearly as much again. The three companies alone (not including their dealers) thus accounted for about half of all newspaper spending on automobiles, and automobile advertising accounted for a little more than one-fifth of all national newspaper ads. For the *Journal*, the picture was even more dramatic: Of the four largest categories of national newspaper advertisings, the *Journal* participated only in automotive; it did not publish advertisements for groceries, alcohol, or toiletries.

This kind of spending yielded a certain amount of influence, and it seemed that influence, the *Journal* now reported, was being used to limit advertising of bootlegged cars. From an auto industry point of view, it was the perfect resolution to the problem of bootlegging: The mechanism used to dispose of excess inventory would remain, but the broader public would not learn of the lower prices. Thus the effect on other or later sales was minimized.

The *Journal* story was sweeping, and painfully specific. *The New York Times,* the *Journal* reported, had changed its advertising policies in late April, just after the Justice Department rejected GM's anti-bootlegging contract language. The *Times* now refused to accept advertising offering new cars for sale by nonfranchised dealers. The *Times*'s advertising director said, "It is our opinion that our readers' interest is best served by doing business with franchised dealers." New cars were defined as those having fewer than 2,500 miles on them. One independent new-car dealer continued to advertise in the *Times,* indicating that its cars for sale had "run over 2,500 miles." But a *Journal* reporter visiting the showroom noted that of the sixty cars on the showroom floor "not one . . . appeared to have run 2,500 miles. Some still had shreds of factory wrapping on them." Mileage indicators on a dozen cars checked by the reporter ranged from 1 mile to 36 miles. A salesman at the independent dealership told the *Journal,* "We don't have any used cars. That's the only way [the *Times*] let us advertise."

Nor was the *Times* alone. The New York *Journal-American* had gone so far as to take out an advertisement of its own in *Automotive News* headlined "No 'Bootlegging' Problems in the New York Journal-American." The *Journal* story reproduced the ad. The classified display advertising manager at the New York *Daily News,* the nation's largest-circulation paper, reportedly acknowledged to an independent dealer that he feared the loss of other business if he continued to accept advertising from bootleggers. "Zone managers [from manufacturers] have told us face-to-face across the table what would happen to us if we took ads from discounters." The dealer had a similar experience with the *New York Mirror,* the city's (and the nation's) second-largest newspaper.

Even before the article was published, the *Journal*'s reporting of the story had an effect. The *Mirror* reversed itself and resumed accepting advertising from the bootleggers. The New York *World Telegram & Sun* declared that it was reexamining its policies. The ad manager from the *New York Herald Tribune,* the most direct competitor of the *Times,* told a *Journal* reporter, "This is a very touchy subject: I understand the F.B.I. is asking some of the same questions you're asking." He added, "I wouldn't say we have a policy."

Industry reaction was swift. On the day the story was published, *Ward's Automotive Reports* canceled the *Journal*'s subscription to the weekly newsletter.

The confrontation between Kilgore's newspaper and Curtice's company was only beginning, however.

On May 28, the *Journal* published another exclusive story, this one the work of Detroit bureau chief John Williams, revealing details of the styling of the 1955 new car models due in the fall. Williams had been a *Journal* reporter since 1947, Detroit bureau manager for two and a half years. Another DePauw graduate, he had been recruited by Buren McCormack and had already run through two tours in New York and one in Washington.

Read today, Williams's story seems innocuous, even perhaps excessively promotional. It began: "Forecast for 1955 auto models: More makes will be thoroughly restyled than ever before in the half-century of automotive history. Under the hoods will be new, more muscular engines." Additional revelations: more makes "joining the wraparound windshield trend," "bigger bumpers, bolder tail lights, plenty of chrome 'gingerbread.' Many a car will stare at you in a different way: its headlamps will be visored." V-8 engines would proliferate, horsepower would continue to grow. Illustrations for the article included renderings of the new Chevvy (then itself rendered with two v's) and Dodge. Making clear throughout that the reporting, which had taken more than a month, was based largely on interviews with industry die-makers, the article detailed projected changes in all eighteen car brands then on the market. The designs were months away from being unveiled but

> *the dies and tools required for creation of the '55's are being made right now; patient prowling in the shops which make these disclose much information. And men within the auto companies will often talk about what competitors have afoot: they make it their business to know.*

Among the GM lineup, only Chevrolet and Pontiac had significant changes in store: Both models, Williams's "patient prowling" revealed, were slated to more closely resemble their cousins at Buick and Oldsmobile.

Williams later recalled, "I worked hard, got my material together, and got lucky. Someone offered me pictures." Pressed by managing editor Henry Gemmill to get reaction from the manufacturers, Williams couldn't get anyone to agree to look at the renderings, save a representative from GM. He remembered,

> *I went to the General Motors headquarters on Grand Avenue [in Detroit]. The press relations man came out of his office to see me and looked at the picture I showed him [of the '55 Chevvy]. When I asked him to comment on its accuracy, he declined rather tersely and returned to his office.*

From an industry perspective there was a problem—a big problem. But the problem wasn't the renderings—it was the story's timing. As the story itself noted, "the alterations are certainly intended to be sufficient so that 1954 models will strike their owners as old-fashioned, once the '55's are in the showrooms; they will stir the itch for a brand-new car." In September or November (the timing of new model releases was also kept a secret), that would be good for business: the '54s would be nearly all sold. Just ahead of June, traditionally (and as recently as the previous year) the industry's biggest sales month, the revelations were thought by the automakers to cause a possible disaster: Sales of the about-to-be-"old-fashioned" '54s could dry up prematurely, as buyers awaited the exciting '55s. The president of Chrysler told Williams he "had put a dagger into the hearts of the dealers."

The automakers had traditionally avoided this problem by briefing reporters well ahead of the new model introductions, but doing so "off the record." But this year the *Journal* had declined to participate in the briefings, apparently recognizing that the information could be derived independently and published earlier. As Kilgore later told *Time* magazine, "For years almost everything in Detroit has been 'off the record.' We just decided not to play it that way. It isn't journalism."

In fact, the *Journal* had been easing away from "playing it that way" for three years. In March 1951, reporter Ray Vicker, who had joined the *Journal* two months earlier upon its acquisition of his employer, the *Chicago Journal of Commerce,* wrote an article on the 1952 model cars which relied heavily on visits to machine tool companies. Vicker was able to determine which engines manufacturers intended to use in which models—V-8s for Dodge and DeSoto, etc.—as well as other changes, such as the introduction of a new automatic transmission for Cadillac and of power steering for Oldsmobile. But Vicker's story had dealt almost exclusively with engineering rather than design.

In August 1953, Williams had taken Vicker's efforts further, and had published a piece on the 1954 model cars quite similar to his later piece on the 1955s. Its lead: "For Buicks and Oldsmobiles: A thorough restyling job, featuring the 'wrap-around' windshield and longer, lower lines." More such detail followed on Cadillacs, Fords, Mercurys, Hudsons, Chryslers, Pontiacs, Chevvies. But there were two key distinctions between this precursor and Williams's later story: First, the article on the 1954 cars lacked illustrations; second, it predicted that, "By and large, 1954 will not go down in automotive history as a year of great model changes." That is, it offered readers no compelling reason to wait for the new models or to stop buying 1953-model cars.

GM's pent-up fury at the bootlegging story and the premature release of the innovative—and illustrated—1955 new car designs quickly exploded. Curtice himself, while running the Buick division, had years earlier personally made the decision to begin advertising in the *Journal. Business Week* later reported that Williams's 1953 story had left GM "particularly incensed," but no action had been taken. Now, however, on the very day the new-designs story was published, GM, acting through five different advertising agencies, canceled all advertising in the *Journal*. The immediate cancellations came to just over $11,000, or nearly $82,000 today, but *The New York Times* estimated that GM had been running ads in the *Journal* at a rate of at least $250,000 annually.

Feemster was traveling in England. When one of the agency representatives told Ted Callis, his deputy, that the *Journal* needed to send someone to Detroit and apologize, Callis, knowing instinctively how Kilgore—his friend of nearly thirty years—would react, said, "You're talking to the wrong department. . . . I will probably go to Detroit one of these days but it won't be to apologize for anything."

GM also cut Williams and his colleagues off from the weekly auto production figures released each Friday. When the *Journal* asked the Associated Press, a newspaper cooperative of which it was a member, to request the figures so it could use them, the AP was denied access as well. The only other source of the figures was *Ward's Automotive*—but that publication had cut the *Journal* off after the bootlegging article.

Meanwhile, private complaints to the *Journal* news staff by the GM public relations staff were rebuffed. Then, a week after the new model story, the *Journal* appeared to rub salt in GM's wounds. Another front-page article by Williams described one Detroit dealer's desperation tactic of offering a new '55 car, when they arrived, to anyone who would buy a '54 model now and accept only wholesale value for their trade-in. Other dealers feared that news of the tactic could pressure prices across the country.

If Curtice had hoped that the editorial page that had leapt to his defense in the antitrust dispute would now turn on its own news columns, he was quickly disappointed. On June 16, in an editorial entitled "A Newspaper and Its Readers," the *Journal* explained that the two news stories "did not make anything happen. They only provided some more information on what was already happening."

The editorial went on to declare that "A newspaper exists only to provide information to its readers. It has no other reason for being." Moreover,

> *in the end the truth about what is happening is the only thing that is of value to anybody. And when a newspaper begins to suppress news,*

whether at the behest of its advertisers or on pleas from special segments of
business, it will soon cease to be of any service either to its advertisers or to
business because it will soon cease to have readers.

Eight letters from readers, seven of them automobile dealers, were published in the *Journal* the same day as the editorial. Thomas Grasso, of Grasso Motor in Bayonne, New Jersey, wrote that the newspaper "of late has acquired a new hobby, namely, running the automobile business into the gutter." Fred Walters, of Fred Walters Oldsmobile in Newark, New Jersey, pronounced himself "disappointed and disgusted." J. R. Sutton, of Sutton Motor in Beaumont, Texas, was canceling his subscription; R. H. Horton, of Horton Chevrolet in Sibley, Iowa, wouldn't be renewing.

The advertising cancellation and press release cutoff remained unknown to the public. General Motors had not announced them, and the *Journal* had not reported the story. But at just the moment the editorial and letters were published, Sid Bernstein, editor of *Advertising Age,* heard of the cancellations at a conference in Montreal. Callis took the call at the *Journal* and referred it to the news department. Kilgore soon confirmed the story to Bernstein's reporter.

Once *Ad Age* issued a press release on its story, GM issued a statement of its own objecting to the publication "of statements and particularly sketches which have as their source confidential information and material divulged in breach of a confidential relationship and in violation of our property rights." The statement continued,

> *While we have no advertising policies as such based on a situation such*
> *as this, we certainly do not believe that we should be placed in the position*
> *of impliedly approving or condoning such a practice by permitting our paid*
> *advertising to appear on one page of a publication which might at any time*
> *on another page of the same issue publish information involving our prop-*
> *erty rights and trade secrets, which have been obtained from sources in a*
> *confidential relationship with us.*

The statement concluded, "To the extent that news releases are issued to the press for general publication, our practice is to make them available to everyone."

The New York Times gave the story wider circulation. Just ten days after attorney Joseph Welch's televised condemnation of Senator Joseph McCarthy with the historic put-down, "Have you no decency?" the *Times* headlined its account "G.M. Blacklisting Wall St. Journal."

Kilgore did not flinch. Perhaps he recalled his first journalistic controversy over the evangelist at DePauw, or his early run-in with General Johnson on the NRA. But whatever the source of his calm and confidence, both were manifest. He tried to take the high road. He issued a statement that concluded, "I find it hard to believe that this represents the policy of General Motors top management, because I do not think that General Motors would use this sort of pressure to express disapproval of editorial or news policies of any newspaper."

On Monday, June 21, rather than report on the matter itself, the *Journal* reprinted the *New York Times* news story on the dispute on its own editorial page, with an introductory note that said, "Since *The Wall Street Journal* is one of the subjects of this story we wanted our readers to have an independent news account."

On the *Journal*'s news pages, the same day's paper carried the weekly article by reporter Williams on automobile production figures. Williams's story had a tone of modest triumph: "While General Motors declined to give this newspaper its weekly production figures, *The Wall Street Journal* obtained estimates of the motor company's output figures which it believes to be accurate. These statistics indicate that Chevrolet, Buick and Pontiac registered relatively minor declines last week from the previous week while Oldsmobile and Cadillac displayed modest advances."

Two days later, the *Journal*'s editorial page again entered the fray, with an editorial headlined "A Difference of Opinion." Following Kilgore's lead, more in sorrow than in anger, the newspaper declared that "we regret our present differences with General Motors Corporation." The editorial said that GM's statement "has, perhaps without realizing it, raised some very basic questions about the business of the press." It canvassed these questions before concluding:

> We do not intend to suggest that a newspaper has the right to demand that a company disclose trade secrets or that it advertise. But our business is publishing information, not withholding it. When there is news available about so vital a segment of our economy as the automobile industry we intend to be free to use our own best judgment about publishing it, undeterred by the fact that it may not be "authorized."
>
> And the fact that a company happily chooses to advertise with us cannot

be allowed to put the newspaper under any obligation to the advertiser
which breaches its obligation to all its readers.

We are sorry there is a difference of opinion about this. But for us to fol-
low any other course would, we believe, make it impossible for us to fulfill
our function as a newspaper.

Kilgore thus drew the lines clearly between himself and Curtice. For him, and for the *Journal,* this was a matter of high principle, a matter of essential institutional identity. For GM, as the *Journal* saw it, it was just a matter of business. The implication: There would be no compromise. Kilgore was prepared to wait out GM, confident that waiting would bring results. He wrote to his father that he thought the controversy "will blow over and I think a big company makes a mistake by getting mad and doing such things."

He was not unaware of the short-term cost, and, as if to underline the point, the *Journal* ran a brief story two days after the editorial setting out the American Newspaper Publishers Association's annual statistics on the largest advertisers in newspapers. GM, of course, was first. Kilgore also told *Time,* "The *Journal* is not mad at anybody. I have a General Motors car—and I certainly don't intend to sell it."

Others were less kind to GM. Ralph Ginzburg, who later gained fame when he was prosecuted on obscenity charges but was then a reporter at *Look* magazine, wrote to GM's Public Relations Department from his home in Brooklyn "as an owner of a General Motors car . . . to express my indignation." He said, "By pulling your advertising out of that paper, you've demonstrated that your own integrity does not measure up to that of *The Wall Street Journal.*"

A letter from the publisher in *Tide* magazine, an advertising trade journal, was even tougher on GM. *Tide* publisher Reginald Clough called GM's reaction "one of those backward steps in the gradually improving behavior of business," and attributed it to "red-headed temper" a thinly-veiled swipe at Curtice personally. *Tide* contrasted GM's behavior unfavorably with that of Ford Motor, which had been angered at a *Journal* story on its finances in late 1953, noting that in Ford's case "no one cancelled any advertising." *Tide* called for an end to the boycott. A *Tide* news story concluded, "Eventually, say some automotive public relations men, GM will have to back down."

Kilgore was not, however, under the illusion that everyone, or even every *Journal* reader, would see it his way. A week after the publication of "A Difference of Opinion," the *Journal* ran ten letters from readers in response to Williams's design story and the *Journal*'s two editorials. The first, from V. C. Marshall of New York City, said, "I believe you rendered the economy a disservice when you stressed the glutted conditions you expected to become rampant throughout the used car markets. Likewise you were grievously wrong to publish advance information about what any one manufacturer was contemplating doing in the way of design for the 1955 car." The letter was published without editorial comment, even though the story had directly predicted no such glut, and had, of course, published advance information about the plans of *all* manufacturers.

From South Bend, Tecumseh weighed in with admiration for the *Journal*'s position, but also some sympathy for GM:

> *No one likes to have their thunder stolen and the edge taken off their big announcements. As I remember it you yourself [were] a bit put out when a news paper in Chicago jumped the gun on your announcement of the purchase of the Chicago Journal of Commerce. After the horse is stolen, however, probably the less said about it the better.*

Letters published in the *Journal* ran seven to two in the paper's favor (with one using the dispute to make a separate point). I. F. Kain of Coshocton, Ohio, called the editorials "most welcome in this decade of conformity and witches." B. F. Davis of San Francisco was more prosaic and direct:

> *I subscribe to your paper because of its fine reporting and for your journalistic scoops.*
>
> *Permitting anyone to dictate to you or censor your columns would be disastrous.*
>
> *Stand your ground! Don't let General Motors or anybody else run your business.*

Mr. Davis was Barney Kilgore's type of guy.

On the same day these letters were published, Kilgore, in a move which has not previously come to light, sought to defuse the escalating crisis.

The vehicle that he chose was another letter from a *Journal* reader. Roy

Brenholts of Columbus, Ohio, had written in support of the *Journal*'s "Difference of Opinion" editorial, and had asked that the *Journal* forward his letter to General Motors. Just three paragraphs in all, his letter included the following:

> *I have two Cadillacs and a Ford. I was considering trading the Ford for a Chevy. Now I will trade for another Ford. I had considered trading one Cadillac for a new one. Until General Motors tells you they will stop their Hitlerite attitude I will not consider another Cadillac.*

Kilgore wrote back to Brenholts himself, saying that, because "you have . . . made some statements I am sure the company would want to know about," he was making an exception to policy and would pass along Brenholts's letter to GM. But he also told Brenholts that "I personally hope that the action of the company with respect to its advertising does not represent the considered judgment of General Motors top management." That said, he also stated that GM's public relations department had "only yesterday" declined to check a "very important story" the *Journal* news department was pursuing. But Kilgore concluded his letter by advising Brenholts against answering boycott with boycott. "Please do not misunderstand me," he wrote. "I appreciate your support of our editorial position. I just don't think that differences of opinion in one particular field should be allowed to spread into others."

Then, clearly by design, and on the very same day, Kilgore turned around and sent both Brenholts's letter and his own reply to Harlow Curtice. He ended his letter to Curtice with something of a plea for reasonableness to prevail:

> *As a newspaperman I don't suppose I should complain about articles published in other newspapers and magazines, but I do feel the publicity about our differences of opinion have tended to prolong those differences and I am particularly aware of the possibility that various members of our own organization may be unduly influenced by published material. The same thing might possibly be true on your side.*
>
> *If you have any good ideas on how we might sort of break this thing up I would appreciate having them.*

For his part, Curtice recognized that he had made a mistake. Bill Kerby recalled it as "an enormous public relations error." Some observers noted that the pending antitrust investigation made the timing of the dispute especially inopportune for the auto company. The ban on the *Journal* receiving GM press releases had been lifted as soon as the controversy became public. On July 1, the day after the second batch of letters appeared in the *Journal,* the newspaper was provided with GM's weekly production figures. The weekly story on industry output appeared in the paper on Friday, July 2. But there was no crowing—the GM figures were mentioned only in the ninth paragraph of the article, and with no reference to the controversy, or to the source of the figures. (By the next week, *Ward's Automotive* had also lifted its collateral ban on the *Journal.*)

The day the weekly production story appeared, Curtice replied to Kilgore. He defended the GM position on the Chevvy blueprints, even as he disclaimed any interest in refusing to cooperate with the *Journal* news department. His letter did not mention GM advertising. But it did invite Kilgore to visit him in Detroit on Wednesday, July 7, following the Independence Day holiday weekend.

Kilgore did not see Curtice's response until Tuesday, July 6. He instantly sent a wire to Curtice, saying that "if your schedule permits," he would arrive at 11:00 A.M. the next morning. At 6:35 P.M., Curtice replied by telegram: "WILL BE GLAD TO SEE YOU TOMORROW MORNING AT ELEVEN AM."

In his memoirs Kerby recalled Kilgore's account of the meeting:

> *"I just told Curtice that as much as we would like to be friends with General Motors and as much as I hated losing all that advertising, I couldn't let anyone dictate what the* Journal *could or couldn't print. Besides that, I told him, if I did what he wanted I'd lose two of the best editors in the United States [presumably Kerby and managing editor Henry Gemmill]. In time I could replace the advertising, but I'd be damned if I knew where to find new editors."*

The two men considered "just letting things take their normal course without a public statement of any kind" but concluded that "a public finish seemed necessary." They hammered out an exchange of letters during the meeting. Curtice's letter to Kilgore was dated the day after the Detrot meeting, and written "in accordance with our discussions." The letter went on to rehearse GM's legal arguments on the impropriety of the *Journal*'s receipt and publication of the rendering of the 1955 Chevvy. GM, he wrote, had had two choices: sue the *Journal* or break off business relations, and had—generously, he suggested—chosen the latter course. The company's public statement had been issued only because of an inquiry from the Associated Press. In future, Curtice warned, GM might choose to sue in such a case.

Having thus supported his more bellicose colleagues and mollified his lawyers, Curtice finally climbed down publicly. His letter concluded,

> *It was never our intention to interfere with your editorial policies, and I am surprised that anyone would seriously think otherwise. I might point out, by way of explanation, not justification, that where such a purpose is sought to be accomplished by a coercive practice, you will generally find that a legal remedy is not available.*
>
> *I regret the misunderstanding that has developed, and trust that our position is now clear to you.*

Kilgore told Tecumseh that both letters "were not particularly brilliant, having been hashed around a good deal, but they served their purpose." Part of that purpose was to tell the troops, on both sides (including *Journal* managing editor Henry Gemmill, who worried that Kilgore had been too conciliatory), that "the war had ended."

It had. The nation's largest corporation, and the newspaper industry's largest advertiser, had capitulated to *The Wall Street Journal*. Kilgore had sought an opening and found one, had shown respect, but had not deferred. The entire incident would be chalked up to a "misunderstanding," and GM did not promise there would not be a recurrence. But the *Journal* would continue to receive production reports, the accuracy of the articles on bootlegging and new model design would stand unchallenged, and GM advertising in the paper would resume.

Kilgore's letter to Curtice in response was dated the next day. Kilgore wrote that he "too, regret[ted] that a misunderstanding has developed and from your letter I think misunderstanding was unnecessary." He noted that the normal flow of news releases had resumed, and matched Curtice's reservation of the right to sue with his own reservation of the right to make editorial decisions, and to use both authorized and unauthorized sources.

On the legal issue of the Chevvy rendering, Kilgore was deft:

> *Before the story and pictures were printed, a reporter from* The Wall Street Journal *met with a member of your public relations department. At*

that time, the legal issue was not raised and perhaps it is unfortunate that neither of the men was familiar with it. Had it been raised, I am sure that the editors of The Wall Street Journal *would have decided that it merited careful consideration.*

Now that it had been raised, Kilgore averred, the Dow Jones lawyers and the General Motors lawyers did not exactly agree. (Kerby recalled that Kilgore "had become convinced that the *Journal* may have been on shaky legal grounds so far as the one sketch was concerned.") But, Kilgore wrote Curtice, the *Journal* did respect property rights, and Curtice had

done the industry a service in defining your position on this matter so clearly. No reasonable definition of property rights will interfere with the independence of editorial and news judgment which we consider the essence of this newspaper. I am pleased that we have reached an understanding on the difference that existed between The Wall Street Journal *and General Motors Corporation.*

Privately, Kilgore told his father, stories on new models would continue,

but I don't think anybody will print company drawings of new cars, and I don't think they ought to if the companies will take reasonable precautions to keep the drawings out of general circulation around Detroit.

Case closed. The *Journal* published the exchange of letters between Curtice and Kilgore on July 12—and did so without comment. Three weeks later, Curtice confirmed in writing that GM had decided not to sue and that the "controversy" was "closed."

Yet, however modestly they portrayed it, the showdown with General Motors had been a turning point for Kilgore and the *Journal*. Kerby wrote that it "firmly established in the public mind, including millions who never had read *The Wall Street Journal,* and presumably never would, that here was a newspaper of unshakable independence and integrity. GM had done us a priceless favor." David Lilienthal, former Tennessee Valley Authority and Atomic Energy Commission chairman (and who overlapped as a student at DePauw with Casey Hogate), wrote Kilgore that it was "a classic in the history of newspapering."

Edward Scharff later concluded that this "new-won reputation was worth inestimably more than the General Motors advertising account." Donald MacDonald, then a junior ad salesman but later head of all sales for the *Journal* and Dow Jones, summed up the implications simply: "Our future was assured."

11

NATIONAL SUCCESS

THE BATTLE WITH GENERAL Motors would, forever after at the *Journal,* be remembered as a watershed, a moment that truly marked "before" and "after" for the newspaper as a business, just as surely as Pearl Harbor had done for it as a news organization. The *Journal* had gained immeasurably in prestige, and was continuing to gain in readers.

Kilgore's correspondence with his father after 1954 has been lost, but the last surviving letter evokes not only Tecumseh's enormous enduring pride in what his son had wrought, but also in how far the *Journal* had come under Barney's leadership.

The letter is dated December 27, 1954, two days after Christmas. Tecumseh thanks Barney for the gift of a new radio. He then notes that the first thing he heard on his new set was an announcer reading the *Journal*'s Christmas editorial, "In Hoc Anno Domini," a parable about liberty based on St. Paul's letter to the Galatians, which was written in 1949 by Vermont Royster and had been published each year since then (and still is). The radio announcer, Tecumseh reports, "praised this editorial quite a bit." Then, he continues, an old friend called to praise another reprint, a Thomas Woodlock column for the *Journal* written during the first Christmas season of the Second World War. Finally, he notes that Arthur Godfrey had quoted the *Journal* on his radio program. The last paragraph of the last letter we have from this remarkable correspondence of a quarter century thus begins, "Well it all shows that *The Wall Street Journal* really gets round these days."

Tecumseh lived another five years before dying suddenly while on vacation in St. Petersburg, Florida, on the Sunday before Thanksgiving, 1959. He was eighty-four. A one-paragraph obituary appeared in *The New York Times; The Wall Street Journal,* which generally avoided obituaries, carried not a word.

The next key innovation of the *Journal*'s boom years was multiplying the number of sites at which the newspaper was printed. In a sense, this was the flip side of faster production at an existing plant, but the net effect was the same: more growth in the number of readers who could be offered early-morning delivery, and more of them becoming new subscribers.

In 1955 a fifth plant was added in Washington, D.C., to serve readers of the Eastern edition well south of New York and as far west as Pittsburgh. *Time* magazine took notice in a piece headlined "From Wall to Main," calling the *Journal*'s rise since the War a "lusty success story" and noting that the size of the paper's staff had doubled, from 700 to more than 1,400 during the first ten years of the postwar period. By year-end *Journal* circulation had hit 365,000, more than ten times what it had been when Kilgore became managing editor, not quite fifteen years earlier.

Laurie Lombard, asked by Kilgore to look at the state of the newspaper and the company—probably as a means of helping Kilgore gauge the mood and preferences of Lombard's clients the Bancrofts—concluded that circulation of one million copies per day was now possible. Lombard agreed with Kilgore than the *Journal* should endeavor, no matter the advertising demand, to keep the paper to a maximum of thirty-two pages per day. Kilgore called this "the right size for us"—it was twice what it had been when he became managing editor.

But while Lombard applauded expansion and growth, he had not forgotten for whom he worked. His report stated that the company, which had paid a dividend of $3.50 per share in 1954 "should pay dividends of $6 per year, and more if earnings justify it." The dividend was promptly raised to $6 per share, or about $7 million today, to be divided largely among the three adult Bancroft family members. This tension between wanting to see the newspaper and the company grow and wanting to take increasing amounts of cash out of it would remain just below the surface at Dow Jones (when not rising above it) for another half century. While Kilgore remained in charge, he consistently proved able to obtain the investment capital he thought he needed; it is not

clear that the same can be said of any of his four successors over the forty succeeding years of Bancroft family ownership under the guidance of Lombard's
successor trustees.

Money was available as well for operating expenses. In February 1956, concerned that too few young men of promise were considering careers in journalism, Kilgore, in a speech at the University of Oregon at Eugene, announced
that the *Journal* was raising starting salaries to an unheard-of $100 per week. It
was about half again more than the national average for such jobs at that time,
and the equivalent of nearly $39,000 per year today. Roughly 800 men applied
for 20 jobs; among the recruits, later stars of journalism R. W. Apple Jr. and
John Noble Wilford, both of whom went on to distinguished careers at *The
New York Times*.

The *Journal* certainly found itself in an enviable position in the mid-1950s.
Another market study by Benson & Benson, the firm Kilgore found in Princeton, concluded in 1956 that the universe of potential *Journal* readers was 4.5
million. Within a target market of men in high-income jobs that made them
"primary prospects," Benson & Benson found about 150,000 who had an interest in the paper, and saw both its value and potential utility to them, but simply lacked local access to the product. These prospects were the low-hanging
fruit whose existence was, by itself, enough to spur continuing the rollout of
new printing locations.

More broadly, the same study confirmed that the *Journal* had made enormous progress in becoming both known and admired. The paper now enjoyed
98 percent name recognition in its potential market, although only 60 percent
could correctly identify it as a daily newspaper. These figures still lagged somewhat behind the equivalent numbers for *Fortune* and *Business Week,* but those
measuring perceptions of product quality did not. Among men with access to
the *Journal* at work, its favorability ratings were 80 percent positive to just 2
percent negative, with 76 percent considering it "very reliable" and 73 percent
"always fair."

By 1957, as larger presses were installed in new offices in San Francisco,
Journal circulation had passed the half million of which Kilgore's consultants
had dreamed just after the war. And the explosion in circulation, Feemster was
delighted to boast, was not at all eroding the demographics of the readership.
A subscriber survey showed the average annual family income of a *Journal*
subscriber to be nearly $22,000 (about $156,000 today)—or better than four
times the national average. Moreover, these new readers were engrossed in the

newspaper, not just toting it as an ornament—another key issue for advertisers. The same survey reported that more than 60 percent of readers spent better than half an hour reading each issue.

In 1958, the *Journal* continued its meteoric rise, gaining nearly 75,000 new readers over the course of just that one year; circulation at year-end was 615,000, more than double what it had been five years earlier, and now nearly twenty times the level when Kilgore had launched his remake of the front page.

It seemed, and seems to have felt, almost effortless. For Barney Kilgore, that was a problem. The young man who had written his first column for nine months, and his next for seven months, who had reviewed scores of books in a single summer, who had completely transformed the newspaper in just twenty-two months as managing editor, had, by 1955, held the same job title for ten years, and had been doing essentially the same job for thirteen. He had set in motion the building of the most successful newspaper in America; if Lombard's circulation projection was right, it might well become the nation's largest—and eventually it did. But it was not enough. Not enough for the company, he knew, because companies must always grow or begin to decline. But, perhaps more imperative, not enough for him.

He had his job down to something of a science in any event. On a typical day, he arrived at the office after the train ride from Princeton and the subway downtown at 9:35. He handed his secretary his heavily marked copy of the *Journal,* with plenty of questions and comments appended. (The most famous of these: "If I see 'upcoming' in the paper again, I'll be downcoming and someone will be outgoing.") He dictated in response to the morning mail from 9:45 until about 10:10, gave out miscellaneous assignments for about five minutes, and was then off to the morning kaffeeklatsch.

Walking around, meetings and lunch came next, followed by signing the morning's yield of outgoing mail, more dictation in response to the afternoon mail, and more walking around, with replies to the afternoon mail signed and dispatched before he left for home at 4:20. If a letter he received made him angry, his secretary recalled, he would take the typed version of what he had dictated in response, and "put the writing in his drawer. Couple days later, he'd redo it, and laugh at his original expression of indignation." As he once told Kerby, "I'm the only one around here who can't afford to lose his temper."

The *Journal* had also grown so large that Kilgore was not always recognized at his own headquarters. One evening he stopped by the copy desk to pick up an early copy of the next day's paper, and a new copy editor, unaware of who he was, refused to give it to him. Never one to pull rank, he simply said okay and headed home.

But he was clearly a bit bored with his routine, and in February 1955, Barney Kilgore purchased his hometown local newspaper, *The Princeton Packet*. At a time when *Journal* circulation was pushing 350,000 daily, the *Packet* had a weekly circulation of 1,000, and was in shaky condition as a business. It would become his hobby, his laboratory, his home away from home.

Pressed later about the purchase, Kilgore acknowledged that "I probably had no business doing it, but I didn't want to see the *Packet* disappear. Besides, it's hard for a newspaperman to resist a chance to get hold of a small town paper." (Feemster had owned a small paper in Indiana since 1946, which may have given Kilgore the idea, or at least encouragement.) "And anyway," Kilgore continued, "you can learn a lot. . . . I've learned you can get called out of bed in the middle of the night, if you've injured some one, for one thing."

Especially at first, there was no task too small for Kilgore to enjoy at the *Packet*. He stopped by the small paper's offices one or more nights nearly every week on his way home from Manhattan. He would sit at the copy desk and mark up copy. Or he would write editorials; he wrote almost all of them, but did warn that "crusading is not usually needed in a town like Princeton, so be careful when you spank." One Saturday morning, the editor he had hired to run the *Packet* arrived at the office to find the proprietor "clad in dungarees and a garish sports short, sweeping the office floor. 'Place is a bit too much like the typical newspaper office,'" Kilgore said.

Just as he marked up each issue of the *Journal* for discussion at the morning kaffeeklatsch, so nothing in the *Packet* was beneath his notice. One such note to a *Packet* news editor became something of a classic around the office:

> *If you could find out who is using the word "signalized" in headlines in* The Packet *to mean honored or some such thing please ask him to stop doing it. I noticed on page 5 this word was used and it was also used the other day in a smaller story. There are lots of words that are better and "signalized" or "signified" which may have been used before are very awkward and almost meaningless.*
>
> *Also, if you could find the typesetter who is splitting words in funny*

fashion, please ask him to stop, too. I notice he split the name "Bishop" in today's issue Bis-hop. There are also a few other badly mangled words.

By this time I am sure you are aware that the photograph on the editorial page doesn't fit the cut lines. There was, alas, some horrible mistake made here and it is too bad because it wastes the space and engraving too.

In general, I think the paper looks neat and newsy.

Best regards,

BK

Even as its president tinkered with his new acquisition, the *Journal's* growth continued, and it pursued the strategy of opening new plants as soon as demand was detected and choice locations could be identified. In early 1959, Kilgore announced that new plants would be opened, first near Cleveland and then close to Springfield, Massachusetts. The Cleveland plant would produce the Midwest edition, relieving part of the burden on Chicago, while the Springfield (actually Chicopee) plant would become the third to print the Eastern edition. The news staff creating the material for all of these copies was nearing three hundred people in 1959. The new plants both came on line in the spring of 1960, bringing the total number of *Journal* printing facilities to seven. By the end of the year, *Journal* circulation had passed 650,000. Kilgore wrote Jane Cochran (formerly Jane Steele), "Sometimes I find some of the figures that we handle in our monthly reports around here hard to believe but it certainly is pleasant while it lasts and I expect it will last quite awhile. Anyway, I hope so."

Recognition of the strength and impact of the *Journal's* coverage was also increasing. In 1961, the paper was awarded its third Pulitzer Prize, the first won by the news (as opposed to editorial) side; the prize was given to reporter (and later editor) Edward Cony for reporting on a scandal in the timber business. Cony won the prize in the category of national reporting; the *Journal's* Louis Kohlmeier won in the same category four years later for reporting on the private fortune of President Lyndon B. Johnson. In the interim, *Journal* reporter Norman "Mike" Miller, later the paper's Washington bureau chief (and another of the $100 per week recruits from 1956), won a 1964 Pulitzer for general reporting. In all, Kilgore's paper was awarded five Pulitzers during his time in charge.

He did not win a Pulitzer himself, of course, having had his last byline in 1944. But in 1961, *Editor & Publisher* magazine, confused by another award

Kilgore had received from Columbia University, credited him with a Pulitzer, alongside those actually won by Grimes and Royster. When *The Princeton Packet* picked up and repeated the error, Kilgore wrote a letter to the editor of his own paper: "Since a newspaper can be presumed to print the truth, although probably not the whole truth about its own publisher, I feel obliged to set the record straight," he began. Referring to Grimes and Royster, his letter concluded, "I wouldn't want them or anybody else to think I was pretending to be a member of their club."

With the printing network significantly expanded, and with the Electro-Typesetter having been commercially available to other newspaper publishers since 1958, Kilgore's attention returned to the efforts at further technological innovation now led by Buren McCormack.

In June 1961, Kilgore announced plans for the *Journal*'s eighth plant, in Riverside, California, a second plant devoted to producing copies of the Pacific Coast edition. At one point, he considered asking Richard M. Nixon, with whom he was friendly and to whose 1960 presidential campaign he had contributed money, to ceremonially open the plant. Nixon's return to politics as a candidate for governor of California in 1962 seems to have prevented this. The need for the Riverside plant reflected a remarkable fact: The newspaper born in and named for the heart of New York's financial district now sold more copies in California than in New York State. This milestone was reached even before California's population passed that of New York, which occurred toward the end of 1962, by Census Bureau estimates.

Riverside was a plant with a difference. It would be the first to deploy facsimile transmission, creating an exact duplicate on presses in Southern California of the pages produced in San Francisco. Following up on Kilgore's 1955 inquiries to Ackell and then McCormack, the technology had been developed and tested in the *Journal*'s New York laboratory. The *Journal* described the new technology this way:

> As each page of the newspaper is set in type in San Francisco, a special page proof will be made and an exact picture of this page will be transmitted over the equivalent of a television channel to the Riverside plant. . . . A complete page will take approximately 41/2 minutes to transmit over the complex of coaxial cable and microwave circuits. . . .

*The electrical image of each page received in Riverside will be repro-
duced on a photographic film. The film, when developed and processed, is
a negative image of the page proof in San Francisco. This film is then
placed on a sensitized metal plate and the picture etched on the plate's surface. The completed semicylindrical plate will be used on a standard newspaper press.*

The new plant went online in May 1962, after several months of dry runs. By
then, total circulation of the *Journal* had grown to 825,000.

Less than a month later, the *Journal* announced plans for another new
plant, this one located in White Oak, Maryland, and a replacement for the
plant in Washington. But the White Oak facility was also needed to house
Barney Kilgore's latest project, the last great idea of his career.

12

A Newspaper with "Flair"

THE IDEA HAD ACTUALLY been kicking around Dow Jones for a long time. As early as 1956, the board of directors had considered the question of how the company might diversify. The *Journal*'s success had been enormous, but it had a couple of troubling aspects: First, the newspaper now accounted for more than 80 percent of the company's profits, and second, while the trend since 1941 had been steadily rising, Kilgore and his fellow directors, as well as his colleagues in management, understood that newspapering generally was a cyclical business, subject to periodic declines, particularly in advertising revenue, and thus profit.

Ideas that were considered and rejected mostly focused, at this early stage, on starting new publications. Among the discards: a national daily newspaper focused on labor-management issues, a magazine devoted to politics, and a weekly financial publication for women.

One diversification possibility Dow Jones did take seriously was the acquisition of *Newsweek*. The largest stake in the magazine had been owed by Vincent Astor, who had, along with Averill Harriman, funded Raymond Moley's *Today* magazine in 1933, and merged it into another magazine called *News-Week* in 1937. (This was the same *Today* for which Kilgore had freelanced often, especially in 1936–37.) Astor died in 1959, leaving control of the publication in the hands of his foundation. When the foundation began quietly shopping *Newsweek* in late 1960, Samuel Newhouse and Meredith Publishing were among those who looked carefully at the property; their interest was publicly reported at the time. Not disclosed was an equally close look taken by Dow Jones. But Kilgore concluded that the magazine would divert Dow Jones too much from the *Journal*, and Kerby agreed that the property, at an asking price of $14 million for all of the shares (nearly $95 million today), was "an indigestible bite."

Soon after deciding not to pursue *Newsweek*, Barney Kilgore became snowbound in Princeton. He used the time to write a memo to his management colleagues seeking to break the logjam, and to move forward on a weekly business magazine. The other executives were largely unmoved; Bob Bottorff still favored the publication for women; Bill Kerby, convinced that the company should buy its way to diversification rather than building toward it, pushed for the acquisition of community newspapers. But Kilgore was undaunted.

In the spring of 1961, as Kilgore continued to nurse his proposal, Bottorff suggested the possibility of a general-interest weekly newspaper as an alternative, and Kilgore was immediately intrigued.

He linked the idea with a notion he had had for years—that an opportunity existed for a publication that would focus on *explaining* the news rather than *reporting* it, emphasizing background and context, stepping back and synthesizing. He had tried to create a team at the *Journal* to do this as early as 1957, and had assigned former managing editor Henry Gemmill and veteran reporter and editor Joe Guilfoyle to lead the effort. Apart from some strong stories out of the Little Rock civil rights confrontation, little had come of the idea, but Kilgore had neither forgotten nor abandoned it.

Soon the general-interest weekly concept was taking shape. The *Journal*'s printing network was largely idle on Friday and Saturday nights; this suggested a Sunday publication day. In a note to himself, Kilgore scribbled, "Nobody in the world could try this out as economically as we can." He dubbed the prospective publication "The National X," and began to think of it as similar to the leading quality British Sunday papers, such as the *The Sunday Times* and *The Observer*.

His colleagues, Bottorff and Buren McCormack aside, remained unimpressed. Feemster weighed in, deeply skeptical of the advertising potential for such a publication. But Kilgore plowed ahead, briefing his board in June 1961 on the Sunday newspaper market in general, and the possibilities for a Dow Jones weekly in particular. He estimated the size of the target market at 35–40 million, many times that for the *Journal*.

Kerby (although not present at the meeting) later described the board's reaction as "far from enthusiastic," but the creation of a small editorial group to explore the concept was authorized. Bottorff and Royster were named to supervise the effort, but this was Barney Kilgore's personal project, and he would lead it for the rest of his working life, devoting more time to it than to anything else.

In late June, with the board having acquiesced, Kilgore sat down and wrote another memo to his executive committee, outlining the idea for the new publication at length. By now he was proposing to call the new paper *The National Observer.*

He termed his note a "screed," and acknowledged that "newspapers are not made by essays; they are made by bright people undertaking trial and error, cut and fit." But he needed to forge a common understanding, and he could best do this, he believed, by writing to his colleagues—nearly all of them, like himself, accomplished professional writers. He ticked off the elements of what he had in mind:

purpose:	*"current information, education, enlightenment and entertainment related to the stream of events"*
format:	that of the newspaper *"which has advantages in manufacture and arrangement"*
schedule:	weekly, *"which is a useful periodicity"*
audience:	*"comparatively young, fairly well educated, reasonably alert and interested in national and international affairs and substantially lacking in information and background"*
content focus:	*"those events which, so to speak, constitute history in the making. . . . But don't slip over this too lightly. Selection is our first major news problem, and it must be done skillfully, firmly and with the attitude that we know what we are about."*
	Start stories with the news ("the news must be newsy"), but assume the reader lacks all background ("For example, a high school senior.")
	As a secondary focus, "the treatment of a news situation that has been running along just below the top category long enough to require a review and exposition—what we might call, in light of our prospective name, an Observation."
	"All the useful Wall Street Journal *writing techniques*

are applicable here, only more so. Take the reader by the hand. But imagine, perhaps, a younger, smaller hand than the horny mitts of the Wall Street Journal *subscriber.*

mix: *"up to a pretty high and fancy fringe of sophistication and down towards pure entertainment and a sprinkle of spice. Newspapers have been built on sensationalism, but I don't think this is our dish."*

tone: *Adopt some of the "know-it-all attitude" that is "another charm of our British cousins."*

"a prestige newspaper, fun to go to bed with."

Then, summing up, he groped for the right term. "I hesitate to use the word 'flair' because an ill-fated publication was once based on it, but it does have some meaning for us here." Kilgore made clear, above all, that he sought through his *National Observer* to instill again in his now-large and successful company the sense of adventure that had permeated the *Journal* when he took command twenty years earlier. He was fifty-two years old now, but he warned his colleagues: "Above all, this project is no haven for tired old men. It has to have enthusiasm and operate in a shower of sparks." The editor selected to lead the *Observer* staff, William Giles, who had been at the *Journal* eleven years, was thirty-four, just two years older than Kilgore had been when he was named managing editor. The average member of the initial staff Giles recruited was in his early twenties.

The project was still proceeding in secret, but Kilgore told department heads in a memo in August that a new group was looking at "various publishing ideas" including "the possibility of publishing a national Sunday newspaper." Giles's team grew to eight men, and prototype issues began to be produced in September 1961. By October, they were churning out new prototypes almost weekly; twelve different prototypes were ultimately printed, an unusually large number then and now. At first, these were only four pages in length; by December they were running as long as twenty-eight pages. Kilgore personally critiqued every one.

He was particularly fascinated by questions of typography in the *Observer.* He hired Edmund Arnold, editor of *Linotype News,* author of the 1956 book *Functional Newspaper Design,* and a recent addition to the faculty of Syracuse University as a graphic design consultant. Arnold had determined that a six-column format was more appropriate for broadsheets than the usual eight-column format, and, perhaps aided by the fact that the *Journal* was published in six columns already, prevailed on Kilgore to make the *Observer* the nation's first major six-column general-interest paper. Such a format, Arnold maintained, when used with 9-point body type, created a layout where each column was exactly as wide as one and one-half times the length of the lower-case alphabet, which Benjamin Franklin and Italian typographer Giambattista Bodoni had first advocated as the optimal width two centuries earlier. (Within fifteen years, the six-column format would be the industry standard.) But the *Observer*'s Plymouth Italic type nameplate reflected Kilgore's personal preference—it was the same type he had chosen years earlier for the nameplate of *The Princeton Packet.*

Nor did Kilgore rely on Arnold alone on typographic matters. As Edward Scharff relates:

> *The basement of [Kilgore's] house in Princeton was strewn with his burgeoning collection of old typefaces, and he fiddled with them late into the night looking for the right combination of type styles for [the* Observer*]. When Kilgore found a combination he liked, he tried it out in* The Princeton Packet, *then took it to the small team of men he had working in secret [at the] Dow Jones [offices] in New York.*

Kerby prepared a budget with its assumptions crafted in light of some of the early prototype work, as well as a projected first-year average circulation of 150,000. These numbers reflected operating costs twice what had been envisioned (and shown to the board) in June, with circulation having trebled. Kilgore was getting carried away with his own enthusiasm, but despite new projections of a loss of $1.1 million ($7.5 million today) in the first year and three million dollars before reaching the break-even point, he took the project to the board for approval in September. That approval was given, although Kerby (again not in attendance) later said that "there was a sort of unofficial deadline that the *Observer* either get in the black or be killed within a relatively short time."

A couple of weeks later, speaking to a seminar in Norfolk, Virginia, Vermont Royster, who had succeeded Grimes as editor in 1958, let slip that Dow Jones planned to publish a national Sunday newspaper to be called *The National Observer.* This was more problematic than an earlier published aside in *Editor & Publisher* that had said Dow Jones was considering a Sunday business publication, both because it was more accurate and because it received wider distribution. One of those in attendance was an Associated Press reporter, and an AP story moved across the national wire the same day, and appeared in *The New York Times* the next day. Kilgore and his team had to scramble to trademark the *Observer* name, which they had not yet done.

The new publication was formally announced in mid-November 1961. The *Observer* was described as "the first of its kind in America." Kilgore had decided that it needed to be based away from the *Journal,* and from New York; its headquarters would be first in Washington, then at the new White Oak plant. The newsstand price would be 25 cents, or about $1.70 today (versus 10 cents for the *Journal*), and the subscription price would be $10 per year, or about $67 today for fifty-two issues, versus $24 for roughly 250 issues of the *Journal*. Publication was slated to begin February 4, 1962.

Clearly, the concept of the *Observer* required some explanation, and Kilgore immediately set about laying out for readers what he had in mind. A full-page advertisement in the *Journal* on the same day as the press release touted the "bouncy, healthy new baby" as "an all-family national weekly newspaper" and stressed that it would be "compact—all in one section," with no more than thirty-two pages (the same length Kilgore had, years earlier, set as the optimal length for the *Journal*). The *Observer* promised that "busy people everywhere will be able to read yet understand much more." Charter subscribers could sign up for nine dollars for the first year.

In the following weeks, a series of clever, small, and repeating house ads in the *Journal* and paid advertisements elsewhere sought to flesh out this approach. The first asked, "Do you find it difficult to cross the Berlin barrier (even mentally)?" It promised that the *Observer* would shy away from "reporting that assumes you are an *expert* on foreign affairs, politics and other complex subjects." Similarly, another ad asked, "When you read about Red China—is it Greek to you?" and followed up by wondering, "Do you find yourself reading more but understanding less?" Another appeal began: "The average medical man has to read so many professional journals, he hardly has time to keep up with other news. Does this remind you of yourself . . . ?" A third was directed to women who "are reluctant to take part in discussions on current events" and promised to arm them to participate. After a year of failure at the Bay of Pigs, the Soviets beating the United States at getting a man into space, tension over the Berlin Crisis, and the civil rights Freedom Rides, another full-page ad in the third week of the campaign promised that the *Observer* would provide "wholesome . . . relief from scare headlines and lurid stories—relief from the excessive playing up of vice and violence, crime and crisis."

These appeals struck a nerve. The plan approved by the board in September had projected an initial press run of no more than 100,000. But within twenty-five days of the initial announcement, more than 57,000 subscription orders had been received. At the thirty-five-day mark, this number had grown beyond 75,000, and before year-end had passed 100,000. Less than three weeks before launch, Dow Jones announced that the printing plants in Chicago and Chicopee would join the Washington plant in printing the *Observer*. The press run for the first issue finally came in at 391,000—nearly four times the projection made just four months earlier. Charter subscriptions numbered 140,000.

The first issue of the *Observer* came in at the maximum 32 pages that had been promised, evenly split between 16 pages of news and 16 pages of advertising. But even at this outer limit, the contrast with other Sunday newspapers could not have been more striking. The same day's issue of *The New York Times* ran more than 400 pages and weighed four pounds; the *Observer* weighed eight ounces. *Time* called its look "clean and uncluttered."

The lead stories in the first issue concerned the latest "thaw" between the United States and the Soviets ("There are times when you might not guess there is a Cold War going on and last week was one"), plans for the projected Manned Spaceflight Center near Houston, a profile of an army general expert on guerrilla warfare, and a look at police scandals across the nation. None of the stories bore bylines. Weekly columns were launched on health, contract bridge, and cooking. The *Observer* had arranged for exclusive U.S. reprint rights from three British papers, the *Daily Telegraph*, the *Sunday Telegraph,* and the *Sunday Times,* and made use of these rights.

The purpose of the paper was further explained in the first of the "Observations," which was entitled "A Word About Ourselves." It again promised "a new kind of publication for this country." While the *Observer* hoped to be entertaining, it warned that "we are not in the entertainment business. A newspaper's chief reason for being is news." On the other hand, the editors understood that "there are times when everyone feels inundated with news. What is hard to find in the flood is understanding."

Three distinctions from other publications were seen as key: The *Observer* would be "a newspaper and not a magazine, a weekly and not a daily, [and] national and not local." Being a newspaper meant getting the news to readers more quickly, "before the avalanche of events relegates it to history." Being a weekly meant that "the news does not come in broken bits and pieces." Being national, in a phrase that would come to stand for one of Kilgore's greatest innovations, meant "We will treat the news exactly the same way for the reader in Portland, Maine, and the reader in Portland, Oregon." The final words of the piece embodied Kilgore's essential creed as a publisher, and optimism about his work: "So . . . here is *The National Observer*. We hope it will be a success. But our first impression is to make it interesting and rewarding. For we know that the only way to success is to put out a good newspaper."

Before turning to the fate of the *Observer,* let us take a few moments to pause and note the incredibly striking similarity between Kilgore's vision of what American readers wanted in 1962 and what the most thoughtful publishers believe they want today.

It will not ruin our story, one hopes, to acknowledge that the *Observer* eventually failed. What is more interesting, and almost certainly more instructive, are the ways in which it succeeded, and the genuine genius of its vision.

First, twenty years before the publishing phenomenon of *USA Today,* Kilgore understood that an economy and polity that had become truly national in scope made possible a national newspaper. Next, more than thirty years before the advent of digital publishing, Kilgore recognized that well-educated professionals were becoming overwhelmed by the amount of information they were being asked to take in, and that a flood of data was actually yielding a drought of understanding. Many years before efforts sprang up to broaden the range of newspapers in an effort to lighten their mix of content and to appeal to readers in their personal as well as public, professional, and civic lives, Kilgore's *Observer* devoted much of its attention to what it called the "business of living." Finally, as we have seen, the promise of such a publication produced a huge number of readers ready to pay for it, sight unseen.

Almost immediately, however, there were notable gaps between promise and performance.

Perhaps the most serious of these came in the mundane but critical realm of distribution. Buren McCormack had been instructed to create a distribution system that would focus on newsstand sales, with delivery to subscribers as a lower priority. Instead, subscriptions mushroomed, and newsstand sales almost immediately fell short of expectations. Most of the subscriptions had to be delivered through the U.S. mail, which meant that subscribers would not receive their copies until Monday or Tuesday, undermining the "newspaper" advantage of timeliness. Initially, even Monday delivery was optimistic, as the system had been designed to get no more than 40,000 copies into the mail. The *Observer* boasted in advertising that it had "the shortest closing news deadline of any national news weekly in the United States," but the relevant time frame was not from copy-closing to printing, but from copy-closing to delivery.

On the content side, *Time*—which, of course, might well have seen the *Observer* as a competitive threat—while acknowledging that it was "the U.S.'s first serious try at a national newspaper," added that the articles were displayed in "no detectable pattern," and backed up the point with a couple of embarrassing examples. The *Time* article concluded with a quote from an anonymous "high-ranking editor" at *The New York Times* (another *Observer* competitor): "If *The National Observer* is worth 25¢, the Sunday *Times* is worth $2.50. I expect the second issue will be a lot different; they'll change it while they still have time."

All of this yielded problems in both circulation and advertising. After the delivery snafus (which became apparent immediately), the first difficulties to surface were on the advertising side. Space in the first issue had been oversubscribed, with Dow Jones turning away five pages in addition to the sixteen it printed. But over the course of the *Observer*'s first year, while news pages remained fixed at sixteen, advertising pages averaged only about six. By December 1962, advertising (even at the height of the holiday shopping season) had fallen to two and half pages in an issue. *Newsweek,* another weekly competitor, sniffed that the *Observer* "often serves up a diet of cold hash and rehash" and derided the editorial "Observations" as "often infuriatingly bland and crashingly dull."

Even before that, by the fall of 1962, Kilgore was fighting back. In a pair of ads aimed at the advertising trade that ran as house advertising in the *Journal* and on a paid basis elsewhere, the questions agencies and clients were raising were taken on directly. "Who *needs The National Observer?*" the first asked. The answer: "The same folks who 'need' color TV; who 'need' wardrobes of the new miracle fibers; who 'need' European vacations; who 'need' new kitchen appliances; who 'need' more life insurance." In other words, affluent readers, *buyers* of high-end goods and services. The second ad posed the flip side of the same question. Its headline: "As an ad man: I want to know: What do readers get

from *The National Observer?*' The answers were detailed in eight crisply numbered items, ranging from greater timeliness to "the equivalent of a dozen cover
stories" to "a welcome relief from stylized cuteness, noisy headlines and artifi-
cially stimulated excitement."

The advertising problems were only exacerbated when more circulation
difficulties began to surface. All those charter subscribers came up for what
publishers call "conversion" (first renewal of their subscriptions) no later than
February 1963. Conversion rates were soon ranging around a paltry 20 percent. The only significant factor masking the problem was additional newsstand sales in New York City and Cleveland where long newspaper strikes
(114 days in New York, 129 in Cleveland), not affecting production of the *Observer,* were under way in late 1962. Dow Jones later estimated that the strikes
had temporarily boosted *Observer* circulation by 85,000 copies per week.
Year-end 1962 total paid circulation was 223,000 copies, which Kilgore was
happy to note exceeded all original forecasts. What he didn't say was that the
subscriber count had actually fallen from 140,000 at launch to 113,000 ten
months later.

But Kilgore made it plain that he was in for the long haul. He insisted to
Time that "we are quite satisfied. We are not amateurs. We know the *Observer*
will be successful, but we don't know what the size of the success will be." He
reminded *Editor & Publisher* in an interview that he had grown *Journal* circulation more than twenty-five-fold in twenty years, and indicated that he was
thinking in terms of at least a ten-year plan for the *Observer.* And he reminded
questioners of his publishing philosophy: "Advertising? First things first. First
comes the product and circulation, then comes advertising."

And he did start to make progress in 1963. The newspaper strikes ended in
April and newsstand sales fell back to fewer than 24,000 by the end of the year,
but the subscriber count rose to a record 167,000. Conversion rates climbed
to nearly 30 percent and renewal rates (second and subsequent renewals) were
nearly 70 percent, close to the levels for the *Journal,* and well above industry
norms. Advertising volume in the first nine months of 1963 exceeded that in
the last eleven months of 1962, but was still under three pages per issue in the
first half of 1964. Although heavy spending on circulation promotion was necessary to accomplish it—more than $2 million in 1964—total paid circulation
continued to grow every quarter through 1964 and into 1965. Riverside, California, was added as a fourth printing plant for the *Observer* in late 1964.

Moreover, the content was strong and getting stronger, as Kilgore and his editors refined their feel for their new audience. At first, Kilgore had thought the *Observer* might not even need its own reporters, that its editors and writers could simply "observe" the reporting of others and add large and intelligent dollops of context and explanation. Very shortly after the paper's debut it became clear that reporting really was the *sine qua non* of a newspaper, and the *Observer* news staff was increased by half again over the course of the paper's first ten months, from twenty-three to thirty-four men. Soon Kilgore dispatched a memo that led to the left-hand slot on the top of the *Observer*'s first page being reserved for "some more or less personalized report on the news."

The prose in the new paper was often sparkling, and the mix was both provocative and eclectic. Pieces ran the gamut from a defense of suburban sprawl to an inquiry into the changing mission of psychiatry, from a brief history of the rise of Billy Graham to a candid look at the sexual revolution on campus, from a rank ordering of attitudes toward TV ("honest snob" nonviewers, "ownership tempered by apology and declarations of rarely watching," "slobs") to an article on Americans' increasing use of Yiddish words and expressions. Kilgore and Giles had attracted a number of the best young reporters in the land. James Perry wrote about politics, from a first-person account of President Kennedy's assassination, with gruesomely detailed reporting from the parking lot of Parkland Hospital to a portrait of a defeated presidential candidate, Senator Barry Goldwater, "a man of quicksilver moods," on election night to Winston Churchill's funeral, "one of the last spectacular flashes of a mighty empire." Hunter Thompson developed a beat his name would later come to define with articles on the decline of the Beatniks, the increasing obstacles to hitchhiking, and expatriate life in Cali, Colombia. Robert Semple contributed powerful coverage of a bus on the way to the civil rights march on Washington.

In the middle of 1963, Kilgore decided the *Observer*'s strengths in explanatory journalism could be parlayed into a new form, a magazine-format report on a single current topic of interest. The reports were dubbed "Newsbooks," and were described as "broader and deeper than a newspaper feature article or series providing background for a major news event—yet more pertinent and timely than a history book." The first Newsbook, devoted to the 1964 presidential campaign generally, was published in April 1964. The second, devoted more narrowly to Goldwater, was written entirely by Perry, ran 159 pages, and was available to readers just twelve days after Goldwater delivered his acceptance speech at the Republican National Convention in

San Francisco. Subsequent topics included Latin America and Religion in Action.

Kilgore continued to commit not only Dow Jones's resources but his own prestige to the *Observer*'s success. He wrote prospective advertisers personally in late 1964 about why he thought the *Observer* "is doing very well and thanks for asking," and then authorized general sales manager Ted Callis to reprint the letter as a full-page ad in the *Journal* "if you want to—but no personal photo, no big headlines."

Callis later recalled that, with *Observer* circulation slated soon to pass 400,000,

> *Barney was really charged up to grow [it] to five hundred thousand. He wanted to get it above the foothills of the magazine world. At three hundred thousand, four hundred thousand—many good publications,* The New Yorker, The Saturday Review of Literature, *and so forth, topped off, and he thought if we could get the* National Observer *up around five hundred thousand, we'd stand above those.*

On the desk in the study in his home in Princeton, Kilgore worked by light from a lamp crafted from a printing press plate of the first page of the first issue of his latest creation.

That is where the *Observer*'s story stood in the spring of 1965. Before picking up this aspect of the story, however, let us double back and briefly review developments at the *Journal* during the *Observer*'s critical early years.

13

INTERRUPTED

Had it not been for the struggles of *The National Observer*, the first half of the 1960s would have constituted something of a victory lap for Barney Kilgore and Dow Jones. The period was not without its complications, but business was strong, recognition for the *Journal* was increasing, and the printing network continued to drive circulation gains.

One difficulty did arise, however, in the executive team Kilgore had built. The presence of Bob Feemster had become problematic. In addition to the demands of Feemster's ego, he was now increasingly distracted by outside business interests, which had expanded beyond the newspaper in Indiana to include a motel in Daytona Beach, Florida. As Kerby later recalled the situation, "For several years . . . Bob had done little or no work up to the point where he had authorized his secretary to sign salary increases, etc., for him." Kilgore had been able to live with this, especially as Ted Callis took up the slack on the advertising side, but, Kerby continued, "he wasn't amused when circulation sales ran into trouble because of Bob's absentee management." It certainly did not help that Feemster continued to oppose the *Observer* and "all but washed his hands of the whole project."

Toward the end of 1962, Kilgore pushed Feemster, who was only fifty-one years old, into retirement—the first and only time, in all of his years running the company, that he essentially fired a senior executive. Even the reduction in Joe Ackell's responsibilities in 1956 had been glossed over, and Ackell remained on staff for ten years thereafter, before retiring at the age of sixty. In Feemster's case, as well, Kilgore tried to be gracious. He and Feemster jointly announced Callis's promotion to general sales manager and appointment to the executive committee in early December. Nothing was said publicly, or even privately, about Feemster's departure; he was, for the moment, "on vacation."

Then, just two weeks into the New Year, Feemster was killed in the crash of a small private plane near Fort Pierce, Florida; his motel manager, who was piloting the plane, also died in the crash. The *Journal* referred to Feemster as "chairman of the executive committee of Dow Jones" and made no mention of his departure weeks earlier. Even Callis remained unaware, then and years later, that his former boss had been forced out.

The *Journal*'s news story referred to Feemster as "one of the leading architects of *The Wall Street Journal*'s rapid growth in the last 20 years." The editorial noting his passing was somewhat more equivocal. It called him "the most successful sales manager in [the paper's] history," but, overall, used the backhanded formulation, "his was no small contribution to our growth."

Just weeks after Feemster's death, Dow Jones reported that revenue in 1962 had reached a record $59 million (nearly $400 million today), with net income of $6.5 million (about $43 million today), down slightly from 1961, as losses at the *Observer* took a toll. Still, profits had only exceeded $1 million for the first time in 1953, and had grown by more than 50 percent in the most recent four years.

The public disclosure of these numbers was much more detailed than at any time in the past—and for a reason. Dow Jones & Company was going public. The vehicle was a secondary offering of shares. In the offering, the Bancroft family sold just over 7 percent of the company for $12.3 million (or about $81 million today); employees of the company had the opportunity to buy shares in the offering at a small discount. The offering valued the company at $175 million, or about $1.2 billion today.

The latest printing facility, in White Oak, Maryland, opened for business five days after the offering. It replaced the Washington printing plant, open since 1955, and, as planned, also housed the *Observer* staff. *Journal* circulation in late 1962 and early 1963 was inflated by sales resulting from the New York newspaper strike, which had not affected the *Journal,* masking the softness produced by Feemster's inattention in his final months, so 1963 saw yet another rise in total paid copies, as had every year since 1941. Kilgore and Mc-

Cormack had seen enough of the New York printers' union, though. Two days after the end of the strike, they announced that they were closing the *Journal*'s New York printing facility, effective ninety days later.

But the circulation growth streak ended in 1964. Without the bounce from the New York strike, *Journal* circulation fell from 880,000 to 843,000. It was just a blip, however—circulation resumed its upward march for more than fifteen consecutive years thereafter. Already, the *Journal* was the nation's third-largest newspaper by circulation. On the paper's seventy-fifth anniversary, in July 1964, Callis publicly predicted that *Journal* circulation would top one million by early 1967. In the event, the milestone was reached in late 1966.

Meanwhile, Dow Jones revenues and profits both reached record heights in 1963 and again in 1964. The board declared a three-for-one stock split in 1964, and raised the quarterly dividend from fifty cents at the time of the offering to sixty cents soon thereafter to seventy-five cents before the split. The annual dividends being paid to the Bancroft family now exceeded the current equivalent of $25 million per year.

And the business continued to be built. A new and expanded plant to replace the one opened in Dallas in 1948 was built in 1964. Plans to replace the San Francisco plant with a new one in Palo Alto were announced in late 1965. That same year, the company moved into new offices at 30 Broad Street, even closer to the New York Stock Exchange, selling the building at which Kilgore had arrived in 1929, and in which Dow Jones had been housed since 1893 (although the place had been thoroughly renovated in 1931). Kilgore had insisted on purchasing a large tract of land in South Brunswick, New Jersey, near Princeton, in 1962, and a new administrative and research facility, initially employing 250 people (of a total workforce of about 2,300) in areas including circulation sales, personnel, purchasing, and accounting, was opened there in early 1965.

Diversification, however, remained an issue for Dow Jones. The *Observer* held out the promise of making the company less dependent on the *Journal* as a property, and less a hostage to the fortunes of the financial markets, but profits from it were years away at best, and even then it was, after all, a second national newspaper. The board was pushing Kilgore for more risk spreading than that, and so, it seems likely, was Kerby.

Consultants were retained in early 1964 to lay out options for how Dow Jones might grow, mostly by acquisitions. Their marching orders limited them to looking at targets that were already profitable, had growth potential, and were related in some way to existing Dow Jones businesses. Textbooks and other business book publishing were identified in advance as a particular possibility. A report delivered in June recommended immediately:

- Buying a book company and augmenting the development of a book division through internal expansion as well (the *Observer*'s Newsbooks were likely pushed forward in this context);
- Expanding the offerings of the Dow Jones News Service into information as well as news;
- Expanding into trade journalism through new publications or an acquisition; and
- Buying community newspapers.

Over the longer term, the report, from Bradford Mills of New York Securities Consulting Corp., suggested:

- Looking into television and radio, but not until uncertainties over the future of pay television and UHF broadcasting were resolved; and
- Perhaps eventually buying a newsprint company.

This plan made perfect sense to people like Laurie Lombard and Bill Kerby, and it would essentially guide the company's strategic direction for more than thirty years, through and beyond the tenures of Kilgore's first two successors as president.

In part as an anticipation of the work ahead, Kerby and Buren McCormack were elected to the company's board in May 1965, while Bob Bottorff, Ted Callis, and Vermont Royster were named corporate vice presidents. These moves may also have been the formal opening move in a vague plan of Kilgore's, hatched in 1964, to have two or three of his lieutenants (Kerby, McCormack, and possibly Bottorff as well) each be given a relatively brief chance to run Dow Jones before age compelled them all to retire sometime during the 1970s.

But while his own tenure continued, diversification of the sort outlined in the Mills report failed to engage Barney Kilgore's imagination. He was still a newspaper man, and the *Observer* remained his dream. The *Observer,* like the *Journal,* continued to grow. But unlike the *Journal,* it did so only at high cost. While the *Journal's* audience almost seemed to seek out the newspaper once it was physically available, the *Observer* audience had to be hunted down. And while Feemster had long since honed an effective pitch for *Journal* advertising, Kilgore and Callis were still straining to persuasively position the *Observer* as an advertising vehicle.

Kilgore was undaunted, however, even optimistic. Then his dream was interrupted.

One day during the summer of 1965, Kilgore was visiting Mary Lou in Princeton Hospital, where she was undergoing tests on an old back injury, when he collapsed with severe stomach pain. Tests indicated some sort of intestinal obstruction; Mary Lou went home, but Barney underwent a long and difficult surgery. His colleagues were told the surgery had been "minor," and that he would be back at work soon. But it had not been, and he would not be.

Barney Kilgore had terminal colon cancer, and he knew it. He was fifty-six years old.

He went off to Palm Springs to recuperate, then returned to work, spending two days a week in New York (now usually commuting by car rather than train and subway), and three days at the new facility in South Brunswick—where he sketched out plans for a much larger building, as well as a new printing plant. He sited the buildings himself, ignoring the cost implications, placing himself increasingly at odds with his board.

Sometime during these months, probably shortly after his return from Palm Springs and before returning to the hospital for a second surgery, he confided in Kerby that he had cancer and did not expect to recover. He would give up the presidency of the company in the spring of 1966, and abandon the notion of multiple short-term successors. While he expected to remain chairman of the board, he would recommend Kerby be elected president, and would confine himself to working in South Brunswick. "You will have a clear field," he promised.

He told Kerby in the same conversation that he intended to "live my life as though I didn't have [the cancer]." And he tried. After recovering from the second surgery, he made a number of business trips in 1965, 1966, and early 1967.

Meanwhile, the plan of succession moved ahead. Kilgore told the staff in a note on January 17, 1966, that he would retire as president at the company's annual meeting on March 15 and that Kerby would become president, McCormack executive vice president, and Bottorff general manager. "This is not a sudden decision," he wrote. "I have been President for more than 20 years and for the last 15 months of so, in consultation with other directors of the company, I have been at work on appropriate recommendations whereby our management team could be expanded and responsibilities more broadly shared." But an era clearly was ending.

In that connection, there was also the matter of Kilgore's contract to resolve. Since 1948 it had provided that, even in the event of his early death, Kilgore would receive the equivalent of what amounted now to the earnings on 150,000 shares for ten years following his death or retirement, following which Mary Lou would receive the same sort of annual payment, based on 75,000 shares, for the duration of her life. Dow Jones had earned $2.07 per share in 1965, so this obligation was likely to amount to well more than $300,000 per year—more than $1.9 million today—for ten years (assuming that earnings continued to rise), and then half that amount for as long as Mary Lou, who was only fifty-four in 1966, survived.

The company's outside lawyers, Patterson, Belknap & Webb, led in these matters by Dow Jones outside general counsel Robert Potter, devised a plan under which the Kilgores would accept a lump-sum settlement of the contract. This gave them use of the money while Barney was still alive, and qualified for taxation as capital gains rather than income. But it also required shareholder approval and thus public disclosure, shining a public spotlight, for the first time, on the fact that Barney Kilgore's work leading *The Wall Street Journal* had made him a rich man. The accountants calculated that $3,503,678 was a fair settlement price, and this was agreed to be paid; it amounts to nearly $22 million today. The amounts were all laid out in a *Wall Street Journal* story on Dow Jones's annual proxy statement, published on February 21, 1966. Kilgore also signed an agreement to remain a Dow Jones consultant, at $25,000 per year. Laurie Lombard defended the agreement at the shareholders meeting, and a threatened lawsuit alleging waste of corporate resources came to naught.

Still, Robert Potter warned Kilgore that the attractive tax status of the deal depended on his no longer acting as an employee of the company after March 15, 1966. He shouldn't use company letterhead (except as chairman of the board) and shouldn't list any company return address. Dow Jones should stop paying his club dues. Bill Kerby would occupy his Broad Street office. Kilgore duly acknowledged the letter.

The scope of Kilgore's consultancy may have been a source of some tension between him and Kerby. After the Dow Jones annual meeting at which he stepped down as president, Kilgore went on vacation to Acapulco. On his return, he had lunch with Bottorff and McCormack; he soon reminded Kerby by memo that "we discussed executive lineup recommendations and you and I explored this the following day or two days later." In future, he undertook to stay abreast of what he called "new equipment stuff," but presumably not "executive lineup recommendations." He asked to be permitted to continue to attend meetings of the American Newspaper Publishers Association and American Society of Newspaper Editors, though not as a formal representative of Dow Jones. Kerby carefully retained the memo in his files. Kilgore was working hard to be deferential to and respectful of Kerby, but the role reversal after thirty years of partnership must have been jarring for both of them.

In the first eighteen months of his illness and retirement, Kilgore was a fixture at industry conferences, speaking at events in Los Angeles in November 1965, New Orleans in October 1966, and Milwaukee in November 1966. As 1966 gave way to 1967, he tried to continue working whenever he had the strength. *The Princeton Packet* started a magazine, and Kilgore bought three additional newspapers in adjacent towns. The local paper that had had a circulation of 1,000 when he rescued it twelve years earlier now was the flagship of a group with 18,000 circulation.

Kilgore joined Kerby to open the *Journal's* Palo Alto printing plant in late February 1967, and later to inspect a new offset printing facility at Highland, Illinois, near St. Louis, which opened the following month. But the last item pasted in his scrapbook was dated January 1967. On April 17, he had yet another operation, this one at Columbia Presbyterian Hospital in New York. Kerby now tried to prepare the staff for the inevitable, and perhaps also to deal with rampant rumors. He described the operation as intended to deal with "the stomach difficulties which have been troubling [Barney] for the past few months. Although it would be medically described as a serious operation, he will be out of the hospital in a week or 10 days."

While Kerby continued to visit him once or twice a week, as did others—Bottorff also called once a week—Kilgore's work was largely at an end. Bottorff described Kilgore during the summer of 1967 as "demolished" and said he would "go down to Princeton to see him and come back all shaken."

Mary Lou later noted that, in the first months of his illness, "he said, well, at least he'd be able to play the piano. . . . But what happened was his illness progressed all through his muscles and he wasn't able to play the piano which bothered him a great deal." His son Jack noted Kilgore's frustration as his body betrayed him. When he made a mistake at the piano one day, he closed the cover over the keys and never played again. When he once dropped his spoon at the table, he ceased taking meals with the family. To some extent, he turned for comfort to religion, spending a lot of time with his local ministers and asking his wife often to read the Bible aloud to him.

Even in the autumn of 1967, he tried to remain engaged. He was particularly frustrated that he could no longer type, yet he dictated a memo in response to an article about the rise of the *Journal* in the American Society of Newspaper Editors *Bulletin* by Warren Phillips, who had become managing editor of the *Journal* in 1957 and was now the company's top editorial executive. Phillips had written, "Kilgore, more than any other, broadened the concept of what constitutes news of importance to *Journal* readers. It also was he who developed the page one leader story. . . ." In his memo Kilgore described how moved he was to see Phillips cite the Kilgore news formula as the root of the *Journal*'s success. He concluded proudly that

> *my role is apparently still meaningful although it has been inactive a long time in the sense of holding the highest news executive job on the paper, as Warren Phillips does today. It means to me that the staff must still understand quite clearly what we are trying to do even though we may not always succeed.*

He sent the memo on to Kerby, Phillips, McCormack, Bottorff, and Royster with a covering note: "My chances these days of writing things about the paper, even for the file, are pretty limited so I thought I'd send you a copy of this. BK"

His last note to Kerby came a few weeks later:

> *WFK:*
>
> *According to everything I hear, things are going fine and I wish you well in your administration.*
>
> *Next time I see you there is one thing I want to ask you about so please remind me of it. I forgot the last time.*
>
> *Saw Fanny [Kerby's wife] briefy the other day. She was looking extremely well.*
>
> *Best regards,*
>
> *BK*
>
> *PS—I got a report on the Palo Alto editorial meeting. Very interesting.*

At the *Journal,* his obituary and a related editorial were going through multiple drafts and edits from everyone up to Kerby himself. The working assumption was that Kilgore would not live to see his fifty-ninth birthday on November 9. But he surprised them. That day he sat in his living room, having blood tests taken, but went through a pile of papers with his secretary. After four hours of this, the secretary, William McSherry, left "with enough work to keep busy for a week."

The "one thing" he wanted to ask Kerby about became the subject of their last conversation. It was *The National Observer.* Kilgore's last words to his successor and friend were "Bill, will my baby make it?" Kerby "assured him the circulation and advertising trends were up. They were."

Late on the evening of Tuesday, November 14, 1967, five days past his birthday and too late for his own newspaper's deadline, Barney Kilgore died at home in Princeton.

His funeral service and burial were private, concluded within seventy-two hours, and limited to family. A memorial service followed on Friday afternoon in Princeton, with Kerby, McCormack, Bottorff, Royster, and Callis—three of the five, men with whom he had attended college—serving as honorary pallbearers. In lieu of flowers, the family asked for contributions to a memorial fund at DePauw. The Dow Jones Foundation immediately sent $100,000, with more to follow.

The New York Times, which was able to scoop the *Journal* on Kilgore's obituary, started it on page one. The headline said that he had "Built *The Wall Street Journal.*" Robert White, the man he had helped install in the failed effort to save the *New York Herald Tribune* (the last trace of which had folded six months earlier), and now the head of Sigma Delta Chi, called him "the publishing genius of our age." Bill Kerby told the staff in a note on Wednesday morning that, while the published obituaries would tend to measure him only by his great reputation as a newspaperman and publisher," he "was, most importantly, a courageous and inspiring leader and a very human, warm and loyal friend. He will be intensely missed—and in a most personal sense."

Letters of condolence flooded in to the *Journal.* One of those which seemed to capture what had been lost came from an advertising executive who wrote to Kerby, "I once asked Barney how he would describe the writing style which helped the *Journal*'s circulation grow so rapidly. He said: 'It's sprightly.' I think that word describes Barney's personal charm. He was sprightly!"

The *Journal* obituary, when it appeared on Thursday morning, included two photographs of Kilgore, the first a head shot inset into the text on page one, the second, a familiar portrait with sleeves rolled up, sitting before a type-writer. The article seemed to focus on another word for Kilgore, calling him a "restless man," determined to ensure that the *Journal* and Dow Jones not stand still while others explored new ideas, a man of "restless energy" who governed through a kaffeeklatsch, a man of "restless interest" who bought the *Packet* and started the *Observer* in his later years. The *Observer* obituary, appearing four days later, was headed simply, "Barney Kilgore, Newspaperman," and told of his "restless drive to achieve excellence in journalism."

Vermont Royster, on the editorial page of the *Journal,* crafted perhaps the most enduring image, a key phrase of it borrowed from the *Observer*'s own debut editorial: "As some men look at rivers and see them spanned by great bridges, he looked at the nation and dreamed of crossing it with a single news-paper that each morning would carry the same news to Portland, Oregon, as to Portland, Maine."

Epilogue

*T*HE *WALL STREET JOURNAL'S* circulation was just about one million when Barney Kilgore died. It kept on growing for nearly fifteen years, topping two million in the early 1980s. The number of the *Journal's* U.S. proprietary print sites peaked at eighteen in 1985, and stands at sixteen today. Satellite transmission of pages, a fascination of Kilgore's in his last years, replaced the Electro-Typesetter. The *Journal* became the nation's largest-circulation newspaper in 1979, and stayed that way until overtaken by *USA Today* in the early 1990s.

Mary Lou Kilgore maintained a home in Princeton the rest of her life. Her children had been fifteen, nineteen, and twenty-two when Barney died. In 1973, she married Robert Beilman, a retired Pan Am airplane pilot, and they split their time between Princeton, the home she and Barney had built in Twin Lakes, Pennsylvania, Nantucket, and two places in Florida. The bargain she and Barney had struck on his Dow Jones pension turned out to have been a very good one for the company, as she lived to the age of ninety-three. In the boom year of 1999 alone, the contract from 1948 would have paid her $2 million, although the payouts would have been highly volatile and unpredictable.

Mary Lou's older son Jim still owns and runs *The Princeton Packet,* which is now the flagship of a nineteen-publication group, with an aggregate circulation of 190,000. Mary Lou was still chairman of the Packet Publications Board when she died in 2005. Kathryn Kilgore became a writer; at one time she was married to Alexander Cockburn, a self-described radical writer who worked for ten years as a columnist for the *Journal*. Jack Kilgore owns and runs an art gallery in New York City.

All of Kilgore's key contemporaries—Buren McCormack, Bob Bottorff, and Ted Callis as well as Bill Kerby—worked at Dow Jones until their retirement. The leading figures in the next generation of the newspaper and the company—Warren Phillips, Vermont Royster, Donald MacDonald, and others—were largely men whom Kilgore and Kerby had identified and groomed during their years together. Other contemporaries of Kilgore spent much of their careers elsewhere. Charlie Robbins, Kilgore's DePauw roommate, sold advertising for *The New York Times* after leaving the *Journal,* worked at Bozell & Jacobs, including on promoting the *Journal,* and founded the Atomic Industrial Forum. Ken Kramer, Kilgore's constant companion during his early days in San Francisco, ultimately became editor in chief of *Business Week*. Eugene Duffield, who coauthored Kerby's series on the defense buildup of 1941 before succeeding Kilgore as Washington bureau manager of the *Journal,* turned down a Kilgore-instigated offer to run the *New York Herald Tribune,* and instead ended up heading *Popular Science* magazine.

Kerby could not figure out how to save *The National Observer,* but he did not have the heart to kill it. Barney Kilgore's dying question—"Will my baby make it?"—was no doubt ringing in his ears. The losses on the *Observer* peaked at $2 million (nearly $13 million today) in 1965, the year Kilgore became ill, before easing. In 1974, Edwin Roberts's commentary won the *Observer* its first Pulitzer Prize, and the losses came down to $300,000. But then, instead of completing the move toward profitability, the losses widened again as the economy weakened. Ultimately, over the years, those losses added up to $34 million.

Satisfying current readers wasn't the problem: Circulation was still above 400,000, and renewal rates remained at 70 percent. A national survey, which found that the *Journal* was the nation's most trusted newspaper (a finding that would never thereafter vary), also found the *Observer* roughly tied with *The New York Times* for second place. But acquiring new readers was difficult and expensive, and attracting advertisers was becoming nearly impossible. The *Observer* had an audience, but it was too small and, even worse from an advertising perspective, couldn't be readily pegged. Advertisers could never figure out what to sell to *Observer* readers, and Dow Jones could never adequately help them do so.

Warren Phillips succeeded Kerby as president of the company in late 1972, and as chief executive officer in 1975. He decided that the July 4, 1977, issue should be the *Observer*'s last. His statement said, "The long effort to make the *Observer* self-supporting has not succeeded and its future prospects do not give sufficient encouragement to continue the battle." More than a few reporters and editors thought Kilgore, sometime during the sixties, would have found a way.

Many of the novel ideas forming the basis of the *Observer*'s approach—its focus on distillation, on analysis, on "less is more," on mixing humor and entertainment into the stew of offerings—are being put forward again as the keys to reinventing newspaper journalism, more than forty years after Kilgore first articulated them. Beyond this, Kilgore's first critical finding, published in that "Dear George" letter seventy-five years ago, that readers seek insight into tomorrow even more than an account of yesterday, may only now be getting through to many editors and publishers.

The Bancroft family, after owning Dow Jones for 105 years since Clarence Barron bought it from Dow and Bergstresser, finally got an offer they thought they couldn't refuse in 2007 and sold the company, and the *Journal,* to Rupert Murdoch's News Corporation. The months during which the bid remained pending were marked by a debate, inside Dow Jones and out, that gave testament to what Kilgore had created. The *Journal,* it was generally agreed, was a national treasure, now at risk. Would it remain journalistically independent under the ownership of a media behemoth? Would its news pages still be a paragon of integrity? Would advertisers and other business partners gain new influence over content?

Murdoch talked bravely of carrying on the Kilgore legacy of independent journalism, but his track record was devoid of any reason to think, for instance, that the General Motors confrontation of 1954 would have played out as it did if Murdoch had been substituted for Kilgore. Lawyers labored to install procedural guarantees of independence, but these were almost instantly revealed as empty.

The reasons for the sale were many, and the roots ran back at least two decades; that tale could (and, in other hands, will) fill a separate book or two.

An important part of the story can be traced through the movements of the price of Dow Jones stock. It went public in 1963 at just above $2 (adjusted for subsequent stock splits). It rose through Kilgore's tenure and into the late 1960s, then fell during the sluggish 1970s, bottoming in 1974–75 not far above the original offering price. When the broader market recovered in the 1980s, Dow Jones soared, reaching a record $57 in 1986. Shares purchased at the time of the public offering, that is, had increased fourteen times in twenty-three years, all while paying a significant dividend. Dow Jones was perennially listed as one of the "most admired companies" in the country.

Then the company's business problems began to mount, and the stock did not regain this 1986 level until 1998. It reached new highs, around $75, amid the Internet boom of 2000, but dropped as swiftly as it had risen when the Internet bubble burst, falling to near $30 in 2002. And these numbers, while alarming on their own, grossly understate the difficulty. When Dow Jones shares peaked at $57 in 1986, the Dow Jones Industrial Average had never reached 2000. By the time the company's stock recovered its high point twelve years later, the broader market index was nearing 10,000. From the beginning of 2005, as awareness of the business crisis in newspaper publishing grew, the stock seemed stuck below $40—even as the DJIA crossed 13,000. That is, until Murdoch made his $60 per share bid in the spring of 2007.

Beyond that, suffice it here to note the following:

- Bill Kerby and Warren Phillips spent their terms at the helm of Dow Jones (through the 1980s) essentially executing the diversification plan laid out in 1964. When that was (quite successfully) done, the small size of the new businesses relative to the old left the company in need of . . . diversification, in particular away from newspapers.
- The most important step then taken in this direction, still fully consistent with the same 1964 plan, was the creeping takeover of an electronic financial data company named Telerate, which was completed in 1990. But the managers of Dow Jones remained newspaper people, top to bottom, with Phillips's successor, Peter Kann, a brilliant writer and Pulitzer Prize–winning reporter, having begun his career in journalism with occasional work at his hometown newspaper, *The Princeton Packet*. At the least, the early 1990s match between personnel and strategy was imperfect.
- The Bancrofts, too, must accept some of the responsibility for any shortfalls. As they had since the death of Jane Bancroft, the dilution of

her fortune, and the advent of Laurie Lombard and successor trustees, the owners tended to underinvest in growing the business and to be too frightened of taking on debt, while paying themselves large dividends. In the end, even after selling more than one-third of the company in the open market in the twenty years after 1986, most of the adults in the family wanted more.

- And, probably most significant, the new century brought unprecedented challenges to newspapering as a business, with outcomes for many once-proud franchises still very much in doubt at this writing. With their confidence already shaken, a noneconomic buyer offering a noneconomic price—and that is what Murdoch was—presented an irresistible temptation to many.

Only time would tell what the full cost was, to *The Wall Street Journal* and to our society.

The South Brunswick, New Jersey, campus Barney Kilgore insisted on purchasing and building up was named the Bernard Kilgore Center in the mid-1980s. It became the company's largest facility, and, for about a year after the attacks of September 11, 2001, closed the Dow Jones building in New York, the temporary corporate headquarters. A statue of Kilgore, caught in the act of rolling up his sleeves, graces the main entrance.

But most of the visitors pass by the simple monument without really taking it in. Employees of Dow Jones who went above and beyond the call of duty for many years were given Kilgore Awards, but that custom lapsed some time ago.

Kilgore was overwhelmingly voted the Business Journalist of the Century in a thorough public process concluded in 1999. The news summary form he pioneered now highlights the front pages not only of the *Journal,* but also of its competitors the *Financial Times* and *USA Today*—and of literally hundreds of other papers around the world. His approach to telling stories in newspapers—with anecdotal leads and nut grafs—is omnipresent. The "click-through" format of "What's News" has become the most common means of presenting news in what looms as the dominant medium of our time.

But beyond the walls of Dow Jones and *The Wall Street Journal,* Barney Kilgore himself is not well known. And this is almost certainly as he would have wished it. *The Wall Street Journal,* on the other hand, still stands—at least for now—at the pinnacle of newspaper publishing. At this writing, it has won twenty-two Pulitzer Prizes in the last twenty-one years. It is the best-respected publication of any kind in the country, the American newspaper more people pay for than any other, the only paper whose content has enabled it to charge readers on the Web. And that, too, is what Barney Kilgore wanted, dreamed of, and worked to achieve.

These two realities constitute not a paradox, but an integrated whole. As *The Wall Street Journal* editorial mourning his death concluded,

> *Thus his work is more famous than himself. If you ask what he did, you need only look at this newspaper you are reading simultaneously with more than a million others in cities and villages all across the land. . . . If you ask what manner of man he was, his friends can only tell you that he had a touch of genius and was to the full measure a gentleman.*
>
> *Such men are rare.*

NOTES

References to authors, unless otherwise indicated, are to their books and articles listed under sources.

Abbreviations

Ad Age	*Advertising Age* magazine
BK	Bernard Kilgore
Bridge	Bridge, John, unpublished manuscript *Dow, Jones, Berg and Us All* and interviews for that work (on file in Dow Jones archives)
DJ	Dow Jones & Company
E&P	*Editor & Publisher* magazine
KCH	Kenneth C. Hogate
LK	Lavina Bodenhorn Kilgore
MLTK	Mary Lou Throop Kilgore (Beilman)
NO	*The National Observer*
NYT	*The New York Times*
PCE	Pacific Coast edition of *The Wall Street Journal*
TK	Tecumseh Kilgore
WSJ	*The Wall Street Journal*

PREFACE

xi BK "really invented modern journalism": Fox News, 5/1/07.

xi Comparing BK with Freud. *Columbia Journalism Review,* 5/21/07.

INTRODUCTION

1 a remarkable meeting: The account of Kilgore's efforts to help salvage the *Herald Tribune* is drawn largely from Richard Kluger, *The Paper,* 545–75.

2   "(No strings attached to this)": BK to Thayer, 8/25/58.

3   "You have got to get the *readers* talking about the newspaper": Notes on Meeting, 8/25/58; emphasis added.

3   "It is not . . . a bad newspaper": BK to Thayer, 1/19/61.

3   "it is a little too much of a newspaper that might be published in Philadelphia": BK to Thayer, 8/25/58.

3   BK on importance of research: Ibid.

3   deadwood: Ibid.

3   A later memo: BK to Thayer, 1/19/61.

3   "This will take two or three good men": BK to Thayer, 8/25/58.

4   Need for shorter stories: Ibid.

4   "the compact model": BK to Thayer, 1/19/61.

4   Whitney . . . didn't take BK's advice: See Kluger, 565–99.

1. HOOSIER BEGINNINGS

5   BK's first name: TK to BK, 5/18/35; James Kilgore to author, 11/12/07.

5   TK taught school in Muncie: TK to BK, 1/7/40.

5   LK was one of his students: TK to BK, 3/31/44, 7/1/54.

5   TK joins Union Central: TK to BK, 6/2/38; TK to BK, 6/7/44.

6   TK at Indiana University: TK to BK, 6/23/34; 12/16/41.

6   Tecumseh's family had deep roots in Indiana: TK to BK, 8/23/36, 5/14/47; TK to Mrs. W.T. Congleton, 1/12/34.

6   BK enjoyed boxing and toy trains: TK to BK, 5/14/34

7   "I can also remember how": BK to TK, 4/6/44.

7   "mooching around among old papers and books": TK to BK, 1/13/40, 11/26/41

7   "that got me a head start in school": BK to TK, 5/11/38, 11/12/40.

7   "Dear Papa": BK to TK, 6/15/14.

7   He built a model railroad, and hitched a sail to his favorite wagon: *South Bend Tribune,* 12/6/53.

7   BK a member of the debate team: BK to TK, 9/9/53.

7   BK creates "owl house" category: Lloyd Wendt, *The Wall Street Journal,* 306.

8   TK convinces LK that BK is ready for college: TK to BK, 6/5/32, 11/14/40.

8   Background on DePauw: This comes largely from Clifton Phillips and John Baughman, *DePauw: A Pictorial History.*

10   Rector scholarships: Phillips and Baughman, 213. The program was eventually broadened to include women and high school students from beyond Indiana.

10   Rector may have kept BK from attending Notre Dame: MLTK (Beilman) interview, Bridge, 10/18/79 at 23.

10   "college work does not seem very hard": BK to LK, 9/17/25.

11   "you have a place to sleep and three meals a day assured you while I have not": TK to BK, 11/16 or 11/17/25.

11   "Buy ribbons for *it* instead of *her*": TK to BK, 12/1/25, emphasis in original.

11   "the most important is English because it is you[r] medium of exchange of ideas": TK to BK, 10/18/25.

11   "Dear Omnipotens": BK to TK and LK, 10/20/25, 11/22/26.

12   the highest grades of any of the young men in his fraternity: BK to LK, 11/2/25.

12   "In fact, I know so": BK to TK and LK, 10/28/25.

12   BK selected for the debate team: BK to TK and LK, 10/28/25.

12   BK's first exposure to journalism: BK to TK, 9/9/53.

12   "I am doing a little bit of something here this year": BK to TK and LK, 10/22/26.

12   "We would like more of them": TK to BK, 11/20/26.

12   TK seeks account of BK's time: TK to BK, 11/22/26.

12   "You will leave the margin a little too close some time and will flunk": TK to BK, 2/19/27.

13   BK elected editor in chief of *The Mirage*: BK to TK and LK, 4/22/27.

13   BK writes two short stories: TK to BK, 5/10/27; BK to TK, 6/8/27.

13   "the third highest position on the paper staff": BK to TK and LK, 5/15/27.

13   "you have always said you would not make it on account of having so much outside work to do": TK to BK, 5/18/27.

13   BK continued to get A's: BK to TK and LK, 6/11/27.

13   BK had first date at DePauw: BK to LK, 9/17/25.

13   BK want to church with her: BK to LK, 11/8/25; BK to LK, 7/12/27.

13   BK's spent the summers . . . in Davenport: BK to LK, 7/12/27; BK to TK and LK, 6/19/29.

13   "when the first slicing machine": *Today,* 9/5/36, 26.

14   "DON'T SPEND YOUR MONEY TILL YOU GET IT AND THEN DON'T SPEND IT ALL": TK to BK, 7/12/28.

14   BK cut his class load: BK to TK, 9/14/27.

14   BK graduates as a captain: BK to TK and LK, 2/25/29.

14   BK selected editor of *The DePauw*: Robbins to Bridge, 8/16/78.

14   "*The DePauw* is coming along": BK to TK and LK, 9/23/28; see also BK to LK, 10/5/28.

14   "You do not know how much": TK to BK, 9/30/28.

14   "I am afraid her college work is over": TK to BK, 7/7/29.

15   "Tigers Score Twice on Powerful Army Eleven": *The DePauw,* 11/5/28.

15   He hoped to stop in New York City and Washington: BK to TK and LK, 10/28/28.

15   His salary of one hundred dollars: BK to TK and LK, 3/1/29.

15   E. Stanley Jones controversy: *The DePauw,* 2/27/29.

15   "I wouldn't be here long if certain professors had anything to do with it": BK to TK and LK, 3/1/29.

15   "one of the most heartening signs I've seen since coming to DePauw": *The De-Pauw,* 3/4/29.

16   "Charles Robbins left": BK to TK and LK, 2/25/29.

16   He failed to secure one of the Rector Fellowships: TK to BK, 1/28/29; BK to TK, 4/28/29; TK to BK, 4/29/29.

16   "I really didn't expect to get one of the things very much": BK to TK, 5/13/29.

16   "I've often thought": BK to TK, 11/12/40.

16   "So . . . that is settled": BK to TK, 5/13/29.

2. A NEWSPAPER'S ORIGINS

17   Around $40 a week: KCH to BK, 5/13/29.

17   Setting a starting date: BK to TK and LK, 5/15/29; BK to TK, undated "Thursday," 6/29.

17   Phi Gam salaries in New York: BK to TK and LK, 5/15/29.

17   A fine break for Robbins: BK to TK, 7/10/29.

18   Room at the Phi Gamma Club: BK to TK and LK, 9/6/29; BK to TK, 9/11/29; BK to TK and LK, 9/15/29.

18   BK's first day at the office: BK to TK and LK, 9/6/29. See Ted Callis interview, Bridge, 1/27/78, 3, for description of building entrance.

19   "Put it in the first line": Winthrop and Frances Neilson, *What's News,* 30.

19   Goodbody: Hamilton, 22.

19   "I never saw him even excited": Hamilton, 21.

19   First of the "corporation analysts": Woodlock in *WSJ,* 6/27/32.

19   Physical descriptions of the founders: Woodlock in *WSJ,* 6/27/32.

20   "we were just there": Wendt, *Wall Street Journal,* 28.

21   Trend to afternoon papers: Frank Mott, *American Journalism,* 447.

21   Front-page advertisements: Mott, 497.

21   One typewriter and one telephone: Woodlock in *WSJ,* 6/27/32.

21 Adoption of the typewriter: Mott, 499.

22 Circulation of the *World*: Mott, 507.

22 "In all things first, and in many things alone": *WSJ,* 3/9/1899.

23 Purchase price for DJ: Contract dated 3/31/1902 in DJ files. Previous published accounts indicating a price of $130,000, with just $2,500 in cash, are incorrect.

23 "Dow's work": *WSJ,* 12/5/1902.

24 "dabbled . . . in Liberal politics": Woodlock, *WSJ,* 6/27/32.

24 "There is only one side to the truth": Edward Scharff, *Worldly Power,* 16.

25 Barron's collapse: Wendt, 97.

25 Barron's salary and expenses: Jon Meacham, *The Beginning of the Journey,* 43.

25 "he initiated the system of financial journalism in vogue today": *NYT,* 10/3/28.

25 South Sea Bubble collection: *WSJ,* 12/22/49.

25 Barron's demands for service: Scharff, 11.

26 Lifetime output of two million words: Meacham, 4.

26 "they didn't work with him": Lissner, "The Big Three," in DJ files, undated.

26 Barron's whereabouts: Royster, introduction to Charles Preston, ed., *The World of the Wall Street Journal,* xvii.

26 Makeup rule in his pocket: *WSJ,* 2/12/47.

27 "Barron did love him": Wendt, 158.

3. "DEAR GEORGE"

29 "So far, so good": BK to TK and LK, 9/6/29.

29 Books on economics: BK to TK and LK, 9/8/29.

29 "we had a great time": BK to TK and LK, 9/15/29.

29 Writing his parents frequently: BK to TK, 9/11/29; BK to TK and LK, 9/21/29; BK to TK, 9/22/29; BK to TK and LK, 9/30/29.

29 an extra three dollars: BK to TK, 10/16/29. Cf. BK to TK and LK, 9/6/29 on cost of food.

30 "Not bad, not bad": BK to TK and LK, 10/20/29; BK to TK, 10/16/29.

30 "I do not know as yet": BK to TK, 10/28/29.

30 Hamilton's view of the market: Hamilton, 8.

31 "hang onto your shekels": BK to TK, 10/28/29.

31 "Everybody starts in again at scratch": BK to TK, 11/10/29.

32 "a six or seven dollar dinner": Ibid.

32 "a mere infant": Ibid.

33 "in truth a national newspaper": Wendt, *Wall Street Journal,* 154.

33   "a chance to work up to something good": BK to TK and LK, 11/29/29.

33   "I LEAVE HERE FRIDAY": BK to TK, 12/3/29.

33   Margaret joined him on the way west: BK to TK and LK, 12/13/29.

33   "more like a real job": BK to TK and LK, 12/15/29.

34   his week's meals for less than ten dollars: BK to TK and LK, 12/22/29, 12/25/29, 12/30/29, 1/2/30.

34   His money worries . . . at an end: BK to TK and LK, 4/20/30.

34   "both of them much older than I": BK to TK and LK, 12/22/29.

34   Hendee: Wendt, 189.

34   First Christmas away from home: TK to BK, 12/25/29.

34   promptly asked for more money: BK to TK and LK, 2/10/30; BK to TK, 2/19/30.

34   "If you have any more like him send them along": TK to BK, 3/24/30.

34   Bottorff his "right hand man": BK to TK, 1/31/45.

35   Hogate hiring Callis: BK to TK and LK, 3/14/30.

35   expressions of love and pride: See TK to BK, 5/15/30; TK to BK, 6/1/30.

35   the time of his life: BK to TK and LK, 6/2/30; BK to TK, 7/10/30; BK to TK and LK, 3/29/31.

35   fooled by the rally: BK to TK and LK, 3/27/30.

35   Bank collapses in South Bend: BK to TK and LK, 6/20/31; TK to BK, 6/22/31.

35   "I probably could go back to New York": BK to TK and LK, 8/1/31.

35   Barney had become pessimistic: BK to TK and LK, 3/29/32; see also BK to TK and LK, 4/27/32.

35   he was no longer flush: BK to TK and LK, 9/1/31.

36   bottoming out . . . in March 1932: BK to TK and LK, 3/29/32.

36   His parents' first radio: TK to BK, 12/25/31.

36   "a wizard in your generation": TK to BK, 4/18/32; see also TK to BK, 6/27/32.

36   "It is all for your benefit": TK to BK, 8/4/32.

36   Margaret was writing nearly every day: BK to TK and LK, 1/28/30.

36   "just about the cats whisker": TK to BK, 12/19/29.

36   "I have got to save money fast": BK to TK, undated "Thursday," circa 10/30.

37   Barney's weight had ballooned: BK to TK and LK, 1/18/32, 2/3/32; cf. BK to TK, 2/3/30.

37   "I fear that the fire has gone out": BK to TK and LK, 1/18/32.

37   Margaret announced her engagement: BK to TK and LK, 2/3/32.

37   Summary boxes: BK to TK and LK, 2/3/32.

37   "it requires a bit of digging": BK to TK, 2/25/32.

37   George Robertson: 11/1/32; all dates are *WSJ,* not PCE.

37   as Hogate had been promising since June: BK to TK and LK, 6/4/32.

37   "*the problems discussed are real*": WSJ, 7/12/32; beginning with the third letter the *Journal* also noted that the letters were reprinted from its own Pacific Coast edition. WSJ, 7/23/32.

38   "They took my headline and all": BK to TK and LK, 7/13/32.

38   "Feed them the figures later": TK to BK, 2/22/32.

38   "just get a little something in every day": BK to TK, 2/25/32.

38   "an uncomprehending friend": Scharff, *Worldly Power*, 52.

39   three hundred letters: Ibid.

39   "willing to learn": BK to TK and LK, 4/13/32.

39   "It is a 'dollar in circulation' ": WSJ, 7/15/32.

40   Columns ranged over the financial landscape: WSJ, 7/23/32; 7/25/32; 7/26/32; 8/3/32; 8/23/32.

40   "havoc with the economic order": WSJ, 8/18/32.

40   "when they are bad they are awful": WSJ, 8/19/32.

40   LaGuardia's evidence: NYT, 4/27/32; WSJ, 4/27/32.

40   Gomber . . . was still with the paper eight years later: WSJ, 11/30/40.

41   "the taxes will come down or they just won't be collected": BK to TK and LK, 4/27/32.

43   five successive columns on the gold standard: WSJ, 9/1/32; 9/5/32; 9/9/32; 9/12/32; 10/6/32.

43   and one on foreign exchange: WSJ, 10/11/32.

43   "a little better standing with the paper": BK to TK, 9/6/32.

43   "the best young man": TK to BK, 6/26/32.

43   Hogate's offer and Kilgore's reply: BK to TK and LK, 9/17/32.

43   Freelancing and radio: BK to TK and LK, 9/11/32; BK to TK, 10/29/32.

43   "more carefully worked out": BK to TK and LK, 9/30/32, 10/29/32.

44   " 'The Perils of Prosperity' ": WSJ, 10/25/32.

44   Kilgore . . . took only one college course in economics: *The DePauw*, 11/17/67.

44   "before there was any microeconomics": Robert Allen, *Irving Fisher*, 12.

44   "the greatest doctoral dissertation in economics ever written": Ibid., 58, 11.

44   "first American to use mathematics in economics": Ibid., 42.

44   Economics Association and Econometric Society: Ibid., 1, 204.

44   "created the national accounting systems": Ibid., 11, 112–14, 13.

44   "the equation of exchange": Ibid., 11.

45   Fisher's index of commodity prices: The *Journal* ceased publishing the index in October 1934.

45   "the triumvirate who established modern economics": Allen, 39n.

45   "one of the most distinguished economists": *WSJ,* 12/30/12.

45   "the greatest economist": Allen, 12, 13.

45   "first of the modern 'monetarists' ": Allen, 253.

45   Fisher had no interest in fiscal policy: Ibid., 254.

45   Fisher's speech in Washington: See, e.g., Maury Klein, *Rainbow's End: The Great Crash of 1929* (New York: Oxford, 2001); *WSJ,* 10/24/29.

45   "notable among them, Professor Irving Fisher": *WSJ,* 10/29/32.

46   "*what those dollars would buy*": *WSJ,* 12/16/32; emphasis in original.

46   Column reference to textbooks: *WSJ,* 4/6/33.

46   Taussig on Fisher's book: Allen, 133.

46   "optimism and wishful thinking": Allen, 10.

46   "we should have a resumption of the bull market": *WSJ,* 1/22/30.

46   Schumpeter's verdict: Allen, 19n.

47   Depression "self-propagating": *WSJ,* 10/29/32.

47   "trouble with a capital 'T' ": *WSJ,* 11/2/32.

47   "Nobody knows": *WSJ,* 11/5/32.

4. COVERING THE GREAT DEPRESSION

48   *Reading the News About Money*: BK to TK and LK, 9/17/32; BK to TK, 9/6/32.

49   a few sample columns: BK to TK and LK, 9/30/32.

49   Second and third sets of samples: BK to TK and LK, 10/10/32.

49   home for Christmas: BK to TK and LK, 11/9/32, 11/18/32, 12/5/32.

49   Buren McCormack: BK to TK and LK, 1/2/33, 1/30/33.

49   BK sends money to his father: BK to TK, 1/6/33, 7/31/33.

49   "Reading the News" debuts: It actually ran first in the January 16 afternoon edition of the *Journal,* where it appeared on the front page. BK to TK, 1/16/33.

49   The first column: *WSJ,* 1/17/33.

50   "King Cotton": Ibid.

50   Broadcasting work "fun, but putting the material together is the real job": BK to TK, 2/22/33.

50   "something as cheerful as possible": BK to TK, 3/21/33.

51   appearances on the NBC Red Network: TK to BK, 4/1/33; *WSJ,* 12/9/33.

51   "Mother was all thrilled to hear you": TK to BK, 4/1/33.

51   BK's optimism: *WSJ,* 1/27/33, 1/31/33, 2/8/33, 3/1/33.

51   TK's warning: TK to BK, 2/1/33.

51   "It's too much like playing around with nitroglycerine": BK to TK, 2/27/33.

51   Gold standard column: *WSJ*, 1/26/33.

52   Tire prices column: *WSJ*, 2/3/33.

52   Auto sales column: *WSJ*, 2/8/33.

52   Bank holidays column: *WSJ*, 2/15/33.

52   Timber column: *WSJ*, 2/16/33.

52   Leather column: *WSJ*, 3/17/33.

52   "The ones I do not like are the ones that seem to be nothing more than a restate-
      ment of the news item": TK to BK, 2/27/33.

52   Bimetallism: *WSJ*, 1/26/33.

52   Sugar prices: *WSJ*, 1/31/33.

52   Industrial production: *WSJ*, 2/2/33.

52   RFC loans: *WSJ*, 2/10/33.

52   British trade practice: *WSJ*, 2/15/33.

53   Money supply: *WSJ*, 2/24/33.

53   Purchasing power: *WSJ*, 2/28/33.

53   Dairy production: *WSJ*, 3/17/33.

53   Agricultural tariffs: *WSJ*, 3/18/33.

53   London conference: *WSJ*, 6/30/33.

53   Banks couldn't find investments: *WSJ*, 2/7/33.

53   J. C. Penney use for cash: *WSJ*, 2/18/33.

53   GM paying a dividend: *WSJ*, 2/11/33.

54   "the building industry": *WSJ*, 2/21/33.

54   "the little dog has six inches of the big dog's tail in his mouth": TK to BK,
      2/27/33.

54   Possibly buying sterling: BK to TK, 2/27/33.

54   "I would get some of my money . . . for your own safety as well as ours": TK to
      BK, 3/2/33.

54   " 'Credit' is just another word for 'confidence' ": *WSJ*, 3/7/33.

55   "Look at the money supply . . . People can't pay for things at a normal level with
      only one-seventh or less their normal money supply": *WSJ*, 3/9/33.

55   DJ failed to make payroll: BK to TK and LK, 3/14/33.

55   "implicit faith in President Roosevelt": *WSJ*, 3/11/33.

55   First "fireside chat": *WSJ*, 3/14/33.

55   "I think the time . . . You started out this way and I hope you will never get away
      from it": TK to BK, 3/19/33.

56   Calling a turn: He commented on a key earnings report: "United States Steel

Corp. lost money in 1932 for much the same reason that the owner of a steam roller would run in the red if he used his machine only to crack nuts. It is just too big to do small business at a profit." *WSJ*, 3/16/33.

56   "He must think the odds are pretty good, however, or he wouldn't sponsor the bill": *WSJ*, 3/18/33.

56   possible experiments, ways to reflate prices: *WSJ*, 3/21/33; 3/22/33; 4/1/33.

56   "No matter how cold . . . just a form of suicide": *WSJ*, 3/24/33

57   "It is becoming more and more apparent . . . sooner or later another lurid chapter in United States financial history will have to be written": *WSJ*, 3/31/33.

57   History in the making: "Historians and economists": *WSJ*, 6/16/33.

57   Three mentions of Fisher: *WSJ*, 5/30/33; 6/15/33; 7/11/33.

57   Comparing commodity indexes: *WSJ*, 5/30/33.

58   "no book [has] yet been written": *WSJ*, 8/1/35.

58   1935 book review: *WSJ*, 5/16/35.

58   GM shareholders: He was wise enough, however, to note that the number-two company in the auto business, Ford, seemed to have little trouble competing, despite having just three shareholders. *WSJ*, 3/18/33.

58   Comparing shareholder groups: *WSJ*, 3/24/33.

58   "stock market 'gambling' ": BK to TK, 6/17/33.

58   "the country had to go off the gold standard for me to make any money in stocks": BK to TK and LK, 6/26/33. Years later, Kilgore would publicly deny ever having speculated. "I've never been in the market. It's all right for others to put money into stocks, but I've always said, 'I don't touch the stuff myself.' " *Ad Age*, 7/6/64.

58   "Footnotes on the News": *WSJ*, beginning 3/29/33.

59   Column from Cincinnati: *WSJ*, 4/18/33.

59   Column from Chicago: *WSJ*, 4/19/33.

59   a measure of renown: TK to BK, 4/30/33, 8/3/33.

59   End of regular run of "Reading the News": The last regular column ran 4/20/33.

59   New articles: *WSJ*, 4/21/33; 4/25/33; 5/25/33; 6/9/33.

59   "friends of mine rather than friends of Mr. Woodlock": BK to TK and LK, 5/22/33.

59   Woodlock "knows a lot of things": BK to TK, 6/17/33.

60   "The dollar's value now depends on what people think of it": *WSJ*, 4/21/33. By the new noncolumn's second week, Kilgore even resumed adding smaller items at the end of his principal essays. *WSJ*, 4/28/33. Once, he even reappropriated the "Footnotes on the News" subhead. *WSJ*, 5/24/33.

60   The most "spectacular and stirring appeal for peace" in "the world's history": *WSJ*, 5/17/33.

60   Accepting Hitler's response: *WSJ*, 5/18/33.

60   End of "Reading the News": The last column altogether ran 8/4/33.

60   "my inclination at the start was strongly skeptical and now is less so": BK to Hogate, 9/1/33.

61   Albany not "notably enthusiastic": *WSJ*, 9/16/33.

61   exemptions from the NRA's codes: *WSJ*, 9/19/33.

61   "The Blue Eagle graces . . . The local NRA chairman described it as a 'corker' ": *WSJ*, 9/16/33.

61   "One way to get . . . go out and ask a lot of people a lot of questions": *WSJ*, 9/21/33.

62   "Your correspondent is a trifle dizzy": *WSJ*, 9/26/33.

62   Taxi prices: *WSJ*, 9/27/33. Kilgore charted the ways in which new jobs were being created, but also how individuals who had been willing to work hard were having their hours cut to make way for others to work limited shifts, how profits were suffering, how labor-management tensions were being exacerbated, how many smaller firms were being put under terrible pressure. *WSJ*, 9/28/33; 10/4/33; 10/7/33.

62   "the NRA is more a matter of psychology": *WSJ*, 9/29/33; 10/3/33.

63   Johnson speech: *WSJ*, 10/12/33; *NYT*, 10/11/33 for full text.

63   Hogate had written the piece personally: BK to TK, 10/10/33, probably actually written 10/11/33.

63   Editorial: *WSJ*, 10/12/33.

64   "because the belief that white labor is superior to colored labor": *WSJ*, 10/19/33.

64   In New Orleans at the Cotton Exchange: *WSJ*, 10/24/33.

64   a month's pay in advance: BK to TK and LK, 10/8/33.

64   The plan "was scheduled to go too far and too fast . . . it never should have been billed as a depression-ending device": *WSJ*, 11/10/33.

65   "It isn't the habit of the writer . . . the very same difficulties which are becoming increasingly apparent now on a large scale": *WSJ*, 5/30/34.

65   Tempering his optimism: *WSJ*, 11/17/33.

65   Stories from Chicago: *WSJ*, 4/3-5/34.

65   Story from Charlottesville: *WSJ*, 7/4/34, 7/6/34.

65   Raise to $95 per week: BK to TK, 3/15/34.

65   BK spending: TK to BK, 12/9/33; BK to TK, 2/23/34; BK to TK and LK, 4/19/34; 1/26/34.

66   "You . . . will simply have to pin a good deal of faith on the foresight, integrity and ability of the men you have sent to Washington": *WSJ*, 1/13/34.

67   "There is an article": Public Papers of the President, 3/14/34.

67   *Herald Tribune* coverage: *New York Herald Tribune*, 3/15/34.

67   "YOU ARE FAMOUS": Grimes to BK, 3/14/34.

67   "More air and sun, and no subways": BK to TK and LK, 8/30/33.

68   "considered as a group . . . But they have lacked and continue to lack any economic philosophy whatever": *WSJ*, 5/9/34.

68   slowing the breakneck pace of change: *WSJ*, 5/12/34.

68   A man "who can back down more aggressively than anyone else in Washington": *WSJ*, 5/10/34.

68   "The opposition . . . lacks leadership": *WSJ*, 5/11/34.

68   *Journal* editorial: *WSJ*, 5/14/34.

68   BK first meeting with Kerby: BK to TK and LK, 8/30/33; William Kerby, *Proud Profession*, 181.

69   Staying at home of Kerby's parents: BK to TK, 5/3/34.

69   Kerby background: Kerby, 9–11, 15–16, 19, 59.

69   Kerbys' maid: BK to TK, 5/3/34.

69   Kerby's father: Kerby, 10–11, 20.

69   Grimes a "friend and golfing partner" of the senior Kerby: Kerby, 33.

69   "You have a job here next summer, but it would be nice if you would just learn to spell": Kerby, 35.

69   Kerby's father pays his salary: Kerby, 36.

70   Kerby interview with Hogate: Kerby, 67.

70   such stories would often be about the weather: Kerby, 21.

5. "WHAT'S NEWS"

71   Total U.S. newspaper circulation: Frank Mott, *American Journalism*, 637, 675.

72   New DJ offices: *WSJ*, 6/27/32.

72   1931 DJ profits: Lloyd Wendt, *Wall Street Journal*, 215.

72   *Fortune* estimates: "The Times and The Times and Their Times," *Fortune*, May 1930, 58.

72   Fiftieth anniversary issue: *WSJ*, 6/27/32.

72   "all he had were a couple of suggestions and said the stuff was interesting." BK to TK, 1/16/33.

73   Suicide of Hugh Bancroft: Jon Meacham, *The Beginning of the Journey,* 58–59.

73   "Don't you and the boys worry about dividends": Meacham, 61–62.

73   Scharff in 1986: Edward Scharff, *Worldly Power,* 14.

74   "maintain . . . their horses and their yachts and so forth": Ann Hogate Hamlet interview, Bridge, 16.

74   "everything would go along just about as in the past": BK to TK and LK, 11/17/33; Hogate remarks, 11/13/33.

75   Kissane nicknamed "Stupid": Scharff, 45.

75   the morning paper was outselling [the afternoon] by a ratio of nine to one: *Time,* 9/17/34.

75   It was apparently Hogate's idea: Wendt, 245–47; Scharff, 53.

75   Other news summaries: Herbert Brucker, *The Changing American Newspaper,* 2, 22, 104.

77   "McCormack is supposed to be learning to write it": BK to LK, 9/14/34. A 1955 memo indicates that Kilgore apparently told his secretary at that time that he wrote the column for "several weeks," but the contemporary account clearly trumps this.

77   BK kept his hand in the column: BK to TK, 8/8/35.

77   Grimes extends the deadlines: BK to LK, 9/14/34.

78   Opening up headline styles: William Kerby, *Proud Profession,* 91–92.

78   Grimes . . . conclusively separated the news and advertising functions: Scharff at 47. One of the people thus forced out of the paper as a result of separation of news and advertising was Charlie Robbins, Kilgore's one-time DePauw roommate. Robbins to Bridge, 8/16/78.

78   "There must be some flaw in his character which I didn't detect all these years." Kerby, 77.

79   Boyle "drank about a quart of whiskey every day for several decades": BK to TK and LK, 12/30/36.

79   the bureau had grown to thirteen: Wendt, 190, 249.

79   Meyer . . . attempted to recruit Grimes: Kerby, 75, 78.

79   He threw clubs in golf, and cards in bridge: Kerby, 76.

79   he . . . yanked the pay phone at the National Press Club out of the wall: Scharff, 45.

79   "Purple-faced . . . tell them to bill me personally": Kerby, 76.

79   "a shy man who spoke so softly he could barely be heard across the width of a desk": *WSJ,* 1/17/72.

80   Walker on weeklies: Stanley Walker, *City Editor,* 33, 35.

80   Kerby on *Fortune*: Kerby, 40.

81   "It is extremely difficult even when one is vacationing in a spot far removed from both Wall Street and Washington": *WSJ*, 8/2/34.

81   "governments almost invariably fix prices at uneconomic levels": *WSJ*, 8/24/34.

81   "even more patently a ring-around-the-rosey game": *WSJ*, 9/6/34.

82   "Business men . . . less and less certain why they don't like it": *WSJ*, 9/28/34.

82   Gains at Cleveland surrendered: *WSJ*, 10/3/34.

82   "If the Administration really wants to plan a recovery all it has to do is to quit planning": *WSJ*, 10/4/34.

82   FDR was more popular in Iowa: *WSJ*, 10/9/34.

82   "You'd be surprised": *WSJ*, 10/15/34.

82   "a sort of 'class' feeling": *WSJ*, 10/22/34.

83   He was also more confident of his own range: *WSJ*, 11/8/34.

83   Reprint offers: *WSJ*, 11/27/34, 11/28/34, 12/3/34.

83   "next to nothing": *WSJ*, 12/29/34.

83   "the foundation has been laid for a boom, not lasting prosperity": *WSJ*, 1/2/35.

83   "boomlets": *WSJ*, 3/16/35; 9/17/35.

83   Limits of confiscatory taxation: *WSJ*, 12/12/34.

84   "he only runs through red signal lights when his brother-in-law asks him to": *WSJ*, 5/10/35.

6. WASHINGTON

85   "a lost man in Washington": William Kerby, *A Proud Profession,* 80.

85   Kerby . . . was refused a raise and left: Kerby's last byline before leaving was 10/22/34.

85   Casey had in mind matching BK up romantically with young Jane: Ann Hogate Hamlet interview, Bridge, 6/17/78 at 32.

86   BK "Hot Oil" column: *WSJ*, 1/9/35.

86   "It was a good job": *WSJ*, 1/10/35.

86   BK gets a raise: BK to TK and LK, 1/28/35, actually 1/29/35 based on "Tuesday" dating.

86   TK delighted but wary: TK to BK, 1/13/35.

86   BK was quick to defend himself: BK to TK, 1/15/35.

87   WSJ memo on FDR interview: Lloyd Wendt, *The Wall Street Journal,* 229; see *WSJ*, 1/25/35.

87   "I intend to try to see him again": BK to TK and LK, 1/"28"/35.

87   First column from Washington: *WSJ,* 3/20/35.

88   Second column: *WSJ,* 3/21/35.

89   Third column: *WSJ,* 3/22/35.

90   "no way of telling the proportions of 'recovery' and 'reform' in its basic formula": *WSJ,* 3/27/35.

90   Freelancing: BK to LK, 9/16/35.

90   "Watch that boy. He isn't through yet": *South Bend Tribune,* 12/6/35.

90   BK encouraged them to call him collect: BK to TK, 2/23/35.

90   Money home in 1935: BK to TK, 8/8/35; 9/11/35; 10/1/35; BK to TK and LK, 8/23/35.

90   "I had three dollars in my pocket and $1.20 in the bank when it came": TK to BK, 10/4/35.

90   Column on thirty-hour week: *WSJ,* 4/23/35.

91   "He can't get away": *WSJ,* 5/22/35.

91   Roosevelt . . . remained strong in Texas: *WSJ,* 5/25/35; 5/27/35; 5/28/35.

91   "Simeon S. Snuffkins": *WSJ,* 3/28/35; 4/19/35.

91   Financial Bookshelf column: "Financial Bookshelf" ran on page 3 of the paper. It was a book review compendium, and each column briefly reviewed from one to three books, often adding short summaries ("Notes on New Publications") on a few others, and merely noting the publication ("Books Received") of yet more. Most of the books reviewed were narrowly financial, and many were published by one or the other of the newly emerging think tanks. Some were as narrow as *Silver and Prices in China,* described by Kilgore as "a report of the Committee for the Study of Silver Values and Commodity Prices appointed by the Chinese Minister of Industries" in February 1934, and *Livestock Under the AAA,* "the fourth of a series of books published by the Brookings Institution as the result of its study of the Agricultural Adjustment Act." *WSJ,* 9/6/35, 9/26/35. But titles by now-former NRA administrator Hugh Johnson, and economists Stuart Chase and future senator Paul Douglas were also included. *WSJ,* 3/28/35, 4/11/35, 9/19/35. Kilgore reviewed a couple of books on relations with Japan, and one on Nazi Germany, which he described as "the story of a diseased economy and a nation gone mad." *WSJ,* 4/25/35.

91   Review of *Handout: WSJ,* 5/9/35.

92   BK fill-in for McCormack in writing "What's News": BK to TK, 8/8/35.

92   "They are nice people in spite of the fact that they are rich": BK to LK, 9/16/35.

92   BK named bureau manager: Ibid.; BK to TK, 9/23/35, 10/1/35. Many years later,

Phelps, having become a stockbroker, would be a neighbor of Kilgore's, and something of a friend. BK to TK, 10/18/46.

93   BK turned down Hearst offer: TK to BK, 6/15/36.

93   Hearst's holdings: "Hearst," *Fortune,* 5/35, at 43, 46, 48, 50.

93   nearly a hundred Hearst employees earned $25,000 or more: Ibid., at 44.

93   "Hogate might be thinking of making an executive out of you instead of a writer": TK to BK, 11/29/35; see BK to TK and LK, 2/7/36, on pay level.

93   "I don't think I would want to remain in New York forever either": BK to LK, 9/16/35.

93   BK on Social Security: *WSJ,* 10/22/35.

93   BK on "permanent" unemployment: *WSJ,* 11/8/35.

94   "Unemployment is the depression": *WSJ,* 1/2/36. See also 7/14/39.

94   "$100 is still a whole lot of money": *WSJ,* 12/27/35.

94   "Probably they wouldn't be Townsendites if they did": *WSJ,* 1/3/36.

94   BK incorrectly predicted that the Supreme Court would overturn the Wagner Act: *WSJ,* 12/31/35.

94   BK consistently overestimated Alf Landon's strength in 1936: *WSJ,* 8/7/36, 8/27/36, 8/29/36, 9/28/36, 10/17/36, 10/19/36.

94   BK Ohio prediction: BK to TK, 10/27/36.

94   BK insufficiently skeptical of Roosevelt's repeated hints: *WSJ,* 1/2/40, 3/13/40.

95   close to the mark in forecasting large Republican gains in 1938: *WSJ,* 11/3/38.

95   BK on Willkie: *WSJ,* 4/30/40, 5/17/40, 5/25/40, 6/20/40.

95   BK on FDR enlarging Court membership: *WSJ,* 7/1/36.

95   Sliced bread article: *Today,* 9/5/36, 15, 26.

95   "on the record at least no one wants to head the ticket": *WSJ,* 7/16/40.

95   Timmons "campaign": *WSJ,* 7/16/40; *Saturday Evening Post,* 11/2/46, 33.

96   BK ignores Perkins tip on Wallace: *New York Herald Tribune,* 9/28/51.

96   "There was one man for me, and one man [FDR] for you": *Saturday Evening Post,* 11/2/46, 32.

96   BK disappointment about Gridiron: BK to TK and LK, 12/17/37.

96   BK delight at Gridiron membership: BK to TK, 4/11/38.

96   Gridiron skit: *NYT,* 12/18/38.

96   Practice for Gridiron dinners: BK to TK and LK, 4/4/39, 12/1/39.

96   BK takes Hogate and Grimes to Gridiron: BK to TK, 12/13/39.

96   BK takes TK to Gridiron: BK to TK, 5/6/49.

96   BK raises, 1935–36: TK to BK, 11/29/35; BK to TK and LK, 2/7/36.

96 BK raises, 1936–37: BK to TK and LK, 11/22/36; BK to TK, 2/4/37.

96 Arrangement with Hogate on freelance fees: BK to TK and LK, 4/8/36, 12/30/36.

97 BK spending: BK to TK, 3/27/36; BK to TK and LK, 4/15 or 4/22/36, 11/22/36.

97 "perhaps someday I will want to live off of it": BK to TK, 2/19/36.

97 "compound interest peanuts": BK to TK and LK, 11/9/36.

97 BK sends money home: BK to TK, 3/27/36, 5/7/36, 10/5/36, 10/30/36; BK to TK and LK, 4/14/36, 11/12/36.

97 "I won't really have to do without anything": BK to TK and LK, 11/12/36.

97 His parents BK's dependents in 1937: BK to TK, 2/13/38; TK to BK, 2/17/38.

97 TK's earnings recover in 1938: BK to TK, 1/10/39; TK to BK, 1/18/39.

97 Skippy and Rosamond: BK to TK and LK, 4/14/36, 4/15 or 4/22/36, 6/25/36, 6/27/36, 9/9/36, 11/9/36, 11/6/37, 11/13/37, 12/5/37.

97 Birthday greetings from Margaret and Vera: BK to TK and LK, 11/9/36.

97 relationship with Rosamond: See, e.g., BK to TK and LK, 11/9/36, 11/13/37.

97 Rosamond moves to Maine: BK to TK and LK, 1/10/38.

98 "this DePauw girl from Greencastle": BK to TK, 8/31/38.

98 BK seriously involved: TK to BK, 9/23/38.

98 "she thought she ought to have another week at home to finish up her job and arrange things": BK to TK and LK, 9/23/38.

98 BK had met her parents briefly: James Throop to TK, 10/4/38.

98 She had never met his parents: BK to TK and LK, 9/23/38.

98 Even after they had been married more than three years, he was unsure of her birthdate: BK to TK, 2/16/42.

98 They had met on a visit by Kilgore back to DePauw: MLTK (Beilman) interview with Bridge, 10/18/79 at 1-2; *South Bend Tribune,* 12/6/53.

98 "She is smart and she can cook": BK to TK and LK, 9/23/38.

98 BK called her Lulu: BK to TK and LK, 6/14/39.

98 BK-MLTK wedding: BK to TK, 9/29/38; TK to BK, 9/29/38.

98 Honeymoon: BK to TK, 10/8/38.

99 BK and Gallup: See, e.g., *WSJ,* 6/25/36.

99 twenty-five-part series: *WSJ,* 7/25/36–8/29/36.

99 "more interested in whether he will have a job next Winter than he is in whether Mr. Roosevelt will have one": *WSJ,* 7/25/36.

99 "On even closer examination, it turns out that the two banks have also stopped": *WSJ,* 7/27/36.

99   "Interviewing farmers . . . is an interesting business": *WSJ*, 8/13/36.

99   BK as a marketable commodity: E.g. *WSJ*, 4/16/37, 6/29/37, 4/13/38, 6/3/38.

99   Full-page ad: *WSJ*, 4/6/38.

100   "they sold a good many subscriptions with the Washington series as bait": BK to TK and LK, 4/18/38.

100   "Business recovery" series: *WSJ*, 5/29/39, 5/31/39.

100   "Is the tide changing in Washington today?": *WSJ*, 4/11/38.

100   FDR's weakness: *WSJ*, 4/14/38.

100   BK sees potential in defense spending: *WSJ*, 11/17/38.

100   "Dixie Highway" diary: *WSJ*, 7/9/38.

101   BK survey method: *WSJ*, 10/26/38.

101   "the Buttonhole Institute of Public Opinion": *WSJ*, 10/27/38.

101   "50,000 straws . . . are not to be sneezed at": *WSJ*, 10/29/38.

102   "aimed at the general public over the heads . . . of the Republican organization leaders": *WSJ*, 5/29/40.

102   Influence of Gallup: *WSJ*, 6/13/40.

102   BK 1938 interview with FDR: BK to TK and LK, 1/10/38.

102   FDR press conference: Roosevelt Presidential Press Conferences, Number 520, 1/24/39, in FDR Library.

103   A "stern[] rebuke": *WSJ*, 1/25/39.

103   "Washington Nightmare": *WSJ*, 1/28/39.

104   "a scatterbrained approach to the recovery effort": *WSJ*, 6/6/39.

104   "The federal budget is simply out of control": *WSJ*, 6/9/39.

104   Offer from McGraw-Hill: BK to TK, 10/19/39.

104   "taking over [McGraw-Hill's] Washington work": BK to TK, 11/10/39.

104   BK gets another raise: BK to TK, 11/3/39.

104   Gallup accompanied him to a Gridiron dinner: BK to TK, 12/13/39.

105   Sunday lunch with Mrs. Roosevelt: BK to TK, 3/9/40.

105   Justice Douglas comes for dinner: BK to LK, 2/29/40.

105   Taft "seemed to have a good time": BK to TK, 8/30/40.

105   Plan with Hogate, Labor Day 1939: BK to TK and LK, 8/10/39.

105   twenty-five . . . for breakfast the morning after the 1940 White House Correspondents Association dinner: MLTK to TK and LK, 3/18/40.

105   BK radio appearances: MLTK to "Family," 12/27/39.

105   Placed Willkie's chances at "better than 50–50 to win": *WSJ*, 11/1/40.

105   "I was fooled by the noise": *WSJ*, 11/7/40.

106   BK on Grimes: BK to TK, 2/23/40.

107   Kerby "suffered a convenient loss of memory": Kerby, 97–98.

107   Third installment of "Washington Wire": *WSJ*, 10/4/40; emphasis added.

107   "We have a lot more readers outside New York than inside": BK to TK, 1/11/41.

7. MANAGING EDITOR

108   Turning down the army: BK to LK, 1/10/41; BK to TK, 1/11/41.

108   never seems to have considered enlisting: See BK to TK, 5/16/42.

109   Hosting Hogate for Friday night dinner: BK to TK and LK, 1/6/41.

109   More columns like "Washington Wire": See BK to TK, 1/11/41.

109   "they are going to try to do more summarizing": BK to TK, 1/24/41.

109   "Mary Lou and I talked it over": BK to TK and LK, 2/7/41.

110   Would have stayed with Grimes if alone: BK to TK and LK, 1/30/41.

110   "I've done about all I can do here now": BK to TK and LK, 2/7/41.

110   "much room for future development": Ibid.

111   1944 story: *WSJ*, 10/19/44.

111   On unreliability of Kerby memoirs, *A Proud Profession,* cf. *WSJ*, 3/14/38, on Austrian crisis with Kerby, 90; *WSJ*, 10/28/38, on development of nylon with Kerby, 110–11. With respect to this time period, for instance, Kerby says that he learned of Kilgore's appointment months in advance, which would have been months ahead of Kilgore, and is thus inconceivable, Kerby, 98. He recalls stories he wrote as being published under Grimes, when they came only after Kilgore's appointment. Cf. *WSJ*, 3/4/41 and 3/28/41, with Kerby, 98.

111   Key personnel changes: Lloyd Wendt, *The Wall Street Journal*, 273; Richard Kluger, *The Paper,* 567; Kerby, 98–99, 101.

111   The "usual hearty cooperation": Hogate to the Staff, 2/14/41.

111   Living off a "due bill": BK to TK and LK, 2/23/41.

112   Move to Brooklyn Heights: BK to TK, 5/8/41, 8/21/41.

112   Snowden: BK to TK, 4/1/42.

112   BK's free hand: See BK to TK and LK, 3/14/41.

112   "Progress of the Week" began 7/29/35, moved to the top of "What's News" on 10/7/35, and took on "Review & Outlook" as a prefix to its name in 1944, see *WSJ*, 1/8/44. The column became a product of the *Journal*'s news rather than editorial staff in 1953 and its name was shortened to "The Outlook." *WSJ*, 7/13/53. The

column was moved to page two from page one when the *Journal* was redesigned in 2002.

112 "What's News" format: *WSJ*, 3/26/41; 4/3/41; 12/12/41 (two columns), 12/15/41 (first use of format in place until 2002).

113 "interesting to a wide assortment of people": BK to TK, 4/3/41.

113 "Commodity Letter": See *WSJ*, 2/8/65, 1/3/66 (last column).

113 First "Tax Report": *WSJ*, 4/2/41.

113 First "Business Bulletin": *WSJ*, 4/10/41.

113 "Business Bulletin" discontinued: *WSJ*, 12/28/2000.

113 Death of LK: TK inscription on BK to TK and LK, 3/14/41.

114 "I want you to be proud of me": BK to TK, 3/22/41.

114 Special "defense edition": BK to TK, 5/23/41.

114 "flashlines": *WSJ*, 7/11/39.

114 "business news embraces everything that relates to making a living": *WSJ*, 7/8/64.

114 "financial people are nice people and all that": *Time*, 6/4/47. This quote would eventually become the lead of Kilgore's *New York Times* obituary. *NYT*, 11/15/67.

115 "from Portland, Maine to Portland, Oregon": *NO*, 2/6/62.

115 Rejecting Scripps-Howard offer: Kerby, 103.

115 "The easiest thing in the world": Ibid., 102.

115 Anecdotal leads and "nut grafs": See, e.g., Scanlan, Christopher, *Reporting and Writing Basics for the 21st Century*, 16; Henry Fairlie, "Press," *Encounter* (June 1966), 79. Herbert Brucker, *Changing American Newspaper*, 75–77, written in 1937, decries the inverted pyramid but cites no examples of newspapers moving away from it. Brucker seems to have been quite current on developments at metropolitan papers, although completely ignorant of those at the *Journal*, which is never mentioned in his book.

116 McCormack rooming with BK: BK to TK and LK, 1/30/33.

116 New Year's 1934–35: BK to TK and LK, 12/30/33, 1/5/35.

116 BK stays with the McCormacks: BK to TK and LK, 9/4/37, 12/14/39.

116 Kerby and McCormack wrote nearly every leder: See Kerby, 101.

116 "Some days I think it is pretty interesting as a paper": BK to TK, 10/30/41.

117 Wire service bulletin: BK to TK, 12/8/41.

117 Planned series on tax rates: Bridge, chap. 12, p. 13.

117 Kerby stories on defense build-up: *WSJ*, 3/28/41, 4/4/41.

117 "defense issue": *WSJ*, 5/16/41.

117 Covering Pearl Harbor: See Kerby, 100.

118 Kerby on Pearl Harbor as "turning point": DJ newsletter "What's News," 2/78.

118 Kerby's last bylines: The advertising stories were published 8/13/42, 8/22/42, 8/26/42. Cf. Kerby, 99.

118 First "Pepper and Salt": *WSJ*, 11/15/41.

119 BK seat-testing story: *WSJ*, 10/24/36.

120 BK Pennsylvania Turnpike story: *WSJ*, 10/14/40.

120 First "A-hed": *WSJ*, 12/17/41.

120 First "London Cable": *WSJ*, 1/10/42.

120 "over a hundred a day": BK to TK, 12/17/41.

120 continued to rise: BK to TK, 2/3/42, 2/22/42.

120 1941 year-end paper: BK to TK, 1/5/42.

120 Survey of readers in Ohio: *Sales Management*, 12/1/42.

121 BK considers offer from *Time*: BK to TK, 1/15/42, 2/3/42, 2/27/42, 3/11/42.

121 "a good deal of deadwood": BK to TK, 2/27/42.

121 KCH in decline for a year: BK to TK, 4/3/41, 5/8/41.

121 Initial reports on KCH stroke: BK to TK, 3/11/42.

121 "the best man around here": Ibid.

121 "some cutting down and some tough management": Ibid.

122 "I really think I'm happier on a daily paper": Ibid.

122 "that clears up all the hocus-pocus": BK to TK, 3/30/42.

122 "laid on the shelf": TK to BK, 4/1/42.

122 "right much worried": BK to TK, 4/3/42.

122 "I went over all the books myself this afternoon": Ibid.

123 "he is still pretty sick": BK to TK, 4/27/42.

123 Expected back in October: BK to TK, 9/17/42.

123 "I hope he will get back fulltime one of these days soon": BK to TK, 11/12/42.

123 Scharff on Ackell: *Worldly Power*, 75.

124 "watch out for my health": BK to TK, 11/17/42.

124 "he'll get sick again I am sure": BK to TK, 12/8/42.

124 Kerby on the evening in Brooklyn Heights: Kerby at 108–9.

125 Kilgores' weekending with the Grimeses: BK to TK, 4/9/41, 5/9/41, 5/16/41, 5/23/41, 7/19/41, 7/25/41, 9/2/41, 9/16/41, 12/15/41, 2/22/42.

125 BK matter-of-factly: BK to TK, 12/31/42.

126   "a fine big office": BK to TK, 1/9/43.

126   Hogate had . . . "something of a set-back": Ibid.

126   BK visit to Hogate farm for wedding: BK to TK, 6/7/43.

126   1944 farm visit: BK to TK, 9/27/44.

126   "he still has trouble in talking however and he gets tired out quickly": BK to TK, 10/4/44.

127   "damage to his nervous system": BK to TK, 5/2/44.

127   "avoided even worrying about it": BK to TK, 5/1/45.

127   Problems with paper supply: BK to TK, 1/9/43.

127   Declines in average issue size: Edward Scharff, *Worldly Power,* 81.

127   Kerby's news formula: William Kerby, *A Proud Profession,* 107.

127   "much better edited, more concise, meatier": Ibid.

128   Tax considerations: See Scharff, 81

128   "There'll be lots of time later to get advertising": Scharff, 82.

128   BK worries about the draft: BK to TK, 5/6/42, 4/27/43, 5/3/43.

128   "it was all done without any fussing or appealing or anything like that": BK to TK, 5/6/43.

129   "that's pretty much that": BK to TK, 6/24/43.

129   Later blood test and X-ray: BK to TK, 10/26/43, 12/8/43.

129   Kerby's relief: Kerby, 119.

129   The "beauty chorus": Kerby, 108.

129   BK on women in newsrooms: Scharff, 84–85.

129   BK considers closing PCE: BK to TK, 2/10/43.

130   "some of the same mistakes": Lloyd Wendt, *Wall Street Journal,* 291.

130   BK visit to San Francisco: BK to TK, 11/26/44.

130   Findings generally encouraging: Wendt, 291.

130   "we are not in a position to go after new circulation": BK to TK, 1/26/44.

130   BK delight at door-to-door sales: BK to TK, 9/12/44.

131   "there isn't much to it": BK to TK, 6/9/43.

131   "mostly luck, but still good to look at": BK to TK, 7/23/43.

131   Move to Princeton: BK to TK, 3/23/43.

131   First three-week vacation: BK to TK, 6/5/42.

131   1943 on the farm: BK to TK, 3/31/43, 6/28/43, 7/7/43, 7/13/43, 7/30/43, 8/5/43, 9/7/43.

131 Kilgores host the Grimeses: BK to TK, 2/10/43, 3/23/43, 7/23/43, 8/20/43, 8/27/43, 12/30/43.

131 BK writes editorials: BK to TK, 6/9/43, 6/24/43.

132 Time off to plant trees: BK to TK, 4/12/45, 4/25/45.

132 Kilgores join a church: BK to TK, 12/8/43.

132 BK as homesteader: BK to TK, 1/17/44.

132 "Thought you would be interested": BK to TK, 2/5/45.

132 Names for a boy or a girl: BK to TK, 5/16/45.

132 BK and baby Kathryn: BK to TK, 6/4/45.

132 "she doesn't get much chance to talk things over with anybody": BK to TK, 1/31/45.

132 Quarterly conferences with Jane Bancroft: BK to TK, 11/19/43, 6/13/44, 9/12/44, 1/31/45.

132 Annual meetings in Boston: BK to TK, 5/15/45.

132 Overnight in Cohasset: BK to TK, 9/18/44.

133 Only making it "official": BK Memo to Executive and Administrative Personnel, 4/1/3/45.

133 *Editor & Publisher* articles: "Wall Street Journal Has Post-War Ideas"; "Dow, Jones Co. Promotes 3 Executives," *E&P,* 5/12/45.

133 KCH management style: Kerby, 123.

133 "I deliberately try not to take on anything that someone else can do": BK to TK, 2/10/43.

133 "most of my working day is spent in somebody's else's office": BK to TK, 9/25/49.

133 Royster on BK management style: Vermont Royster, "Life With Barney at *The Wall Street Journal,*" *WSJ,* 3/16/87.

134 "This is being done": BK to TK, 10/2/45.

134 BK misses writing: BK to TK, 10/2/45.

134 Out of respect for Hogate: BK to TK, 11/23/45.

135 "Business is booming": BK to TK, 3/14/46.

135 "the most readable front page of all U.S. newspapers": *Kiplinger,* Feb. 1948, 28.

135 Subscription promotions: One of the men to whom Feemster assigned the promotional work was former Kilgore roommate and *Journal* reporter Charlie Robbins, now at Bozell & Jacobs. Robbins to Bridge, 8/16/78. On mailings, see *E&P,* 8/3/46. A mailing of the same scale to today's population would entail ten million pieces per year.

135 half a million someday: Scharff, 90.

135   Ending front-page advertising. The last day of front-page advertising was Mar. 29, 1946. Feemster considered this a sign of strength to the marketplace, and an important expression of confidence in the newspaper's commercial future. Front-page advertising would not return until 2006, and would then, while lucrative, be widely viewed as one among many confessions of industry weakness.

135   Spring 1946 ad rate increase: *E&P,* 8/3/46.

136   Lombard's recommended changes: Wendt, 297–98.

136   Selling Hogate on the plan: *Time,* 2/7/44; BK to TK, 11/4/46, Wendt, 298.

136   BK learned of the proposals: BK met with Hogate and Mrs. Bancroft jointly at Hogate's home in Scarsdale in December 1945, and with Hogate alone in April and again in August 1946. BK to TK, 12/28/45, 4/23/46, 8/4/46, 8/9/46.

136   "His chief handicap is difficulty in speaking": BK to TK, 8/9/46.

137   Lombard recommends excluding BK: Wendt, 298.

137   first meeting of new trustees: BK to TK, 11/4/46.

137   "most newsmen burn out young": *Time,* 2/7/44.

137   "he is a fine fellow": BK to TK, 11/4/46. On persistent misspelling, see also BK to TK, 5/12/47.

137   Boeschenstein came "for a visit": BK to TK, 11/29/46.

137   Circulation over 100,000: *Newsweek,* 2/24/47.

137   KCH obituary: *WSJ,* 2/12/47 One idea that seems to have died with Hogate was consideration of changing the name of the *Journal.* At almost the very moment Hogate was suffering his final attack, Kilgore was sending him a memo elaborating on a marketing study by a polling firm in Princeton. The firm, Kilgore noted, had concluded that the newspaper's name "is a handicap to our growth." Both "Wall Street" (with its narrowly financial and Eastern connotations) and "Journal" (evocative of magazines) were said to be problematic. Kilgore offered "World's Work" or "North American Journal" or "Business Day" as possibilities; he said Grimes had suggested "The National Journal." (Wendt at 301). But the memo has likely been misread over the years. It is phrased as offering Kilgore's own suggestions, but was clearly intended as a follow-up to an earlier discussion, perhaps during Kilgore's last meeting with Hogate, in early December 1946, just before he left New York for California. See BK to TK, 11/29/46. During that discussion, Hogate had proffered the name "Financial America" (Wendt at 301). Kilgore's memo is better understood as a gentle rebuttal to this suggestion. Perhaps this entire idea of a name change had been, in some way, another product of Hogate's illness. In any event, two things happened just after the memo was written: Hogate died, and the name change idea was quietly dropped. Had the idea been Kilgore's, it seems

only logical that the discussion of changing the newspaper's name would have intensified.

138   Pulitzer Prize to Grimes: The award was given for Grimes's body of work for the year, but observers took special notice of one editorial, published Mar. 7, 1946, which, *The New York Times* reported had "received wide attention" (*NYT,* 5/6/47). Writing just two days after Winston Churchill's "Iron Curtain" speech in Fulton, Missouri, Grimes took America to task for "losing its faith." American weakness was emboldening Stalin. The "criminal decision at Yalta," he warned, meant that "we have abandoned the tradition that peoples have the right to work out their own destiny." Headlined "Apathetic and Pathetic," the editorial had concluded, "We are apathetic. We are rapidly growing pathetic." It was tough stuff, but not nearly so pointed as another Grimes gem from 1946, headed "Justice," which read, in its totality: "Henry Wallace has become editor of *The New Republic*. We suggest it serves them both right." (10/15/46)

138   Redesign while Grimes on holiday: Wendt, 317.

138   BK 1944 campaign story: *WSJ,* 10/19/44.

138   BK belief that Dewey would win in 1944: BK to TK, 10/9/44, 10/18/44, 10/31/44, 11/6/44.

138   BK 1946 editorial analysis: *WSJ,* 10/17/46.

138   "I wish I had more time to write politics but there are too many other things to do": TK to BK, 10/20/46; BK to TK, 10/16/46, 10/24/46.

138   Closing the *Boston News Bureau:* Wendt, 299. In its last issue, the sixty-year-old Boston paper, two years older than the *Journal,* and C. W. Barron's own creation, closed its note to subscribers this way: "So the old man retires in favor of the lusty son. We believe that you will like the boy. We want you to. But if sometimes you have a moment to indulge a pleasant memory of the oldster, we will not be sorry." *Boston News Bureau,* 4/5/47.

138   Lombard recommends Southwest edition: Kerby at 131.

138   BK sends Ackell to scout locations: Wendt, 302.

139   *Journal* announcement: *WSJ,* 10/6/47.

139   Southwest edition debuts: Wendt, 302–03.

139   Southwest edition matches PCE: BK to TK, 4/16/48.

139   "about as nice a newspaper plant as I have ever set eye on": BK to TK, 6/9/48.

139   "to tend to the social side of it": BK to TK, 4/16/48.

139   BK and baby James: BK to TK, 5/13/48.

139   working less hard: During the summer of 1947, he, Mary Lou and Kathryn spent nearly two months, from June 21 until August 11, in Bermuda. BK to TK,

6/11/47, 7/28/47. In February of 1948, the elder Kilgores (without child) vacationed for eleven days near the Grimeses in Delray Beach, Florida; in 1949, they extended this Florida trip to three weeks. BK to TK, 2/3/48, 2/1/49, 2/10/49.

140   1946 bonus: BK to TK, 12/9/46.

140   1947 shareholdings: BK to TK, 12/8/47.

140   1948 incentive contract: BK to TK, 1/29/48.

140   Payment to KCH widow: BK to TK, 12/8/47.

141   Truman remarks: Public Papers of the President, 9/29/48, 10:45 A.M.

142   Ackell named business manager: Wendt, 307.

142   Feemster background: See Scharff, 92, 95.

142   Feemster leaving the wrong impression: Scharff, 93.

142   Feemster interview with *E&P*: *E&P,* 7/10/48.

143   Feemster's early rise: Scharff, 96–97; Callis interview, Bridge, 1/27/78 at 15.

143   Feemster roomed with BK: BK to TK and LK, 11/17/33.

143   the couples often socialized: They weekended together at Atlantic City and Plum Point, Maryland; the Kilgores sometimes stayed with the Feemsters in New York during Barney's later years as head of the Washington bureau, the couples later traded visits to their respective homes in Princeton and Westchester County, the wives traveled together back home to Indiana; the foursome spent Christmas together in 1943, and planned to do so again in 1944. BK to TK, 11/28/38, 6/28/39, 8/30/40, 6/26/41, 1/9/43, 6/9/43, 12/21/43, 2/25/44, 12/13/44, 12/28/44.

143   Scharff on Feemster: Scharff, 105; brackets in original.

144   "the only national business daily": Scharff, 98.

144   "over the hump": BK to TK, 9/29/49.

144   "probably do the whole organization some good": BK to TK, 10/18/49.

144   In Boston for Mrs. Bancroft: Wendt, 314.

144   Lombard statement: Statement to Employees of Dow Jones Businesses, 12/28/49.

145   "She was a very great lady": DJ Board resolution, 1/26/50.

145   Pew approach to Kerby: Kerby, 148.

145   "Grandfather's company is not for sale to anybody—at any time, at any price": Scharff, 90.

145   "Mother was so fond of you, Barney": Jane B. Steele to BK, 1/19/50.

145   "It really seems absurd that I should be paid anything": Jane Steele to BK, 5/16/51.

145   "intangibles": BK to Jane Steele, 5/23/51.

145   Steele letter: Edwin Steele to BK, 9/20/51.

146   BK response: BK to Edwin Steele, 9/25/51.

9. THE BOOM BEGINS

147   *Journal of Commerce* history: Peter Leach, "Turning Back the Years."

148   Lacking committed owners: Raphael Govin, according to the paper's official his-
        tory, fronted as owner of the *Journal of Commerce* in the mid-1920s for Charles
        Stoneham, who was better known for his interests in racehorses and the New
        York Giants baseball club. Govin had managed the trick, rare in the twenties in
        New York, of shrinking his newspaper's profits, in part perhaps by insisting that it
        include more sports coverage. Leach.

148   Offices remained on Park Row: *Time,* 9/27/48.

148   Situation at 1927 purchase: *NYT,* 1/1/27.

148   Value of AP franchise: *Time,* 1/10/27.

148   Willis clash with Ridders: Leach; *Time,* 5/25/31.

149   Windfall from reprints: Leach.

149   Founding of *Chicago Journal of Commerce*: *NYT,* 11/18/47.

149   Near purchase by Hogate: BK to TK, 12/17/41.

149   Ridder purchase in Chicago: *Time,* 11/24/47.

149   Finally vacating Park Row: *NYT,* 11/23/47.

149   First reactions to Ridder offer: William Kerby, *Proud Profession,* 137.

149   Conversation at Gridiron: Ridder, *Journal of Commerce,* 11/17/67.

149   BK approach to *Chicago Daily News*: Lloyd Wendt, *Wall Street Journal,* 319.

150   BK alerts his father: BK to TK, 10/2/50.

150   "We wouldn't sell it today for twice what we paid for it": *Time,* 8/25/52.

150   News of the negotiations: See *NYT,* 11/3/50.

150   "as quickly as we can get it organized": BK to TK, 11/16/50.

150   The Ridder family used the proceeds: *Time,* 8/4/52.

150   *Journal of Commerce* drops coverage overlaps: Leach.

150   "one of the most readable of U.S. newspapers": *Time,* 1/08/51.

150   "the only company check he signed in his entire career": Kerby, 139.

151   BK's potential successor: *WSJ,* 3/16/87.

151   "the only word of commendation I ever heard": Bridge, chap. 13 at 3.

151   "Use the enclosed only if you can't manage any other way": Kerby, 159.

151 " 'I'm on my way to ruin Dow Jones and put all these people out of work' ": Kerby, 139.

152 Kilgore joined them for two weeks: BK to TK, 1/31/51, 2/14/51.

152 "having themselves a ball": Wendt, 330.

152 "I will never forget those four guys sitting down on the rim of the desk": McWethy interview, Bridge, January 1978, 4.

153 BK had rejected a first draft: Kerby to Bridge, 3/21/79 at 6.

153 chunks . . . reprinted more than half a century later: *WSJ*, 6/6/07.

155 "Mary Ann": Kerby, 126. The same Sixth Avenue offices would much later serve as the temporary home of the *Journal*'s New York news operation following the 2001 attack on the World Trade Center across the street from the *Journal*'s headquarters.

155 "about as complicated as changing a couple of electric light bulbs": *WSJ*, 12/16/52.

156 a deal with the ITU: Kerby, 126–27; Edward Scharff, *Worldly Power*, 116–17.

156 Underscoring the point: *WSJ*, 12/16/52.

156 An agreement was soon reached and ratified: *WSJ*, 4/27/53.

156 First use two months later: *WSJ*, 6/30/53.

156 In full use by May 1954: Wendt, 343.

156 RCA would commercialize the Dow Jones patents under license: *WSJ*, 10/8/58.

157 McCormack replaces Ackell: BK Notice to the Staff, 1/9/56; Kerby to Bridge, 3/21/79 at 11; Wendt, 350–51.

157 McCormack's abortive appointment to editorial page: Wendt, 350.

157 "a good man and a fast mover": BK to TK, 11/15/46.

157 Royster's Pulitzer Prize: The Pulitzer Board, at the height of the cold war, cited Royster's "ability to discern the underlying moral issue, illuminated by a deep faith and confidence in the people of our country." *WSJ*, 8/5/58.

158 "getting enough papers printed in time to keep the customers happy": BK to TK, 3/17/53.

158 Feemster's innovations: Scharff at 98, 100, 102–3.

158 "linage": Lines—volume—are thought to be the best measure because newspaper circulation is generally conceived of as roughly flat, and as not varying with economic cycles, while advertising *revenue* reflects not only volume but also price, which tends to rise with inflation (or, during a depression, fall with deflation). At the *Journal,* then in a six-column format, 1,776 lines comprised a page—296 per column, times six columns. (Classified advertising was published in an eight-column format, resulting in 2,368 classified lines per page.)

158 Ad pages in 1930: The page figures assume that classified ads were 10 percent of the mix in the period through World War II; that proportion grew later.

158 Ad volume in 1938: Wendt, 354.

159 Ad volume grew five times: Ibid.

159 Discontinuing the Saturday edition: The last Saturday issue of the *Journal* was published 6/27/53; Saturday publication resumed 9/17/05. Before moving to end Saturday publication, Kilgore had, characteristically, commissioned a survey from Benson & Benson of Princeton. It had revealed that 22 percent of all Saturday copies were being delivered to closed offices, and that only a minority of readers were actually getting the Saturday paper on Saturday. Moreover, Benson & Benson predicted that no more than 2 percent, and probably many fewer, would cancel their subscriptions if Saturday publication was discontinued. Benson & Benson Survey, 11–12/52.

159 Summer home in Milford: BK to TK, 9/14/50, 10/2/50.

159 Bohemian Grove: Peter Martin Phillips, "A Relative Advantage: Sociology of the San Francisco Bohemian Club" (diss., University of California, Davis, 1994).

160 Birth of Jack Kilgore: BK to TK, 5/4/52.

160 Move to Pretty Brook Road: BK to TK, 4/23/52, 5/11/53, 4/12/54.

10. "A CLASSIC IN THE HISTORY OF NEWSPAPERING."

161 Automotive market shares: WSJ, 4/15/54, 4/19/54.

162 Curtice, an avid *Journal* reader: Edward Scharff, *Worldly Power*, 97.

162 GM's Motorama: *WSJ*, 4/23/54.

162 *Time* on Curtice's lifestyle: *Time*, 1/2/56.

162 *WSJ* editorials attacking antitrust investigation: *WSJ*, 4/16/54; 4/30/54.

163 GM proposal on bootlegging rejected: *WSJ*, 4/26/54.

163 Auto company 1953 newspaper advertising: *WSJ*, 6/25/54.

163 Of the four largest categories of national newspaper advertising: Statistical Abstract of the United States, 1954, at 889–90.

164 Williams's background: Scharff, 124.

165 the reporting . . . had taken more than a month: Bridge, chap. 25, 7.

165 "Someone offered me pictures": Lloyd Wendt, *Wall Street Journal*, 346.

165 "he declined rather tersely and returned to his office": Ibid., 347.

166 "a dagger into the hearts of the dealers": Ibid.

166 "It isn't journalism": *Time*, 6/28/54.

166 Vicker 1951 story: *WSJ*, 3/9/51.

166   Williams's 1953 story: In fact, Williams's 1953 article, based on the long lead-time of tool orders, predicted that "wide changes" would only come again with 1955 models. *WSJ*, 8/24/53.

166   Curtice personally decided to advertise in *WSJ*: Scharff, at 97.

167   "particularly incensed": *Business Week*, 6/26/54 at 25

167   Value of cancellations: *Ad Age*, 6/21/54. Advertising was also canceled in at least two local newspapers that reprinted the *Journal* story, the *Des Moines Register and Tribune* and *The Youngstown Vindicator*, although those cancellations were soon rescinded. *Ad Age*, 7/19/54.

167   "it won't be to apologize for anything": Callis interview, Bridge, 1/27/78, 34.

167   Cut off from production figures: *Ad Age*, 6/21/54.

167   Williams story on desperation tactic: *WSJ*, 6/4/54.

168   Callis took the call: Callis interview, Bridge, 1/27/78, 35.

168   BK confirmed the story: *Ad Age*, 6/28/54.

169   "I find it hard to believe that this represents the policy of General Motors top management": *NYT*, 6/19/54.

169   "A Difference of Opinion": *WSJ*, 6/23/54.

170   "I think a big company makes a mistake by getting mad and doing such things": BK to TK, 6/23/54.

170   WSJ story on annual advertising: *WSJ*, 6/25/54.

170   "I have a General Motors car—and I certainly don't intend to sell it": *Time*, 6/28/54. In fact, his latest purchase had been a Ford. BK to TK, 1/5/54.

170   Ginzburg letter: Ginzburg to GM, 6/28/54. Ginzburg sent a copy of his letter to the *Journal,* and almost instantly received a response sent to his office at *Look* by Kilgore. The letter asked Ginzburg to send along whatever reply he received from GM. "We know that they are getting a good deal of mail from readers of *The Wall Street Journal* and others but we do not have any idea what they are saying as to their side of the story. They are having very little to say to us directly these days, I am sorry to report." BK to Ginzburg, 6/29/54.

170   "GM will have to back down": *Tide,* 7/13/54.

171   WSJ Letters to the Editor: *WSJ*, 6/30/54.

171   Tecumseh weighs in: TK to BK, 7/1/54.

172   Brenholts letter: Brenholts to *WSJ*, 6/24/54.

172   "I just don't think that differences of opinion in one particular field should be allowed to spread into others": BK to Brenholts, 6/30/54.

172   BK's letter: BK to Curtice, 6/30/54.

172   "an enormous public relations error": William Kerby, *Proud Profession*, 153.

173   Timing relative to antitrust investigation: See *Tide*, 7/31/54.

173   Ban on press releases lifted: *Ad Age*, 6/28/54.

173   *Ward's* lifts its ban: *WSJ*, 7/8/54.

173   Curtice reply: Curtice to BK, 7/2/54.

173   BK wire: BK to Curtice, 7/6/54.

173   Curtice telegram: Curtice to BK, 7/6/54.

173   Kerby recollection: Kerby, 154.

173   "a public finish seemed necessary": BK to TK, 7/28/54.

173   Exchange of letters: The copies of the letters in GM's files were typed in the identical format, apparently on the same typewriter. Kilgore's letter went through four drafts. See Kerby, 154; the drafts are in Kilgore's file.

174   Curtice conclusion: *WSJ*, 7/12/54.

174   "they served their purpose": BK to TK, 7/28/54.

174   "the war had ended": Gemmill interview, Bridge, 6/27/78, 41–42; TK to BK, 8/1/54.

175   "shaky legal grounds": Kerby, 514.

175   BK to Curtice: *WSJ*, 7/12/54.

175   "but I don't think anybody will print company drawings of new cars": BK to TK, 7/28/54.

175   the "controversy" was "closed": Curtice to BK, 8/2/54.

175   "GM had done us a priceless favor": Kerby, 155.

175   "a classic in the history of newspapering": Lilienthal to BK, 7/7/54.

176   Scharff conclusion: Scharff, 129.

176   "Our future was assured": Wendt, 348.

11. NATIONAL SUCCESS

177   Reprint of a Woodlock column: *WSJ*, 12/24/54.

177   Tecumseh's last letter: TK to BK, 12/27/57.

178   Tecumseh's obituary: *NYT*, 11/24/59.

178   a "lusty success story": *Time*, 11/14/55.

178   "the right size for us": Lloyd Wendt, *Wall Street Journal*, 349.

178   Dividend raised to $6 per share: Ibid.

179   $100 per week jobs: Edward Scharff, *Worldly Power*, 162–163.

179   Benson & Benson study: Benson & Benson, "Market Profile and Attitude Survey for *The Wall Street Journal*," January 1956.

179   Subscriber survey: *WSJ* house ad, 9/4/57.

180   If a letter he received made him angry: William McSherry memo, "Personal Assessment of Bernard Kilgore," undated.

180   "I'm the only one around here who can't afford to lose his temper": William Kerby, *Proud Profession,* 159.

181   Never one to pull rank: Scharff, 155.

181   "you can learn a lot": *Indianapolis Star,* 5/10/60.

181   " 'Place is a bit too much like the typical newspaper office' ": *Princeton Packet,* 11/15/67.

181   One such note to a *Packet* news editor: Ibid.

182   Cleveland plant: *WSJ,* 1/9/59.

182   News staff nearing three hundred: *Time,* 10/12/59.

182   New plants online: *WSJ,* 5/9/60.

182   "it certainly is pleasant while it lasts": BK to Jane Cochran, 10/26/59.

183   BK credited with Pulitzer: *E&P,* 8/26/61.

183   Letter to his own paper: *Princeton Packet,* 10/12/61.

183   Correspondence with Nixon on plant opening: See Nixon to BK, 9/15/61, 10/6/61; BK to Nixon, 9/25/61.

183   More copies in California than New York: *WSJ,* 5/29/62.

183   California's population passes New York's: *Los Angeles Times,* 7/15/62.

183   *Journal* description of facsimile transmission: WSJ, 6/1/61.

184   *Journal* circulation at 825,000: WSJ, 5/29/62.

184   Announcement of White Oak plant: WSJ, 6/27/62.

12. A NEWSPAPER WITH "FLAIR"

185   *Journal* now accounted for more than 80 percent of the company's profits: *WSJ,* 7/8/64; William Kerby, *Proud Profession,* 166.

185   Among the discards: Edward Trayes "*The Observer,*" 2.

185   Ownership of *Newsweek:* *WSJ,* 3/10/61.

185   Newhouse and Meredith among those considering purchase: *Time,* 1/27/61.

186   "an indigestible bite": Kerby, 166. *Newsweek*'s management was ultimately outbid for the magazine by the Washington Post Co., which paid $15.5 million, or more than $104 million today. *Time,* 3/17/61.

186   BK was undaunted: Kerby to Bridge, 3/21/79 at 10; Kerby, 165.

186   Bottorff alternative: Trayes, 3, refers to a "daily" newspaper, but even in the context of his paper, this must be a misunderstanding.

186   *explaining* . . . rather than *reporting*: Gemmill interview, Bridge, 6/27/78, at 58–62.

186   "The National X": Trayes, 3.

187   "far from enthusiastic": Kerby to Bridge, 3/21/79 at 10.

187   Bottorff and Royster named to supervise: Trayes, 4.

187   BK memo: BK to Executive Committee, 6/27/61.

188   "flair": Ibid. *Flair* magazine was published for just twelve issues in 1950–51 by Fleur and Gardner Cowles.

188   average member of the initial staff . . . in his twenties: William and Frances Neilson, *What's News*, 135.

188   "the possibility of publishing a national Sunday newspaper": BK to staff, 8/15/61.

188   churning out new prototypes: Trayes, 7, 13–14.

188   Arnold on typography: New York *Sun,* obituary of Arnold 7.

189   "The basement of [Kilgore's] housed": Edward Scharff, *Worldly Power,* 176.

189   Operating costs twice what had been envisioned: Trayes, 23–25.

189   "there was a sort of unofficial deadline": Kerby to Bridge, 3/21/79 at 10.

189   an earlier published aside in *Editor & Publisher*: *E&P,* 8/26/61.

190   Associated Press story: *NYT,* 10/31/61.

190   scramble to trademark: Trayes, 26.

190   Announcement of plans: *WSJ,* 11/13/61.

190   A full-page advertisement: *WSJ,* 11/13/61.

190   "Berlin barrier" house ad: *WSJ,* 11/20/61, emphasis in original.

190   "Red China" house ad: *WSJ,* 12/19/61.

190   "Medical man" house ad: *WSJ,* 12/1/61.

190   House ad directed to women: WSJ, 12/4/61.

190   "wholesome . . . relief from scare headlines and lurid stories": *WSJ,* 12/1/61.

191   Increased demand and production: Trayes, 29–30; WSJ, 1/18/62.

191   "clean and uncluttered": *Time,* 2/16/62.

191   *NO* arranges for reprint rights: *WSJ,* 2/2/62.

191   First-issue "Observation": *NO,* 2/4/62. The Portland, Maine/Portland, Oregon, phrasing seems to have been an echo, perhaps unconscious, of this about the *Journal* from *The Christian Science Monitor* of 3/27/56: "With minor exceptions . . . the paper, whether you pick it up in Richmond, Va., Richmond, Calif. or Richmond, Ind., will be the same."

193   Only designed for 40,000 mailed copies: Kerby, 166.

193   "shortest closing news deadline of any national news weekly": *WSJ,* 3/16/62.

193   *Time* assessment of first issue: *Time,* 2/16/62.

193   1962 advertising results: *Time,* 2/16/62; *E&P,* 2/9/63; *Time,* 12/7/62.

193   "often infuriatingly bland and crashingly dull": *Newsweek,* 1/28/63.

193   "Who *needs The National Observer?*": *WSJ,* 10/19/62, emphasis in original.

193   "What do readers get from *The National Observer?*": *WSJ,* 11/19/62.

194   Conversion rates of 20 percent: Callis interview, Bridge, 1/27/78 at 45.

194   Circulation levels: *E&P,* 2/9/63; *WSJ,* 2/4/64.

194   "We are not amateurs": *Time,* 12/7/62.

194   BK's ten-year plan: *E&P,* 2/9/63.

194   "Advertising? First things first": *Ad Age,* 7/6/64.

194   Conversion rates climbed: Callis interview, Bridge, 1/27/78, 45–46.

194   Advertising increased: *WSJ* ad, 12/12/63.

194   Circulation growth 1964–65: *Ad Age,* 7/6/64; WSJ, 11/2/64; 3/10/65.

194   Addition of fourth printing plant: *WSJ,* 11/2/64.

195   the *Observer* news staff was increased: Cf. Trayes, 16, with *Time,* 12/7/62.

195   "some more or less personalized report on the news": *NO,* 11/19/67.

195   Sparkling *NO* prose: Charles Preston, *The Observer's World.*

195   BK developed new form. *NO,* 11/19/67.

195   "Newsbooks" announced: *WSJ* ad, 4/23/64.

195   Second Newsbook: *WSJ* ad, 7/28/64.

196   "no personal photo, no big headlines": *WSJ* ad, 12/14/64.

196   "if we could get the *National Observer* up around five hundred thousand, we'd stand above those. "Callis interview, Bridge, 1/27/78, 44.

13. INTERRUPTED

197   "he wasn't amused when circulation sales ran into trouble": Kerby to Bridge, 3/21/79, 12.

197   "all but washed his hands of the whole project": William Kerby, *Proud Profession,* 165.

198   Joint announcement of Callis promotion: *WSJ,* 12/10/62.

198   Feemster's death: *E&P,* 1/19/63.

198   "chairman of the executive committee of Dow Jones": *WSJ,* 1/15/63.

198   Even Callis remained unaware: Kerby to Bridge, 3/21/79 at 12.

198   WSJ news and editorial pieces on Feemster: *WSJ,* 1/15/63; 1/16/63.

198   DJ revenue and earnings: *WSJ,* 2/4/63, 7/8/64.

198   DJ goes public: *WSJ,* 5/29/63.

198   Opening White Oak plant: *WSJ,* 6/3/63.

199   Closing New York printing facility: *NYT,* 4/13/63.

199   Callis's prediction: *Ad Age,* 7/6/64.

199   DJ revenue and profits: *WSJ,* 1/22/64, 2/4/64, 3/10/65.

199   New Dallas plant: *WSJ,* 2/20/64.

199   Plans for Palo Alto plant: *WSJ,* 10/7/65.

199   New offices at 30 Broad Street: *WSJ,* 4/7/64, 2/23/65.

199   South Brunswick facility: *WSJ,* 2/4/63, 7/8/64, 2/15/65.

200   Bradford Mills report: *Proposed Diversification Program for Dow Jones & Company, Inc.,* June 1964.

201   BK surgery: Wendt, 378.

201   Surgery "minor": Kerby, 179; Wendt, 378.

201   "You will have a clear field": Kerby, 179.

201   "This is not a sudden decision": BK to Staff, 1/17/66; *WSJ,* 1/18/66.

202   Potter warned BK: Potter to BK, 3/7/66.

202   BK acknowledgment: BK to Potter, 3/16/66.

202   BK memo to Kerby: BK to Kerby, 4/11/66.

203   Growth of *The Packet: Princeton Packet,* 11/15/67.

203   BK trips with Kerby: Kerby, 180; *WSJ,* 2/27/67 (Palo Alto); *WSJ,* 12/29/67 (Highland).

203   "he will be out of the hospital in a week or 10 days": Kerby to Staff, 4/18/67.

203   "demolished": Bottorff interview, Bridge, 8/26/78, 36.

203   he ceased taking meals with the family: Jack Kilgore, conversation with the author, 10/22/07.

204   BK turns to religion: MLTK (Beilman) interview, Bridge, 10/18/79, 5, 45.

204   frustrated that he could no longer type: Kerby, 180.

204   *ASNE Bulletin* article: Phillips, 4, 8.

204   "my role is apparently still meaningful": BK Memorandum, 10/4/67.

204   Last note to Kerby: BK to Kerby, 10/25/67.

205   McSherry left "with enough work to keep busy for a week": Lloyd Wendt, *Wall Street Journal,* 382.

205   "Bill, will my baby make it?": Kerby, 166.

205   BK funeral: *WSJ,* 11/16/67; undated notes in Kerby files.

205   *NYT* headline: *NYT,* 11/15/67.

205   "the publishing genius of our age": *WSJ,* 11/16/67.

205   "He will be intensely missed—and in a most personal sense": Kerby to the Staff, 11/15/67.

205   "He was sprightly!": John Caples to Kerby, 11/16/67.

205   WSJ obituary: *WSJ,* 11/16/67.

206   *NO* obituary: *NO,* 11/19/67.

206   "the same news to Portland, Oregon, as to Portland, Maine": *WSJ,* 11/16/67.

EPILOGUE

208   But acquiring new readers was difficult and expensive: William Kerby, *Proud Profession,* 166–167.

209   "The long effort": *WSJ,* 7/1/77; *NYT,* 7/1/77.

212   "Thus his work is more famous": *WSJ,* 11/16/67.

SOURCES

I read all of Kilgore's bylined articles in the *Journal* from 1932 until 1941 (and one in 1944) as well as countless other stories from the *Journal* over the years. I also read all of the coverage of Kilgore and his career from *The New York Times* and *Time* magazine, both of which are, helpfully, available online. I also had extensive access to the corporate archives of Dow Jones & Company and *The Wall Street Journal*, including an unpublished 1979 manuscript by John F. Bridge, *Dow, Jones, Berg and Us All*, as well as the transcripts of interviews Bridge conducted in 1978 and 1979 in the preparation of this work.

As noted elsewhere, the single most valuable source, aside from the *Journal* itself and the Dow Jones archives, is the correspondence between Barney and Tecumseh Kilgore. These letters are cited in the notes by date (where, as in almost all cases, the date can be determined). I also had the invaluable opportunity to canvass voluminous scrapbooks kept by both Tecumseh and Barney Kilgore.

In addition, the following published sources proved especially useful:

Allen, Robert. *Irving Fisher: A Biography.* New York; Blackwell, 1993.

Bloom, Murray Teigh. "Everyman's *Wall Street Journal.*" *Esquire,* November 1957.

Brooks, John. "*The Wall Street Journal* Woos the Eggheads," *Harper's Magazine*, March 1959.

Brucker, Herbert. *The Changing American Newspaper.* New York: Columbia University Press, 1937.

Elson, Robert (Norton-Taylor, Duncan, ed.). *Time Inc.: The Intimate History of a Publishing Enterprise 1923–1941.* New York: Atheneum, 1968.

Fairlie, Henry. "Press: Anglo-American Differences." *Encounter,* June 1966.

Halberstam, David. *The Powers That Be.* New York: Alfred A. Knopf, 1979.

Hamilton, William Peter. *The Stock Market Barometer.* New York: John Wiley, 1998. First published 1922.

Kerby, William. *A Proud Profession: Memoirs of a Wall Street Journal Reporter, Editor, and Publisher.* Homewood, Ill.: Dow Jones-Irwin, 1981.

Kerby, William. "The Making of America's 'Most-Trusted' Newspaper." *Michigan Business Review,* November 1971.

Klein, Maury. *Rainbow's End: The Great Crash of 1929.* New York: Oxford University Press, 2001.

Kluger, Richard. *The Paper: The Life and Death of the New York Herald Tribune.* New York: Alfred A. Knopf, 1986.

Leach, Peter. "Turning Back the Years," www.joc.com/history.

Loomis, Carol. "One Story *The Wall Street Journal* Won't Print." *Fortune,* August 1971.

Meacham, Jon. *The Beginning of the Journey.* New York: Dow Jones [privately printed], 2002.

Mott, Frank. *American Journalism: A History of Newspapers in the United States Through 250 Years 1690 to 1940.* New York: Macmillan, 1945.

Neilson, Winthrop and Frances. *What's News—Dow Jones: Story of The Wall Street Journal.* Radnor, Pa.: Chilton Book Co., 1973.

Phillips, Clifton, and Baughman, John. *DePauw: A Pictorial History.* Greencastle, Ind.; DePauw University, 1987.

Phillips, Warren. "How the *Journal*'s Fully-Textured News Stories Get That Way." *ASNE Bulletin,* October 1967.

Preston, Charles, ed. *The Observer's World: People, Places, and Events from the Pages of The National Observer.* Princeton, N.J.: Dow Jones Books, 1965.

Preston, Charles, ed. *The World of The Wall Street Journal: Main Street—and Beyond.* New York: Simon & Schuster, 1959.

Royster, Vermont. *A Pride of Prejudices.* New York: Alfred A. Knopf, 1967.

Scharff, Edward. *Worldly Power: The Making of The Wall Street Journal.* New York: Beaufort Books, 1986.

Schumpeter, Joseph. *Ten Great Economists: From Marx to Keynes.* New York: Oxford University Press, 1951.

Trayes, Edward. "*The Observer:* Prototype for American National Newspapers?" Paper presented to Association for Education in Journalism Convention, August 1968.

Walker, Stanley. *City Editor.* Baltimore: Johns Hopkins University Press, 1999. First published 1934.

Wendt, Lloyd. *The Wall Street Journal: The Story of Dow Jones and the Nation's Business Newspaper.* New York: Rand McNally, 1982.

Wilner, Isaiah. *The Man Time Forgot: A Tale of Genius, Betrayal, and the Creation of Time Magazine.* New York: HarperCollins, 2006.

Writing for Fortune: Nineteen Authors Remember Life on the Staff of a Remarkable Magazine. New York: Time Inc., 1980.

Yagoda, Ben. *About Town: The New Yorker and the World It Made.* (2000) New York: Da Capo Press, 2001.

ACKNOWLEDGMENTS

This is my fourth book, but it still amazes me how generous people generally are when approached for help on such an endeavor. This is where I get to thank them, and it is a special pleasure to write these words.

The research for this book was aided by any number of strangers. Bill Hooper, archivist at Time Inc., was consistently generous; Peter Costiglio facilitated this when we worked together. Mark Mandle, librarian at Crain Communications, went above and beyond the call of duty. Larry Kinsel of General Motors communications, and his boss Steve Harris, did not hesitate to aid an effort to shine new light on what is certainly not one of GM's finest hours; they are models of how writers wish corporate officials would (but often don't) approach questions of history. Coletta Hagan of Kiplinger tracked down an old article. Nancy Lyon, archivist at the Yale University Library, found Kilgore memos in the papers of Richard Kluger. Alycia Vivona, archivist at the FDR Library, enabled me to tell the story of Kilgore's Amlie misadventure for the first time. At DePauw University, Linda Butler, archives assistant, was helpful with files, while Wesley Wilson, coordinator of archives and special collections, and Butler did yeoman work with photographs. Not all avenues of research prove fruitful, but Alison Bridger of the Bancroft Library at Berkeley helped me confirm that the William Randolph Hearst papers were a "dry hole" as far as Kilgore was concerned.

Not all of the research assistance came from strangers, of course. Sam Boyer provided valuable research assistance. Zobbie Potter and Charlie Feldman provided essential endorsements of my ability to carry this project through. Marilyn Machlowitz put me in touch with Ned Scharff, and Ned was friendly and generous; his book remains the best written on Dow Jones. Stewart Griesman, physician and friend, helped sort out a medical puzzle. Steve Howe of the *Financial Times* and former *Journal* colleague, helped make sense of advertising linage numbers. George Melloan, a longtime stalwart of *The Wall*

Street Journal editorial page, took time from his own work on the history of Dow Jones to help me establish the history of "The Outlook" column.

At Dow Jones itself, Naomi Praveen spent hours copying files, each minute of that work saving me valuable time. Howard Hoffman was responsive, thoughtful, and always welcoming.

My friends Carll Tucker and Jonathan Alter read a draft and offered a number of perceptive comments. Steve Adler, Marcus Brauchli, and Paul Steiger, friends, distinguished business editors in the Kilgore tradition, and sometime colleagues all, provided kind words and encouragement. Peter Kann, Barney Kilgore's able successor as leader of *The Wall Street Journal* and its business operations, offered a critical early vote of confidence, useful thoughts throughout, and a calming influence during a difficult moment. Karen House, Peter's successor as *Journal* publisher, helped me talk through a tricky but important passage. Gordon Crovitz, yet another former *Journal* publisher and dear friend, was a constant support during a tough season for us both, providing unbounded enthusiasm about the subject, access to invaluable research material, an important sounding board and a crucial endorsement as I sought a home for this book.

Phil Revzin, former colleague and longtime friend, agreed to take a first look at the manuscript, and then generously agreed to take a second look. His editing strengthened and tightened the volume you are reading; his confidence made it possible for you to read it.

My greatest debt in the research of this volume is owed to Barney and Mary Lou Kilgore's three children, Kathryn, Jim, and Jack. The Kilgores entrusted me with the correspondence between their father and grandfather and almost entirely resisted the temptation to direct how this story should be told. Jim spent hours helping me better understand his father, and also provided access to scrapbooks and photographs. Kathryn overcame initial concerns, and ultimately offered scores of suggestions. Jack provided a telling anecdote and moving account of his father's final days. All three Kilgores read the manuscript in draft and enabled me to minimize the numbers of errors in it. Those that inevitably remain are my responsibility alone.

As always, loved ones make all the difference in the solitude of writing. My father provided encouragement, as he never fails to do, and he and my brother Larry offered me a research home at a critical juncture. My mother continues to guide and comfort me, as she always will. Jeanne Straus read every word of this book and improved it in countless ways. Our marvelous children, Rachel Straus Tofel and Colin Straus Tofel, continue to be the readers whose ultimate approval I most crave.

Finally, this book is dedicated to Janice Nittoli, who inspires me in this and all things.

—R.J.T.

New York

August 2008

INDEX